Shifra Stein

GETAWAYS LESS THAN TWO HOURS AWAY

SHIFRA STEIN'S

DAYTRIPS®

FROM **CINCINNATI**

Sixth Edition

DAVID HUNTER
revised by
KAREN EYLON

The
Globe
Pequot
Press

GUILFORD, CONNECTICUT

Dedicated to my loving husband and beautiful daughter, who make the travels of life so captivating.

—*Karen Eylon*

Copyright © 1984, 1991 by Shifra Stein
Copyright © 1994, 1997, 1999, 2001 by The Globe Pequot Press

All rights reserved. No part of this book may be reproduced or transmitted in any form by any means, electronic or mechanical, including photocopying and recording, or by any information storage and retrieval system, except as may be expressly permitted by the 1976 Copyright Act or by the publisher. Requests for permission should be made in writing to The Globe Pequot Press, P.O. Box 480, Guilford, Connecticut 06437.

Day Trips is a registered trademark.

Cover image: Dubé Studio
Cover design: Saralyn D'Amato

Library of Congress Cataloging-in-Publication Data is available.

ISBN: 0-7627-1199-X

Manufactured in the United States of America
Sixth Edition/First Printing

CONTENTS

SOUTHWEST

SOUTH

SOUTHEAST

DIRECTORY

The prices and rates listed in this guidebook were confirmed at press time. We recommend, however, that you call establishments before traveling to obtain current information.

PREFACE

Welcome to the Ohio Valley. This great basin, carved by the continent's only major westward-flowing river and its many tributaries, played an important role in American history. The Ohio River was the link between the original American colonies and the vast continental interior—a natural highway bound for the West.

To this mighty river came French explorers and trappers, British scouts, and the rawboned Virginia frontiersmen. Battles associated with the American Revolution were fought here, and after that war veterans were given land grants in what was then known as the Western Reserve. No sooner had the smoke of battle cleared than the floodgates sprang open to westward migration, and across the Alleghenies they came.

The rowdy Flatboat Era and the colorful Steamboat Age had their birth on the Ohio River and saw migrants by the thousands, many headed for St. Louis to outfit for wagon treks to the Wild West and many others to make their homes and settlements along the Ohio's fertile banks.

Their legacy is easily found today among the towns and farmlands that lie along the Ohio and along tributaries reaching far into Ohio, Kentucky, and Indiana—the area covered in this book—and most or parts of seven other states.

The thickly wooded hills and, to the west, the grassy plains contribute a pleasant scene to any trip, and if you know where to look, you can find great gorges, natural bridges, caves, and waterfalls.

You will find that not all of today's industry is modernized, that there still are small, family-run operations that follow time-honored ways, from the shaping of pottery to the curing of fine hams. There are splendid old homes, many excellent restaurants, charming inns, country fairs and festivals, and many other things to see and do.

We ask that you bear several things in mind:

Driving Time: Individual trips are designed as one-day, round-trip excursions, with the farthest points being within a two-hour drive from Cincinnati's periphery, not including time spent sight-seeing or dining. Admittedly, we have stretched this limit a little in a couple of cases—the Abraham Lincoln birthplace and related sites, for instance—because they are not that much farther and because, frankly, we just couldn't bear to leave them out.

There are a few trips that, in all practicality, would be more leisurely and comfortable with an overnight stop. We must leave it to you to set your own pace.

Maps: While we have included maps to make your trip easier, we suggest taking along state maps for further detailed information. Or contact the state departments of travel and tourism for maps.

Highway Designations: Federal highways are designated "U.S.," Ohio state routes as "O," and Kentucky state routes as "K." Indiana state routes, however, are designated "Ind." and Interstate routes are designated "Interstate" to avoid any confusion.

Time Zones: From the first Sunday in October to the last Sunday in April, all the territory covered in this book is on Eastern Standard Time, or "Cincinnati time." The rest of the year, Ohio and Kentucky switch to Eastern Daylight Time, while most of Indiana does not. Therefore, Indiana points of interest in this book will be one hour earlier than "Cincinnati time" in summer. Indiana towns directly across the Ohio River from Louisville, Kentucky, stay with Louisville and "Cincinnati time" all year.

Restaurants: Restaurants, as well as hotels, are mentioned in the main text only if they are an inseparable part of the atmosphere of a place. Other restaurants are listed in the directory. The symbol $ means less than $8.00 per person; $$ means $8.00–$15.00 per person; $$$ means more than $15.00 per person, not including beverage, tax, or tip. ◻ denotes that major credit cards are accepted. No ◻ denotes that cards are not accepted.

Combining Trips: These trips are arranged so they may easily be combined into an excursion of two or more days or possibly even a week. In several cases you can take one trip out and another trip back simply by reversing the order of the second trip.

The Directory: Besides listing restaurants, the directory in the back of this book also describes campgrounds at state parks.

Festivals and other special annual events are listed month by month. If you take one of these trips, be sure to check these listings to find out what's going on in an area. A phone number is included for each so you can call for specific dates.

The "Additional Information" section lists area tourism offices, which can supply you with maps, brochures, and other free information.

Phoning Ahead: It is always advisable to telephone ahead for details or for reservations before embarking on a trip, to avoid disappointments on the road. Since a book such as this must be prepared months in advance of publication, it is inevitable that some details—days or hours of operation, prices, and so forth—may change before publication. Phoning ahead is sincerely urged so that you have a pleasant and carefree trip.

We always welcome your suggestions for our future editions.

Day Trip 1 Northwest

0	10	20	30 miles

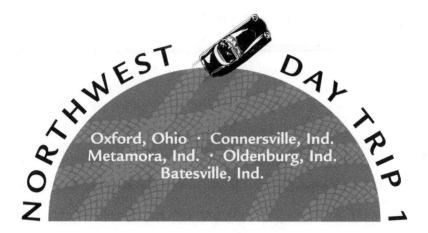

NORTHWEST DAY TRIP 1

Oxford, Ohio · Connersville, Ind.
Metamora, Ind. · Oldenburg, Ind.
Batesville, Ind.

Our first trip is an easy swing through nearby Ohio and Indiana farm country, highlighted by a visit to the old Whitewater Canal, a ride on a steam-powered or diesel train, and perhaps a swim at Brookville Lake beach, topped off with some good country cooking. In between are many glimpses of life as it used to be in nineteenth-century rural America.

The train leaves Connersville at 10:00 A.M. or high noon, depending on the day. If you're not an early riser, you may wish to skip the Ohio portion of this trip and proceed directly to the depot. If so, take Interstate 74 west from Cincinnati to the Brookville exit and go north on Ind. 1 to Connersville. Turn left at the first traffic light, then left again at the next light onto Ind. 121 (southbound).

Please remember that during daylight saving time, noon in Connersville is 1:00 P.M. Cincinnati time.

OXFORD, OHIO

Leaving the city on U.S. 27 (north), one arrives on the rural scene soon after crossing into Butler County. The highway crosses a plateau that offers frequent vistas of gently rolling farmland, patterned in summer by rows of corn and silky fields of hay. Oxford is 23 miles from the county line.

Named for the venerable English university town, Oxford is itself an academic center and a picture-postcard American community with tree-shaded streets, colonial-style store fronts, tranquil residential areas, and, in its midst, the beautiful campus of Miami University, a highly regarded state institution of learning for some 16,000 undergraduate and graduate students from all over the world. Walking- and driving-tour information is available at the Oxford Chamber of Commerce, 118 West High Street. Call (513) 523–5200.

WHAT TO SEE

Miami University. High Street and Campus Avenue. A campus stroll by all means should include the university's formal gardens, the Kumler Chapel, the Shriver Center student union, the Western campus, the Ice Arena on High Street, the Center for the Performing Arts, and the new Recreation Sports Center. The main attraction, however, is the *Miami University Art Museum,* a stone-and-glass edifice designed by architect Walter Netsch, creator of the Air Force Academy Chapel in Colorado. The museum has five galleries of per- manent and changing exhibits and includes the world's largest public collection of Leica cameras, which can be viewed by appoint- ment only. Open 11:00 A.M. to 5:00 P.M. Tuesday–Sunday. Closed hol- idays and most of August. Call (513) 529–2232.

McGuffey Museum. Spring and Oak Streets. Your grandparents may remember the ocher-colored schoolbooks with elaborate black decorations on the cover and engraved illustrations inside. No Amer- ican schoolbooks have ever evoked such nostalgia or become such collector's items as *McGuffey's Eclectic Readers.* Full of quaint and charming tales and poems, this series was the work of William Holmes McGuffey, a nineteenth-century Miami faculty member. His restored home contains period furnishings, his library, the octag- onal desk at which he worked, and, of course, a complete collection of his famous readers. Open 2:00 to 4:00 P.M. Saturday and Sunday, other hours by appointment. Call (513) 529–2232.

Pioneer Farm & House Museum. Doty and Brown Roads, at the south entrance to Hueston Woods State Park. (Brown Road is an extension of Oxford's College Avenue.) Maintained by the state park and the Oxford Museum Association, this 1835 farmhouse contains period furniture, clothing, appliances, and even toys collected from throughout southwestern Ohio to reconstruct the lifestyle of a working Ohio family before the Civil War. In the fall visitors can watch apple butter being made here in forty-gallon kettles stirred over open fires. It is for sale, as are homemade doughnuts, cider, maple syrup, Indian corn, gourds, and pumpkins. Open 1:00 to 4:00 P.M. Saturday, Sunday, and holidays Memorial Day–September. For information call (513) 523-6347.

Hueston Woods State Park, O-732 north of Oxford. Nearly 3,600 acres in size, Hueston Woods features 200 acres of virgin woodland for hiking and exploring. With its spectacular ninety-four-room, A-frame lodge with dining room and fifty-nine cabins, plus campsites, the park caters to all tastes. Sailing and a beach are available at the park's Acton Lake, in addition to fishing, an eighteen-hole golf course, an indoor-outdoor pool, an impressive nature center, and picnic areas. Call (513) 523-6381 or (800) 282-7275.

WHERE TO SHOP

Fairhaven, Ohio. This tiny hamlet is noted for its antiques, on sale by residents, who open a dozen or more little shops on Saturday and Sunday along Main Street. Take O-732 north from Oxford to O-177, then go north 6 miles on O-177 to Fairhaven, just past the junction of O-725. As you leave Oxford on O-732, watch for the Black (or Pugh's Mill) Covered Bridge just outside town.

CONNERSVILLE, INDIANA

To reach Connersville from Oxford, follow U.S. 27 north 14 miles to Liberty, Indiana, and Ind. 44 west 12 miles. From Fairhaven return a half-mile to O-725, turn right, and proceed 18 miles through Liberty to Connersville. Note that O-725 becomes Ind. 44 when it crosses the state line.

When in Liberty—if you're in the mood for a swim or a hike—take Ind. 101 south about 2.5 miles to Whitewater State Park and its fine sand beach along Whitewater Lake. You can also rent a canoe or boat, fish, picnic, or camp in this beautiful state park. The Hornbeam Nature Preserve is especially lovely in the spring, with wildflowers everywhere. Call (765) 458-5565. Return the same way to Liberty and turn left on Ind. 44 to reach Connersville.

John Conner (1776-1826), for whom the town was named, was born in Ohio and grew up in the frontier region of Detroit, where his father had a large farm. As an adult he became a licensed fur trader with the Indians and established a trading post on the site of Connersville in 1808. The town was platted in 1813, three years before Indiana's statehood, and Conner was its first sheriff, first miller, and first merchant. He was also an Indian-language interpreter for General William Henry Harrison in the War of 1812, a member of the commission that selected Indianapolis as the site for the state capital, and, later, a member of the Indiana House of Representatives and the State Senate.

Connersville's heyday was as the chief community along the old Whitewater Canal, a human-made waterway linking Hagerstown, some 25 miles north, with the Ohio River, 50 miles south. Horse-drawn canal boats brought central Indiana farm goods and passengers along this route from 1836 to 1866 to connect with Ohio River steamboats. The canal crisscrossed Indiana, incorporating parts of the West Fork of the Whitewater River and, south of Brookville, the Whitewater itself. While driving this trip, you may still see several abandoned canal locks and a feeder dam.

Railroads not only choked off the canal-boat trade but also, in this case, eventually bought and used the old canal towpath as a bed for the tracks.

WHAT TO SEE

Canal House. 111 East Fourth Street, Connersville 47331. Built in 1842, this was the original headquarters for the Whitewater Valley Canal Corporation, a stock company created to extend the canal north to the National Road at Cambridge City. It has been purchased and restored by Historic Connersville, Inc. Its four Doric columns symbolize the stature of the early canal industry. The building is listed on the National Register of Historic Places and is considered by some to be the purest example of Greek Revival architecture in Indiana. Open by appointment only. Donations encouraged. Call (765) 825-2744 or 825-5325.

Fayette County Historical Museum. 103 South Vine, Connersville 47331. Located on the corner of State Road 44 and Vine Street, the museum features a variety of exhibits, including one highlighting area schools. (The first marching high school band hailed from Fayette County.) The museum also includes exhibits from the pioneer and

Civil War eras, Indian artifact displays, and products of industrial Connersville. Open 2:00 to 5:00 P.M. Sunday. Admission free. Call (765) 825-5325, (765) 825-0490, or (765) 825-0708.

WHAT TO DO

The Whitewater Valley Railroad. Ind. 121 on the south city limits, opposite Elmhurst. There is no longer any regular passenger rail service through Connersville—and, indeed, throughout most of the Ohio Valley—so retired railroaders and volunteers have collected vintage locomotives and cars and resurrected the old Whitewater Valley Railroad.

When the whistle blows (at 10:00 A.M. or noon, depending on the day), No. 25 chugs away from the station loaded with sightseers headed for Metamora, many laden with picnic lunches. This is a 32-mile round-trip that follows the old canal to Metamora, a restored canal town, returning to Connersville about six hours after it leaves the station.

No. 25 is a 108-ton diesel built in 1951 in Lima, Ohio. First used at Cincinnati's Union Terminal, it later was owned by Lake City Railroad in Florida and purchased by Whitewater Valley Railroad in 1973. Used alternately is the old No. 9339, which is also a diesel engine. It was built in 1948 by the American Locomotive Company of Schenectady, New York, for the Procter and Gamble Company, which donated No. 9339 to the Whitewater Valley Railroad in 1985.

The coaches, admittedly a bit dilapidated, are Erie Stillwell and New York Central cars. Several other old cars and engines are stationary displays at the depot, which also houses a small collection of railroad memorabilia and a gift shop.

A two-hour layover in Metamora affords an opportunity to visit attractions there.

The train runs Saturday, Sunday, and holidays, departing at 12:01 P.M. Spring Adventure trips depart every Wednesday, Thursday, and Friday in May at 10:00 A.M. Fall Foliage train rides are offered Thursday and Friday at 10:00 A.M. through October. Holiday trips take place the four weekends after Thanksgiving in conjunction with the Metamora Christmas Walk, with advance paid reservations required. Generally, though, reservations are unnecessary except for large groups. Fare charged. For information call (765) 825-2054.

The Whitewater Valley Railroad offers a train-to-dinner that leaves the station in Connersville at 6:00 P.M., for Laurel, Indiana, a one-hour ride 150 years into the past. The Laurel Hotel was built in the 1840s as a canal hotel and later became a railroad hotel. Now it is a restaurant specializing in pan-fried chicken. The dinner train runs the first and third Friday of each month, May–October. $$$. ☐. Reservations required. Call (765) 825-2054.

METAMORA, INDIANA

This old canal town fell into decline with the advent of the railroads. By the middle of the century, a tired gristmill and about twenty buildings were all that remained of the original—and flourishing—community. In the past thirty-five years, though, progressive, creative minds have restored the mill, hauled in log cabins, and reopened a 14-mile section of the old canal, including its locks and wooden aqueduct. Listed on the National Register of Historic Places, the Whitewater Canal State Memorial opened in 1973 and absorbs thousands of visitors each year into the rustic pioneer times of the early 1800s.

If you're not taking the train from Connersville, continue south on Ind. 121 from the train station 15 miles to U.S. 52 and turn left (east). Follow U.S. 52 for 2.5 miles to Metamora. The direct route from Cincinnati is Interstate 74 west to U.S. 52 and then north for 22 miles to Metamora. If your pace is leisurely, it's worth your time to make a brief stop in New Trenton as you travel north on U.S. 52. New Trenton's expansive antiques mall and the one-of-a-kind Sacksteders Interiors offer a memorable shopping break. Right next door, Bonderheid's Grocery is known for excellent deli sandwiches. Continue north 15 miles to Metamora. (The complex is open mid-April to mid-December, but most shops are closed on Monday, except Memorial Day and Labor Day. Open July 4.)

WHAT TO SEE

The Gristmill. The big waterwheel and huge stone buhrs (grinding stones) are turned by the flow of the canal. Built in 1845, the mill burned and was rebuilt in 1900. Now it again produces cornmeal, whole wheat flour, and grits, and bags these grains for sale. The mill has produced as much as six tons of meal a day in peak season. Visitors can watch the grinding process. The mill is open March 16 through December 31, 9:00 A.M. to 5:00 P.M. Wednesday–Saturday and 1:00 to 5:30 P.M. Sunday. Closed Monday, Tuesday, Thanksgiving, and Christmas. Open Memorial Day, Labor Day, and July 4. No admission fee. The information number for the entire historic site is at the Gristmill; call (765) 647–6512. Shops and other attractions on the grounds do not have telephones.

Metamora Merchants Association. This is the collective name of some 120 small shops housed in cabins and other buildings in Metamora. The array of shops includes potteries, snackeries, antiques collectors, jewelry stores, cheese shops, broom makers, candle shops, and artists of every ilk. Shops raise flags to indicate they are open for business. Call Metamora's Welcome Line at (765) 647–2109 year-round.

Wooden Aqueduct. Built in 1848 to carry the canal over Duck Creek, this is the only known wooden-covered aqueduct in the United States in operating condition.

WHAT TO DO

The *Ben Franklin.* This replica canal boat takes passengers on a twenty-five-minute cruise along the canal, through the aqueduct, and to the restored Millville Locks. It is pulled by a horse on the towpath, as in times gone by. The boat operates May–October on the hour noon to 4:00 P.M. Wednesday–Friday and on the hour 11:00 A.M. to 4:00 P.M. Saturday and Sunday. A fare is charged. Call (765) 647–6512.

Hiking. The state memorial is a way-stop on the Shawnee Trail, a marked hiking trail from Laurel Dam, northwest of the park, 5 miles southeast to Boundary Hill, an Indian-treaty reference point. Use of the trail is free.

WHERE TO EAT

Several places to eat in Metamora are all clustered within the village.

The Hearthstone Restaurant. At the east end of town on U.S. 52. This is Metamora's oldest continuing business. It features fried chicken and country-cured ham and will prepare carryout picnic lunches. Open 11:00 A.M. to 9:00 P.M. Tuesday–Thursday, 10:00 A.M. to 10:00 P.M. Friday and Saturday, and 10:00 A.M. to 8:00 P.M. Sunday. Call (765) 647–5204. $$. ◻.

The Mounds. U.S. 52, 11 miles east of Metamora. Follow the highway through Brookville toward Cincinnati. The restaurant is 3 miles east of Brookville.

This family-run roadside restaurant has drawn regular customers from as far as 50 miles away since the 1930s. Its secret: just plain, good country cooking. Food is served from platters and bowls placed on long, family-size tables. There are country ham, steak, or pan-fried chicken, cod, heaps of vegetables, hot biscuits with cream gravy, and desserts. $$. Closed Monday unless it's a holiday. Also closes the first Sunday before Christmas for the winter, reopening the first Saturday in March. For hours call (317) 647-4111.

If you're returning to Cincinnati from here, continue east on U.S. 52 to Interstate 74 east, and take it back to the city.

OLDENBURG, INDIANA

Oldenburg, locally called the "Village of Spires," is a little snip of Europe cupped in the hills of southeastern Indiana. The road approaching it from Metamora is flanked by croplands, and in a good August, corn growing 10 feet tall crowds to the very edge of the highway, blocking all else from sight. The rest of the year, you can see Oldenburg from afar, looking very much like a village of northern Germany.

From Metamora drive half a mile west on U.S. 52 to Ind. 229; then turn left and proceed south 10 miles to Oldenburg.

This town remains much as it was in 1837, when it was laid out in 16 equal blocks. There are still only four main streets and four cross-streets. Originally, parcels were sold to German immigrants in Cincinnati, who turned out to be predominantly Catholic. In 1844 Father Franz Josef Rudolph and Mother Theresa Heckelmeier came here from Vienna, Austria, to establish a school and an orphanage. Oldenburg Monastery was established by Franciscan friars in 1851 as the principal seminary for their order. The seminary operation moved to Cincinnati in 1978, and only a few friars remain in Oldenburg to run the parish.

German settlers built most of Oldenburg's handsome homes from bricks they fired themselves. Their descendants, the present townsfolk, remain 95 to 98 percent Catholic and are so proud of their German heritage that they persuaded city fathers, more than fifteen years ago, to translate all street names into German. Thus, Water Street became Wasserstrasse and Main Street, Hauptstrasse. Some merchants followed suit by translating company names, too.

WHAT TO SEE

Convent of the Immaculate Conception. Hauptstrasse 229, Oldenburg 47036. Mother Theresa's original school and orphanage is now the motherhouse for the order she founded, the Third Order of Sisters of St. Francis of Oldenburg, Indiana, now numbering some 400 nuns assigned posts throughout the Midwest. The complex includes a girls' academy, a novitiate for inviting women to consider religious life, the convent proper, a retirement home, and an infirmary for members of the order.

The sisters offer tours at 10:00 A.M. and 1:30 P.M. Tuesday–Saturday. They advise travelers who wish to tour the grounds to make arrangements by calling the convent at (812) 934-2475.

The sisters also operate **Michaela Farm,** located 2 blocks from the convent. In 1854 the farm was started to provide food for the hundreds of sisters, students, and orphans of Immaculate Conception. Today, the 300-acre farm provides meat, produce, milk, and herbs for use by the sisters and the farm community. In addition to raising food, Michaela Farm is a tool for growing spirituality and environmental stewardship. Educational programs and tours highlight organic gardening and also advocate using herbs, whole foods, massage, and other natural-health practices to promote well-being. A tour of the farm takes visitors through beefalo pastures, a barn, vegetable gardens, orchards, a children's garden, a contemplation house, and beehives. A more extensive tour takes you down the reservoir nature trail, where wood ducks, turtles, frogs, and a host of bird species are frequently spotted. Free tours are offered, 1:00 to 4:00 P.M Sunday May through October. Drop-ins are welcome to register and take a limited self-guided tour 9:00 A.M. to 2:00 P.M. daily. Group tours are offered for a small fee. Call (812) 933-0661.

WHERE TO EAT

Koch's Brau Haus. Wasserstrasse, Oldenburg 47036. Pronounced "Cook's" Brau Haus, this is a favorite spot locally for quaffing beer and loading up on fried chicken, shrimp, steaks, pizza, or sand-wiches. $. ☐. Open daily for lunch and dinner; Sunday breakfast buffet. Closed Easter, Thanksgiving, and Christmas. For hours call (812) 934-4840.

Wagner's Tavern & Family Restaurant. Hauptstrasse, Olden-burg 47036. More good home cooking is available at this restaurant, noted for pan-fried chicken. $. ☐. Open daily for lunch and dinner. Call (812) 934-3854.

SPECIAL EVENTS

Freudenfest (Fun Festival). The town erupts in a Teutonic frenzy in late July, with German food, dancing, and music. No phone.

BATESVILLE, INDIANA

Continue 2.5 miles south on Ind. 229 past the junction of Interstate 74 and follow the signs to the Sherman House, an inn since 1852.

WHAT TO SEE

Weberding's Carving Shop. 1230 Ind. 46 East. Decorative and elaborate hand-carved woodwork fills this custom woodworking shop. While visitors are allowed in only one of the dozen buildings that make up Weberding's, there is plenty of wooden wonder to appreciate. Watch as three generations of Weberding craftworkers carve custom furniture, fireplace mantels, entertainment centers, one-of-a-kind stair railings, and more, mostly by hand, one piece at a time. Weberding's carves for both homes and public buildings. A number of Cincinnati churches, businesses, and breweries are adorned with furniture and decorative accents made here, such as the carved eagle moldings that grace the Cincinnati Federal Building. Tours stop in the showroom, which is brimming with uniquely carved pieces, including a spectacular 2-foot mahogany replica of England's royal coach; a 4-foot-tall knotty pine camel; and a refurbished, hand-painted, antique, wooden carousel horse. The gift shop offers reproductions of Weberding carvings. Open for tours 8:00 to 10:00 A.M. and 12:30 to 3:30 P.M. Group tours offered by appointment. Call (812) 934-3710.

WHERE TO EAT AND STAY

The Sherman House. 35 South Main Street, Batesville 47006. Founded in the decade before the Civil War, the Sherman House is a typical inn of the period, with a restaurant on the first floor and guest rooms upstairs. Since it continues to enjoy a fine reputation in the area, it seldom is short of customers. Therefore, we suggest reservations, especially on weekends. Sherman House specialties include lobster from the tank, Wiener schnitzel, steak Diane, peppersteak, and a fine salad bar with homemade relishes. $$. ☐. Open 6:30 A.M. to 8:45 P.M. Monday–Thursday, 6:30 A.M. to 9:45 P.M. Friday and Saturday, and 6:30 A.M. to 7:45 P.M. Sunday. Closed Christmas and New Year's Day. Call (812) 934-2407 or (800) 445-4939.

From Batesville you can return to Cincinnati via Interstate 74 eastbound, or you can continue your travels with Trip 2 of this chapter.

SPECIAL EVENTS

Batesville Music and Arts Festival. Held the third week in June at the Batesville High School. This celebration of musical entertainment has been a Batesville tradition for more than twenty-six years. Entertainment begins on Wednesday with the Cincinnati Pops and fireworks and continues in grand style through Friday. Performances nightly from 7:30 to 10:00 p.m. No admission fee. (812) 934-7675.

Apple Fest. Held the last weekend in September in Liberty Park. Celebrate the food guaranteed to keep the doctor away. Enjoy local crisp, juicy apples, cider, and sweet apple butter. Family fun, games, music, fine arts, crafts, food, and entertainment. No admission fee. (812) 933-6103.

INDIANAPOLIS

70

485

52

Morristown

Connersville

27

74

9

44

121

37

Metamora

229

Oldenburg

52

Greensburg

46

Batesville

74

Bloomington

Nashville

Columbus

275

46

Gnaw Bone

CINCINN

Belmont

INDIANA

Belleview

338

Big Bone
Lick

Rabbit
Hash

65

Markland
Dam

42

156

Vevay

Madison

36

56

42

Warsaw

Carrollton

227

7

62

OHIO RIVER

KENTUCKY

Jeffersonville

Clarksville

LOUISVILLE

Frankford

64

31W

31E

60

1638

44

Otter Creek
Park

Fort Knox

Day Trip 2 Northwest

0   10   20   30 miles

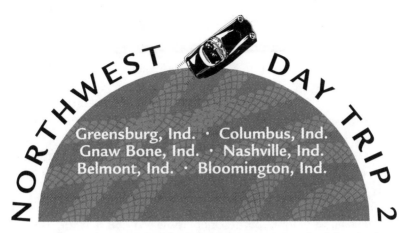

Greensburg, Ind. · Columbus, Ind.
Gnaw Bone, Ind. · Nashville, Ind.
Belmont, Ind. · Bloomington, Ind.

When they said, "Head for the hills!" this area must have been what they meant. We speak of the south-central Indiana highlands centering upon Brown County, rising incongruously from the broad, relatively flat plain around them.

For nearly two centuries these hills collected trappers, frontiersmen, renegades, hermits, and others seeking solitude. It is said that many Brown Countians are descended from men who came here to avoid military conscription during the Civil War.

Little backwoods communities with names like Gnaw Bone, Stoney Lonesome, Bean Blossom, and Scarce O'Fat Ridge slumbered unmolested in the forested highlands until the 1920s, when they were discovered by artists. Some of the paintings done here achieved international recognition and prompted thousands to come see this Midwestern Shangri-la where handsomely antlered deer browse by the roadsides and rocky creeks tumble through the hollows. Brown County was no longer alone.

Our route passes through Columbus, Indiana, with its growing collection of top-name architecture; visits Brown County; and continues to Bloomington, the university town that was the setting of the bicycling film classic *Breaking Away*.

GREENSBURG, INDIANA

From Cincinnati take Interstate 74 west past Batesville and then 16 miles to the Greensburg exit. Please note commentary in Trip 1 of this chapter on Batesville's Sherman House.

Greensburg is known in southern Indiana for two peculiar arboreal and historical quirks. The first is the large-toothed aspen growing boldly out of the top of the handsome Decatur County Courthouse. No one drives through Greensburg without stopping to gaze upon or photograph the tree. It simply is the thing to do. The tree has been here for at least fifty years. After it was mentioned in Ripley's nationally syndicated column, "Believe It or Not," townsfolk began enjoying its prominence. It is listed as a landmark on some state maps.

The second unique—but less noticeable—landmark is the "Center of U.S. Population" monument located just south of Greensburg. The story goes that in 1890, U.S. engineers in Washington examined westward expansion, calculated the center of our national population, and landed a finger right on Decatur County, Indiana. More than 10,000 people descended upon the village for the dedication of the 9,500-pound Bedford stone monument. Greensburg claimed the unusual title for only one decade, of course, until the next census report showed that the center of the U.S. population had moved even farther west.

In Greensburg pick up Ind. 46 westbound, the main route for the remainder of this trip.

COLUMBUS, INDIANA

Columbus, a city of 37,000 seated on flatlands 28 miles west of Greensburg, styles itself the "Athens of the Prairie" because of its formidable, and growing, collection of buildings designed by top-name architects.

The city is home to Cummins Incorporated, one of the largest diesel-engine manufacturers in the world. In 1938 the congregation of the First Christian Church hired the renowned Finnish architect Eliel Saarinen to design a new church. To encourage high-quality architecture, the Cummins Foundation paid for the design of other public buildings. Since then, more than sixty such buildings have been built and more are planned. Besides Eliel Saarinen, noted architects have included his son, Eero Saarinen, designer of the Gateway Arch in St. Louis, and I. M. Pei, Kevin Roche, Eliot Noyes, John Carl Warnecke, Harry Weese, Richard Meier, and Cesar Pelli.

In the midst of all this concrete, stainless steel, and glass, it is interesting to reflect upon the first building in this county, a log cabin built about 1810 on the banks of the White River by General John Tipton. In 1829 Tipton donated twenty acres for a county seat, and for a while the growing town was called Tiptona. Changing political winds, however, renamed it Columbus. Tipton distinguished himself throughout the state, and Indiana named both a city and a county after him.

WHAT TO SEE

Columbus Visitors Center. 506 Fifth Street, Columbus 47201. The center is housed in a restored nineteenth-century home and has exhibits, a laser audiovisual presentation about the city, a Chihuly chandelier, and a gift shop. Bus tours are available by reservation only. The center provides walking- and driving-tour maps for self-guided tours. The center is open 9:00 A.M. to 5:00 P.M. Monday–Saturday and 10:00 A.M. to 4:00 P.M. Sunday, March–November. Call (800) 468-6564, or visit www.colombus.in.us.

First Christian Church. 531 Fifth Street, Columbus 47201. Designed by Eliel Saarinen and opened in 1942, this was the first edifice built by a world-class architect and was one of the first churches in the nation built in contemporary style. The church office is open 8:00 A.M. to 5:00 P.M. Monday–Friday. Closed holidays and during church services. Call (812) 379-4491.

The Commons. 302 Washington Street, Columbus 47201. This downtown public building entirely encloses a shopping mall, a children's playground, kids commons, the Indianapolis Museum of Art-Columbus Gallery, movie theaters, and restaurants. It was designed by Cesar Pelli. The mall's centerpiece is a huge, motorized "sculpture in motion" entitled *Chaos I,* by the Swiss artist Jean Tinguely. A Rube Goldberg–type contraption with pullies, mobiles, spindles, armatures, and wheels, all moving at various speeds, it is engrossing. The artist said the sculpture is intended to reflect the motion of human activity. The area arts council offers many excellent and free family entertainment programs throughout the year. For hours and information on programs, call the Columbus Arts Council at (812) 376-2535.

Eero Saarinen Buildings. The Gateway Arch creator made two notable contributions to Columbus. His first, in 1954, was the *Irwin Union Bank & Trust Company* building at Fifth and Washington Streets—the first all-glass bank building in the United States. Added later were a three-story glass arcade and courtyard. The bank is open from 9:00 A.M. to 4:30 P.M. Monday–Friday and from 9:00 A.M. to noon Saturday. Call (812) 372-0111. Ten years later Saarinen designed the *North Christian Church* (Tipton Lane just off U.S. 31), a hexagonal building with a gleaming, 192-foot metal spire. He has said he was exceptionally pleased with this church and considered it one of the best examples of his work. Visiting hours vary. Open for services only on Sunday. Call (812) 372-1531.

Irwin Gardens. Fifth and Lafayette Streets. These private, formal gardens reflect an early interest in design. They were created in 1910 by Henry A. Phillips and center upon an Italianate waterfall-pond and an ancient well. The well was unearthed and brought here from Pompeii, the Italian village that was buried by an eruption of Mt. Vesuvius in A.D. 79. Open seasonally to the public 9:00 A.M. to 4:00 P.M. Saturday and Sunday only. No phone.

Otter Creek Clubhouse and Golf Course. 11522 East County Route 50 North, Columbus 47203. Harry Weese designed the clubhouse to complement Robert Trent Jones's championship course, site of the 1991 U.S. Public Links championship. Nine new holes were designed by Rees Jones in 1995. Open all year. Call (812) 579-5227.

WHERE TO EAT

American Cafe. In the Ramada Inn, Ind. 46 at Interstate 65. A popular restaurant featuring steak Diane, seafood, and prime rib. Weekend reservations suggested. $$. ☐. For hours call (812) 376-3051.

Zaharako's Confectionery. 329 Washington Street, Columbus 47201. Across from the Commons, this is the ultimate ice-cream parlor, with homemade ice cream and other goodies. A 40-foot marble counter with onyx pillars, stained glass, and mahogany set the stage for the massive pipe organ, which entertains with Gay Nineties music. Open 10:00 A.M. to 5:00 P.M. Monday–Saturday. Call (812) 379-9329.

WHERE TO STAY

The Columbus Inn. 445 Fifth Street, Columbus 47201. Basically a large bed-and-breakfast—thirty-four rooms and suites—located in the elegantly restored 1895 City Hall. Directly across from the visitors center, the inn is a nice contrast to all of Columbus's contemporary architecture. Call (812) 378-4289.

GNAW BONE, INDIANA

Backwoods country begins almost as soon as you pass the junction of Interstate 65, 2 miles west of Columbus. Ind. 46 begins to rise into the hills, and for the next 35 miles few paved roads intersect it. The rest are gravel or dirt trails that wind through the forested hills and hollows. Exploring them is not particularly recommended, and, in fact, we must warn you against it on rainy days, when such roads are subject to deep mires and flash floods.

Gnaw Bone, 12 miles west of Interstate 65, is a corruption of the French name Narbonne, reportedly bestowed by eighteenth-century French trappers. There is virtually nothing to do in Gnaw Bone, but the name is so intriguing that it's fun to tell friends you have visited there.

WHAT TO SEE AND DO

Sorghum Mill. Just off Ind. 46. Watch for signs, starting about a mile before you get to Gnaw Bone, that will direct you a short distance from the highway, where roadside stands have been set up for the sale of sorghum molasses. Nearby you can watch farmers pressing sugar cane in a horse-driven mill. The sap is boiled down in troughs in a cooking shed, while the delicious scent spreads through the woods. Also sold is sugar candy. Recipes are available for making sorghum candy and cookies at home. Sorghum Mill operates from late summer through the fall, or until all the sorghum is made. There's no phone out there in the woods, so you'll have to play this one by ear.

NASHVILLE, INDIANA

The 6 miles between Gnaw Bone and Nashville take you past the entrance to Brown County State Park on the south (left) side of Ind. 46. This is the northern extremity of the 200,000-acre Hoosier National Forest. From the park's roads and overlooks, there are broad vistas over the highlands, with the great hardwood forest fading away blue in the distance, unmarred by traces of humans. In the valley below are occasional glimpses of Lake Monroe, which was created by a dam on the White River. So many log cabins have been found in these hills—more than 500 by local count—that Brown County is sometimes called "Log Cabin Country."

Nashville, the county seat, has some fine homes and a courthouse, but until a few decades ago, its business district was little more than a general store and a gas station at the crossroads.

In 1907 artist T. C. (Theodore) Steele moved to Brown County, and other artists followed him. Together, they founded the Brown County Art Gallery Association in 1926. Steele's paintings gained international attention and brought attention, too, to these scenic hills. Drama students at Indiana University in nearby Bloomington established their summer playhouse here. The Nashville House opened, and the general store added a fine country restaurant. Now visitors come to Nashville in droves.

Today this little town of 900 souls offers more than 250 specialty shops, a number of antiques stores, boutiques and art galleries, sixteen restaurants (excluding twelve shops dedicated solely to ice cream and candy), and more than 100 lodging sites, including hotels, motels, bed-and-breakfasts, and cabins. On any given summer day, these sites are brimming with visitors, who typically outnumber the town's own population.

In October, when fall spreads glorious color across the hills, crowds are extreme and Nashville is overwhelmed. While you certainly will not be alone if you head to Nashville during this seasonal outburst, the community is sensitive to visitors' needs and constantly reviews what it can do for tourists. Your stay is sure to be pleasant, even when there's a crowd.

Late spring is ideal. Summer is good, though late summer is better, and September is also a good choice. Winter draws tourists too, because of skiing opportunities.

WHAT TO SEE

Brown County Convention and Visitors Bureau. Main and Van Buren Streets, Nashville 47448. The bureau has information on what to see and do and where to stay in Nashville and the surrounding area. Open 9:00 A.M. to 6:00 P.M. Monday–Thursday, 9:00 A.M. to 8:00 P.M. Friday and Saturday, and 10:00 A.M. to 3:00 P.M Sunday. Call (800) 753-3255 or (812) 988-7303, or check out www.browncounty.com.

Brown County Art Gallery. One Artist Drive, Nashville 47448. There are many art displays in Nashville, and this exhibit is among the best. It is operated by the original Brown County Art Gallery Association. Permanent and changing exhibits include works by T. C. Steele and other early Brown County artists, plus contemporary Hoosier artists. The gallery is open 10:00 A.M. to 5:00 P.M. Monday–Saturday and noon to 5:00 P.M. Sunday. Open weekends only in January and February. Closed Thanksgiving, Christmas, and New Year's Day. Admission fee. Call (812) 988-4609.

Brown County Art Guild. Van Buren Street, Nashville 47448. The fine exhibit here on the main thoroughfare features early and current Brown County Guild members and is regularly changed. In addition, the permanent collection of Marie Goth is housed here. The works are for sale. Open March–December 10:00 A.M. to 5:00 P.M. Monday–Saturday and noon to 5:00 P.M. Sunday, except Thanksgiving and Christmas. Open in January and February on weekends, 10:00 A.M. to 5:00 P.M. Saturday and noon to 5:00 P.M. Sunday, or by appointment during the week. Call (812) 988-6185.

Brown County Playhouse. Van Buren Street, Nashville 47448. As they have for more than fifty years, Indiana University students and professional actors perform Broadway musicals and dramas, children's plays, and original productions. Admission fee. Performances are held Wednesday through Sunday, mid-June through August, and Friday through Sunday, mid-September through mid-October. Two special matinees are presented during the season. All other performances are at 8:00 P.M. For information call (812) 855-1103 or (812) 988-2123 (June–October).

Country Time Jamboree. 2887 West Ind. 46, Nashville 47448. This 400-seat theater-in-a-barn is the setting for live country music by the Country Time Jamboree Band. The band plays a variety of country, bluegrass, and gospel music, interspersed with comedy. Call (812) 335-9895.

Melchior Marionette Theatre. West side of South Van Buren. Don't miss this one-of-a-kind, twenty-minute live show featuring nearly life-sized, hand-crafted marionettes. Performances take place in a small outdoor theater. Admission is charged. Performances are held Saturday and Sunday at 1:00 P.M. and 3:00 P.M. June, July, September, and October. Additional performances are held in October and December. Call (800) 849-4853.

Little Nashville Opry. Three-quarters of a mile southwest of Nashville on Ind. 46. The biggest names in country music perform here during the March-to-November season. Shows are at 6:00 and 9:30 P.M. Saturday only. Tickets are available from the Opry 9:00 A.M. to 5:00 P.M. Tuesday through Thursday, and 10:00 A.M. to 10:00 P.M. Friday and Saturday. Little Nashville Express, the house band, performs from 8:00 to 11:00 P.M. on Friday. Admission fee. For tickets by mail, write P.O. Box B, Nashville, IN 47448. Call (812) 988-2235.

Alexander Carriage Rides. North Van Buren, Nashville 47448. Enjoy a romantic ride through Nashville. For hours call (812) 988-8230.

Ski World Recreation Area. Located on Ind. 46 west of Nashville. This center for family recreation activities is open year-round. Call (812) 988-6638. Don't miss their newest addition, the **Pine Box Musical Theatre.** It features the "Good Time Gals and Guys" and offers a variety of music and fun-filled antics. Open February through December. For show information call (800) 685-9624.

WHERE TO SHOP

Some folks compare Nashville to Gatlinburg in terms of the number of places to shop, but the emphasis here is more upscale, with many shops offering unusual craft items such as pottery, weaving, and furniture that are often difficult to find elsewhere.

Nashville House Country Store. Van Buren and Main Streets. Built of local sandstone and log, this is the town's original general store. It has enticing aromas of herbs, teas, and spices. Nashville House sells a wide array of old-fashioned goods, including iron cookware cast by a foundry in Tennessee, kitchen crockery and stoneware, glassware, candles, stone-ground meal, hard candies, molasses, honey, and preserves. There is enough here to outfit a complete pioneer kitchen, including pots designed for use on the hearth. Open 11:30 A.M. to 8:00 P.M. daily except Tuesday. Open seven days a week in October. Call (812) 988–4554.

Brown County Craft Gallery. 58 East Main Street, Nashville 47448. Local artisans bring their wares here for display and sale. You will find beautiful baskets, jewelry, pottery, wood crafts, and stained-glass art. For hours call (812) 988–7058.

WHERE TO EAT

Nashville has many places to eat, and the restaurants are primarily tucked in between the shops that line Main Street and Van Buren. These are two of the best.

Nashville House. Van Buren and Main Streets. The most popular place in town is annexed to the old general store and features all the local specialties: fried chicken, hickory-smoked ham, barbecued ribs, fried biscuits with homemade apple butter, and fresh vegetables in season. The Nashville House bakery supplies both store and restaurant with homemade breads, cobblers, and pies. No alcohol is served, $$. ☐. Closed Tuesday except in October. Weekend reservations strongly recommended. Reservations available every month but October. For hours call (812) 988–4554.

The Ordinary. Van Buren Street, Nashville 47448. This restaurant features colonial dishes in a colonial atmosphere, with wild game the specialty. The menu includes pheasant, turkey, roast pork, loin of beef, and seafood. $$. ☐. Closed Monday, except in October. Closed Thanksgiving, Christmas Eve, Christmas Day, New Year's Eve, and New Year's Day. Reservations recommended. For hours call (812) 988–6166.

Calories. Calories. Calories. Nashville also has more than ten stores that sell candy, treats, and great junk-food snacks. Among them are **Jack & Jill Nut Shop** on South Van Buren (812–988–7480) and **Schwab's Fudge, Inc.** on Calvin Place (812–988–6723). **The Candy Emporium,** 58 West Main Street, offers fudge, old-fashioned candy, more than a hundred kinds of licorice, and an intriguing selection of teas and tea accessories. Call (812) 988–1488.

WHERE TO STAY

The Convention and Visitors Bureau lists privately owned cabins and cottages that can be rented in the Nashville area, and can also recommend several bed-and-breakfasts. Six campgrounds and many area motels offer a variety of accommodations.

Brown County Inn. South end of Van Buren Street (junction of Ind. 46 and Ind. 135). A colorful, long-established inn resembling a forest lodge, this popular hostelry is usually well-booked, and on weekends in October, sold out. It is wise to make reservations. The inn features an indoor-outdoor pool, a playground, a full-service restaurant, tennis, miniature golf, and Friday- and Saturday-evening entertainment. Golf privileges nearby. Open all year. Call (812) 988–2291 or (800) 772–5249.

Abe Martin Lodge. Two miles east on Ind. 46 in Brown County State Park. Situated on a hilltop overlooking the forest, this modern lodge has guest rooms and a dining room, plus duplex cabins scattered on the brow of the hill. The cabins are basic, just a notch better than "primitive," although modern family cabins have cooking facilities. Standard state park rates generally are half to two-thirds what you'd pay at neighboring commercial establishments. Open all year. Call (812) 988–7316 or 988–4418.

BELMONT, INDIANA

Belmont is 8 miles southwest of Nashville on Ind. 46.

WHAT TO SEE

T. C. Steele State Historic Site. Follow the signs in Belmont to the historic site, which is 1.5 miles south of town on T. C. Steele Road. The state maintains the home, studio, and grounds of one of its most prestigious artists here and exhibits more than 150 of his paintings, including landscapes that brought him international attention. His studio, with huge windows overlooking the Hoosier National Forest, has been kept precisely as he left it. Viewing Steele's works enriches the understanding of Brown County's natural beauty and therefore makes this an especially worthwhile stop. Nature trails and picnicking facilities are available. Open mid-March through mid-December

Tuesday–Saturday 9:00 A.M. to 5:00 P.M. and Sunday 1:00 to 5:00 P.M. Closed Thanksgiving. No admission fee. Call (812) 988-2785.

BLOOMINGTON, INDIANA

If you get the feeling you've been here before, perhaps it's because you saw the movie *Breaking Away,* which was filmed here. The town and the campus of Indiana University were the backdrop for the story of bicycle racing because the Little 500 Bicycle Race is held here annually in late April.

Bloomington, 17 miles west of Nashville on Ind. 46, was founded in 1815 and owes its early development to gristmills and limestone quarries. West and south of town lie the state's great quarries, which produce limestone slab for architectural facings. Many, if not most, of Washington's public buildings and many of New York's and Chicago's skyscrapers as well as many of Bloomington's own buildings are sheathed with Indiana limestone.

WHAT TO SEE

Indiana University. Five blocks northeast of the Public Square. IU is one of four state-supported universities. It was founded in 1820 as the Indiana State Seminary and has more than 35,000 students. The university's massive buildings—built with Indiana limestone, of course—lie on a hilly, beautifully wooded campus and include several points of interest for visitors. Of particular interest are the glowing Thomas Hart Benton murals in the IU auditorium, Woodburn Hall, and the magnificent trees all over the campus. For information call the Bloomington Convention and Visitors Bureau at (812) 334-8900 or (800) 800-0037.

Musical Arts Center. IU Campus, South Jordan Avenue, Bloomington 47401. This 1,460-seat auditorium was built in 1972 in a contemporary style. It stages more than one hundred opera, ballet, and symphony performances each year. Call (812) 855-7433.

The Lilly Library. IU Campus, Fine Arts Plaza, East Seventh Street, Bloomington 47401. Named for the wealthy Indiana pharmaceutical family that endowed it, this library houses more than 400,000 rare books and some six million manuscripts, including medieval writings, Lincoln papers, and a Gutenberg Bible. Open 9:00 A.M. to 6:00 P.M. Monday–Friday and 9:00 A.M. to 1:00 P.M. Saturday. Tours available upon request. Call (812) 855-2452.

Indiana University Art Museum. IU Campus, Fine Arts Plaza, East Seventh Street, Bloomington 47401. One of the most modern museum structures in the nation, the IU museum was designed by the noted architectural firm of I. M. Pei, which also designed the contemporary wing of the National Gallery in Washington, D.C. The $11 million IU museum opened in the fall of 1982 and consists of two striking triangular buildings linked by a 3-story, skylighted atrium.

More than 30,000 items of artistic, historical, and anthropological interest are contained on four gallery levels. They include African, Oceanic, and early American art, as well as a large collection of nineteenth- and twentieth-century art. A particularly fine collection representing ancient Mediterranean cultures includes some 5,000 pieces of ancient jewelry. No admission fee. Open 10:00 A.M. to 5:00 P.M. Tuesday–Saturday and noon to 5:00 P.M. Sunday. Call (812) 855-5445.

Indiana Memorial Union. 900 East Seventh Street, Bloomington 47405. The world's largest college union, the historic Indiana Memorial Union (IMU) houses an impressive collection of more than 1,200 paintings, sculptures, and other works of art. A full-service luxury hotel is also located here. Stop by the front desk to pick up directions for a walking tour of the art collection. Several restaurants, a billiard room, hair and barber salons, an IU gift shop, and other amenities call IMU home. Just outside the union, Beck Chapel and the Dunn family graveyard, the final resting place for members of a family of IU benefactors, are interesting historic university sites. Call (800) 209-8145.

Assembly Hall. Seventeenth Street, Bloomington 47401. A visit to IU, where basketball is almost a religion, is not complete without stopping by Assembly Hall, home of one of the richest traditions in college basketball. This $14 million, 17,500-seat basketball arena was considered state-of-the-art upon its completion in 1971. Trophy cases house IU basketball memorabilia, and the Big Red Gift Shop offers IU logo gear and gifts. Just a couple of free throws to the east, Memorial Stadium is home to IU football. Both facilities employ a unique egg-shaped design that places most seats between the ends of the floor or field. Call (812) 855-2794 for hours or (800) 447-GOIU (4648) for event tickets.

Oliver Winery. Seven miles north of Bloomington on Ind. 37. If you're heading on to Indianapolis, this stop is on your way. Now consider this for a special and inexpensive date: Enjoy free samples in the impressive 2,400-square-foot tasting room, then indulge in an inexpensive picnic and bottle of wine as you wander the beautiful grounds—giving full meaning to the courtship line, "A loaf of bread [or cheese and crackers], a jug of wine, and thou."

The tasting room, where you can sample the seventeen wines made here, is open during business hours, and the winery staff offers tours on Friday, Saturday, and Sunday afternoons or by appointment. Open 10:00 A.M. to 6:00 P.M. Monday–Saturday and noon to 6:00 P.M. Sunday. Closed Thanksgiving, Christmas, New Year's Day, and Election Day. Call (812) 876-5800 or (800) 25-TASTE.

Visitor Information. For information contact the Bloomington Convention and Visitors Bureau, 2855 North Walnut, Bloomington 47404. Call (812) 334-8900 or (800) 800-0037.

The Lake Monroe Visitors Center, 3 miles east of Bloomington on Ind. 46 and 5 miles south of Ind. 446 at Paynetown State Recreation Area, also has information on water sports, camping, and other lake activities. Call (812) 837-9546.

WHERE TO EAT AND STAY

Because so many of IU's students are from all over the world, Bloomington is blessed with a variety of ethnic restaurants. The visitors center can help you select one, but these campus traditions are worth mentioning.

Mother Bear's. 1428 East Third Street, Bloomington 47401. It's just pizza, but generations of students swear by it. $. Call (812) 332-4495.

Nick's. 423 East Kirkwood, Bloomington 47408. Its dark paneled walls are festooned with more than fifty years of IU memorabilia, and the atmosphere and menu are classic college town. Good sandwiches and subs. $. ☐. Call (812) 332-4040.

Lennie's Brewpub. 1795 East Tenth Street, Bloomington 47408. Bloomington's only microbrewery, Lennie's offers a good selection of potables brewed on the premises. Order the brew sampler to taste them all. A full menu features unique appetizers and salads, including tasty grilled veggies on focaccia. $. ☐. Call (812) 323-2112 for hours. **Scholars Inn Dessert Cafe and Wine Bar.** 801 North College Avenue, Bloomington 47404. The clubby, academic feel of this 150-year-old mansion is blended with ultra-modern decor, classic poetic wine references, and a piano bar to create an unusual gathering place that's fast becoming a Bloomington hot spot. Scholars Inn's appetizer-size entrees, such as shrimp scampi and beef tenderloin sandwiches, mirror the architecture: classic favorites with a funky, eclectic touch. The menu of indulgent desserts includes renowned Bananas Foster. Order one of the popular "flights" of wine for a sampling of three vintages for the price of a glass. In warmer months, the French porch and a patio provide ample alfresco dining. Right next door, Scholars Inn Bed-and-Breakfast offers equally interesting overnight accommodations. $. ☐. Call (812) 332-1892.

Grant Street Inn. 310 North Grant Street, Bloomington 47408. Period antiques and reproductions fill this 1880s home. The twenty-four rooms were renovated, and guest cottages and an annex were added when this historic house was moved across town to avoid the wrecking ball. Lovely suites feature Jacuzzis and fireplaces. All guests are treated to a lavish breakfast buffet. Call (800) 328-4350 for reservations.

Fourwinds Resort and Marina. 8 miles south of Bloomington on Ind. 37, then 3 miles east on Smithville Road and another 3 miles south on Fairfax Road. Situated on the shores of Lake Monroe overlooking the Hoosier National Forest, this quiet hideaway is reminiscent of out-of-the-way hostelries tucked away in the English countryside—except for its range of activities. Guests and campers on the grounds have access to beach swimming, boating, tennis, golf, a whirlpool bath, an indoor-outdoor pool, and in-room movies. Fourwinds' signature restaurant, **Tradewinds,** gives diners an extraordinary view and an interesting menu that features ever-changing regional and seasonal specialties. A champagne brunch is offered on Sunday. $$. ☐. For hours and reservations, call (800) 538-1187 or (812) 824-9904.

You can go back to Cincinnati by returning along the same route that brought you here, Ind. 46 east to Greensburg and Interstate 74 east to Cincinnati, or you can continue to the next trip, Indianapolis, via Ind. 37 north, a divided highway.

Indiana's capital, and its largest city, is 106 miles northwest of Cincinnati via Interstate 74, almost exactly a two-hour drive. Indianapolis's metro area sprawls across nine counties on the broad, flat plains of central Indiana.

Interstate 74 dead-ends at Southeastern Avenue. To reach the city's center, bear right onto Southeastern and follow it onto U.S. 40, with which it merges. U.S. 40 (Washington Street) then leads into the downtown area.

From Bloomington follow Ind. 37 north to Interstate 465, which circles the city; go east on Interstate 465 to Interstate 65; and then follow 65 north to the Washington Street (U.S. 40) exit.

INDIANAPOLIS, INDIANA

Like Washington, D.C., Indianapolis was founded specifically as a capital. When the state of Indiana was carved from the Northwest Territories in 1816, its first capital was established at Corydon, near the Ohio River and only a few miles from Louisville, Kentucky. Steamboats had started plying the Ohio just five years earlier. Being near that traffic linked Corydon to the life and times of the nation.

But Corydon was, in fact, farther from Indiana's northern shores along Lake Michigan than it was from Ohio, Illinois, or even Tennessee. The hardship of traveling the entire length of Indiana to do business in Corydon prompted state founders to set up a ten-member commission to find a more suitable site for a permanent capital. The commission did its job well. Indianapolis, laid out in 1820, is smack dead-center in the middle of the state.

Day Trip 3 Northwest

0   10   20   30 miles

The city has grown to fill every corner of Marion County—a perfect square—and is now one of the largest cities in the Midwest and consistently selected as one of the most livable cities in the United States. It is an important manufacturing, high-technology, sports, insurance, grain, and livestock center. Its name is a combination of *Indiana* and the Greek ending *polis,* meaning "city." Since 1979 the city has staged more than 400 national and international championships. With such scheduled events as the World Basketball Championship, the World Gymnastics Championships, and the World Swimming Championships, the city will continue to shine in the sports world. Indianapolis also is home to numerous national sports-governing bodies, including the National Collegiate Athletic Association. The NCAA's campus features the Hall of Champions, an interactive museum saluting the student-athlete experience. Indianapolis also commands the sports world's attention with the Indianapolis 500 in late May, the Brickyard 400 every August, and the United States Grand Prix Formula One event in September. These three races represent the world's three largest sporting events. On race weekends, upward of 400,000 fans witness the thrilling "Drivers, start your engines" and enjoy day-long events.

GETTING AROUND

Indy, as the Hoosiers affectionately call it, is flat as a board, and all the streets lie in easy-to-follow patterns. Main thoroughfares converge like the spokes of a wheel, after the design of Washington, upon the Soldier's & Sailor's Monument, the center of town.

Meridian Street (U.S. 31) runs north-south, neatly splitting the city into halves. Washington Street (U.S. 40, the Old National Road) is the major east-west artery, intersecting Meridian 1 block south of the monument. Addresses are designated "east" or "west" from Meridian Street and "north" or "south" from Washington Street. DIRECTION DOWNTOWN signs direct visitors to each of the four quads in the downtown area. Our references in this chapter to the city "center" refer to Monument Circle, the visual and geographic center of the city, 1 block north of that intersection.

Visitor Information. If you have a couple of weeks before heading into Indianapolis, we urge you to contact the Indianapolis Convention & Visitors Association to request a copy of its most recent seasonal guide for the city. The association is located at One

RCA Dome, Suite 100, Indianapolis 46225. Call (800) 468–INDY or visit www.indy.org. Once in the city, if you have time, you really should visit the Indianapolis City Center in the Pan Am Building, 201 South Capitol Avenue. The City Center is an attraction in itself, with brochures, maps on everything there is to see and do in the Circle City, discounts on some attractions, and a lovely gift shop. Open 10:00 A.M. to 5:30 P.M. Monday–Friday, 10:00 A.M. to 5:00 P.M. Saturday, and noon to 5:00 P.M. Sunday. Call (317) 237–5200 or (800) 468–INDY.

WHAT TO SEE DOWNTOWN

Soldier's & Sailor's Monument. Meridian Street at Monument Circle. This recently refurbished colossus of sculpted stone rises 284 feet above the circle and is floodlit at night. It has images of the state's heroes, and fountains streaming into pools at its base. The lower level houses a Colonel Eli Lilly Civil War museum. An elevator leads to a glass-enclosed observation deck at the top that offers a fine panorama of the city and surrounding communities. (Note to summer travelers: For health reasons the observation deck is closed when the temperature in it exceeds ninety-five degrees.) During the Christmas season the monument is strung with thousands of colored lights for the annual Circle of Lights Celebration. Open 9:00 A.M. to 6:00 P.M. Wednesday–Sunday. Closed Monday, Tuesday, and major holidays. No admission fee. Call (317) 232–7615.

World War Memorial Plaza. A 5-block complex along Meridian Street beginning 6 blocks north of the monument at New York Street. This is the hub of civic activities and is dedicated to those who died in the nation's wars of this century.

Proceeding from south to north, the first block is an area of greenery known as University Park. Dominating the complex in the center of the next block is the World War Memorial Shrine, a large colonnaded building of limestone and granite. It contains a military museum downstairs and a shrine room upstairs with a 20-by-38-foot American flag on display. Open 9:00 A.M. to 6:00 P.M. Wednesday–Sunday. Closed Monday, Tuesday, and major holidays. Call (317) 232–7615. No admission fee. Near the shrine is a bronze statue, 24 feet high, entitled *Pro Patria,* and representing the spirit of the American soldier.

The central, or third block, has an illuminated fountain. And, proceeding north, are a black obelisk and the flags of all fifty states. The national and state headquarters of the American Legion are also located on this site.

Indiana State Capitol. Washington Street and Capitol Avenue, 2 blocks west of the city's center. It took ten years, from 1878 to 1888, to build this Indiana limestone edifice, a splendid building that has a gleaming copper dome and rises 234 feet above the street. Corinthian in style and refurbished in 1988, it houses the governor's offices, both legislative houses, the state appellate and supreme courts, and other state offices. Tours are by appointment only, 9:00 A.M. to 3:00 P.M. Walking tours (times posted daily) are also available. Open daily except weekends and holidays. Call (317) 233–5293.

American Cabaret Theatre. 401 East Michigan Street, Indianapolis 46204. Relocated to Indianapolis from New York in 1990, this theatrical organization now resides at the renovated theater in Indianapolis's Athenaeum. Call (317) 631–0334.

Indiana State Museum. 202 North Alabama Street, Indianapolis 46204 (at Ohio Street, 1 block north and 3 east of the city's center). The museum building itself is as interesting as the collection it houses. Formerly City Hall, it is listed on the National Register of Historic Places. The exterior is Greek Ionic in style. Inside the spectacular rotunda, massive blue-and-green marble columns support four floors of glowing, hand-carved Indiana walnut, rising 85 feet to a stained-glass dome.

If you have never seen a Foucault pendulum, here is one of three in our travel area. Suspended from the dome, the pendulum appears to trace out a constantly advancing pattern on the floor, but that is an illusion. "Free-hanging," meaning not influenced by its connection at the top, the pendulum actually swings a constant, true line. It is the floor—and the building and the earth it rests upon—that actually moves. By this device the French scientist demonstrated the rotation of the Earth. The other pendulums are in Louisville, Kentucky, and Columbus, Ohio.

The museum is a showplace for Indiana's history, business, art, nature, and popular culture. Exhibits detail everything from an ancient glacier to 1910 Indiana streets to an 1870 black "living history" settlement called Freetown Village. National traveling exhibits in addition to the collections of Indiana sports memorabilia and the radio broadcasting history exhibit are fascinating. Open 9:00 A.M. to 4:45 P.M. Monday–Saturday and noon to 4:45 P.M. Sunday. Free. Call (317) 232–1637. Note: The New Indiana State Museum, expected to open in May 2002 in downtown's White River State Park, with triple the exhibit space as well as the existing IMAX Theater.

The City Market. 222 East Market Street, Indianapolis 46204. This Old World–style marketplace, dating to 1886, is housed in a big brick building that was enlarged in 1977 as part of an urban renewal project. Akin to Cincinnati's Findlay Market in style, it features more than thirty market stalls that purvey meat, fish, poultry, cheeses, pickles, eggs, fruit, vegetables, candy, and bakery goods—most of the businesses having been a family specialty for many years. Shoppers can find interesting ethnic specialties here, and ice is available for your cooler if you want to take some groceries home with you. The complex includes several restaurants. City Market is open 6:00 A.M. to 6:00 P.M. Monday–Saturday. Closed holidays. Call (317) 634–9266.

Indiana Repertory Theater/Indiana Roof Ballroom. 140 West Washington Street, Indianapolis 46204. Saved from the wrecker's ball in 1984, this one-time luxurious 3,000-seat movie palace featuring an intricate terra-cotta facade and auditorium was divided into three stages. Now home to the Indiana Repertory Theater, a professional resident theater, the building also houses the Indiana Roof Ballroom on its top floor. This beautifully restored ballroom is designed to resemble the plaza of a Spanish village and is capped by a 40-foot domed ceiling of stars, able to create snow, fog, bubbles, or a thunderstorm. Performances are held Tuesday through Sunday, September through May. Tours of both facilities by request. Call (317) 635–5277.

WHAT TO SEE AND DO NEAR DOWNTOWN

Lockerbie Square. A 6-block area bounded by New York, College, Michigan, and East Streets. The Lockerbie neighborhood is a restored oasis of nineteenth-century calm close to the downtown area. Cobblestone streets, old-fashioned lighting, and elegant home restorations bring the past to life. A tour of homes is held in June of even-numbered years. Call (317) 488–7752.

Scottish Rite Cathedral. 650 North Meridian Street, Indianapolis 46204. After its completion in 1929, this Tudor/Gothic-style cathedral was judged by the International Association of Architects to be one of the world's seven most beautiful buildings. The Gothic tower rises 212 feet above street level and includes an enormous carillon with fifty-four bells. Tours offered weekdays from

10:00 A.M. to 3:00 P.M. No admission fee. Closed Saturday and Sunday. Call (317) 262-3100.

The Splatter Zone. 620 South Capitol Avenue, Indianapolis 46225. Two blocks south of the RCA Dome. If you're looking for a break from the ordinary, play paintball, "capture the flag," speedball, and other games. Reservations essential. For reservations and hours call (317) 262-8838.

James Whitcomb Riley Home. 528 Lockerbie Street, Indianapolis 46204. Three blocks north and 5.5 east of the city's center. The home of Indiana's beloved poet is in the middle of the charming Lockerbie area and is considered one of the most perfectly preserved Victorian houses in the United States.

Riley was so fond of this neighborhood that he wrote a verse to Lockerbie Street. He lived in the fine brick Victorian house at No. 528 the last twenty-three years of his life. Riley died in 1916 at the age of sixty-seven, and for the past eight decades, the home has been preserved as he left it. Open 10:00 A.M. to 4:00 P.M. Tuesday–Saturday and noon to 4:00 P.M. Sunday. Last tours daily at 3:30 P.M. Closed Monday and major holidays. Admission fee. Call (317) 631-5885.

Pres. Benjamin Harrison Home. 1230 North Delaware Street, Indianapolis 46202. Twelve blocks north and 2 east of the city's center. The grandson of William Henry Harrison, Benjamin was born in North Bend, Ohio, a western suburb of Cincinnati, and took up the practice of law in Indiana. He was a Civil War general and later served Indiana in the U.S. Senate.

When he ran for the presidency in 1888, the front porch of this house was the focus of national political attention. It was here that he gave many of his speeches, talked to reporters, and regaled all who would gather to listen about the wasteful ways of his opponent, Grover Cleveland. The real Harrison flair, however, was for short tenure. Grandfather William Henry Harrison had the shortest term of any president, dying of pneumonia after only one month in the White House. Benjamin served a full term, but became the only candidate to beat an incumbent and then be defeated by the same man in the following election. Thus, Cleveland is listed as the twenty-second and twenty-fourth president, with Benjamin Harrison figuring in between as the twenty-third.

Sixteen rooms of the Harrison home have been restored, including the one in which Harrison died in 1901 and a third-floor ballroom, now a museum of the president's personal belongings. After hiking the stairs, one is too tired to dance anyway, Hoosiers say. Some of the first White House china Mrs. Harrison commissioned is on display, and occasionally her gowns and family quilts are displayed as well. Also restored are the herb and rose gardens. The home is open 10:00 A.M. to 3:30 P.M. Monday–Saturday and 12:30 to 3:30 P.M. Sunday. Closed holidays. Admission fee. Call (317) 631–1898.

Indianapolis Zoo. 1200 West Washington Street, Indianapolis 46222. The $64 million zoo opened in 1988 and has been wildly successful. Within walking distance of downtown and one of only a few new zoos to be built from the ground up, it is designed around four biomes, which place animals from various continents in similar habitats—the deserts, the waters, the plains, the forests.

The "cageless" zoo features more than 2,000 animals and one of the world's largest whale and dolphin pavilions, as well as a spectacular viewing area to watch polar bears swim. The unique desert biome represents the world's desert climate and has a spectacular botanical collection. This zoo is also a national leader in breeding endangered species, and is the nation's only tri-accredited facility (as zoo, botanical gardens, and aquarium). Don't miss the Siberian tigers. Open 9:00 A.M. to 4:00 P.M. daily. Hours extended in the summer. Admission fee. Call (317) 630–2030 or visit www.indianapolis. org.

White River Gardens. 1200 West Washington Street, Indianapolis 46222. This stunningly beautiful, 3.3-acre landmark botanical attraction continues the Indianapolis Zoological Society's mission of connecting animals, plants, and people. More than 1,000 plant varieties are on display in this glass-enclosed conservatory. The facility features several themed design gardens and water gardens, a wedding garden for outdoor ceremonies and other events, a resource center, and a gift shop. Admission fee. For hours call (317) 630–2001.

Eiteljorg Museum of American Indians & Western Art. 500 West Washington Street, Indianapolis 46204. A world-class museum that spotlights American Indian and Western art and artifacts, the facility and collection of Indianapolis businessman Harrison Eiteljorg is considered one of the finest of its kind. Highlights are the architecture, its permanent collection of Taos artists, works by Charles Russell and Frederic Remington, groundbreaking special exhibitions, and a wonderful museum store. Open year-round 10:00

A.M. to 5:00 P.M. Tuesday–Saturday and noon to 5:00 P.M. Sunday. Closed Monday (except Memorial Day through Labor Day), Thanksgiving, Christmas, and New Year's Day. Admission fee. Call (317) 636-9378.

Madame Walker Theater and Center. 617 Indiana Avenue, Indianapolis 46202. The theater in this four-story building has been restored to breathtaking beauty, embellished with the African and Egyptian motifs beloved by Madame C. J. Walker, America's first female self-made millionaire, who was also black. Once the center of jazz concerts by Louis Armstrong and Dinah Washington, the Walker Theater and Center are the core of a new renaissance in small jazz clubs and restoration along Indiana Avenue. "Jazz on the Avenue," a rebirth of an old tradition, occurs here every Friday. Tours by appointment. Business office open 8:30 A.M. to 5:30 P.M. Monday–Friday. Call (317) 236-2099.

WHAT TO SEE AND DO: SUBURBAN

The Children's Museum. 3000 North Meridian Street, Indianapolis 46208. Two miles north of the city's center; enter on Illinois Street. Whether you're traveling with children or not, it is worth a trip to Indianapolis just to see this place—the largest children's museum in the world and, many believe, the best, since it opened a huge new wing in 1989. And you needn't be a child to enjoy it. There are countless interesting things you are invited to touch and to tinker with, and who can resist that?

The Welcome Center houses the world's largest water clock, the first in the United States, and the SpaceQuest Planetarium, which takes visitors on a 3-D space voyage. In mid-1990 the Lilly Center for Exploration opened to rave reviews. Designed by adolescents for their peers, the attraction lets youngsters explore "focal topics," such as the environment and waste disposal.

Most kids are fascinated by a fifty-five-ton locomotive and caboose parked at a reassembled turn-of-the-century depot. Then they can relish model trains clattering through a miniworld of mountains, forests, villages, and even a circus. The new, interactive ScienceWorks gallery features a climbing wall, fossil dig, construction site, and sewer room. Elsewhere, there is a life-size dinosaur, as well as a pterodactyl sailing awesomely overhead. You can ride a carousel of hand-carved horses, goats, giraffes, reindeer, lions, and other animals, then

visit an incredible collection of toys and dolls, and the recently renovated carousel gallery. You can explore a simulated limestone cave,
climb aboard an airplane, a space module, or a racing car, and pet
live animals in a minizoo. When you visit Ancient Egypt, you can
stop and say hello to Wenuhotep, a very real and very dead 3,000-
year-old mummy in a reconstructed tomb.

Right next to the Children's Museum, the CineDome houses the
nation's first I-WERKS cinema. This 76-foot domed, large-format
theater is equipped with a state-of-the-art sound and video system
that seems to transport visitors on a host of adventures, from a trip
inside a volcano to a ride on an eagle's wings. The CineDome has a
separate admission fee. Spacequest Planetarium, a 130-seat theater,
features family programs on the universe. Here, high-tech computer
graphics create a world of space-related special effects. A new
museum store encourages hands-on exploration of its different
zones, such as science, arts and crafts, and kid stuff. The renovated
Reflections restaurant offers sandwiches, snacks, and ice-cream.
Open 10:00 A.M. to 5:00 P.M. Tuesday–Sunday. Closed Mondays from
Labor Day to March 1, Thanksgiving, and Christmas. Admission fee.
(Free the first Thursday of each month 5:00 to 8:00 P.M.) Call (317)
334-3322 or visit www.childrensmuseum.org.

Indianapolis Museum of Art. 1200 West 38th Street, Indianapolis 46208. About 3.8 miles north on Meridian Street from
Monument Circle and 1.25 miles west on 38th Street. The museum
is just past Crown Hill Cemetery.

This complex of museum buildings is a former 152-acre estate
purchased in 1932 by the Lilly family and given to the city art association. One of the oldest art museums in the country, the IMA
underwent a massive renovation and expansion in 1990, adding the
new Hulman Pavilion (which houses the Eiteljorg collection of
African art) to the existing Lilly Pavilion of Decorative Arts. The
Krannert and Clowes pavilions house the museum's other comprehensive collections, featuring outstanding Oriental, Renaissance,
and Neo-Impressionist works. A theater, concert area, restaurant,
greenhouse, and shops complete the museum. Open 10:00 A.M. to
5:00 P.M. Tuesday, Wednesday, Friday, and Saturday, 10:00 A.M. to
8:30 P.M. Thursday, and noon to 5:00 P.M. Sunday. Closed Monday
and major holidays. Tours available and recommended. No admission fee. Call (317) 923-1331.

Indianapolis Motor Speedway. 4790 West 16th Street, Indianapolis 46222. On Meridian Street 1.3 miles north of the city's center
and 4.5 miles west on 16th Street. Located in Speedway, an indepen-
dent city entirely surrounded by Indianapolis, this is the home of the
annual Indianapolis 500 in late May, the Brickyard 400 in August, and
the United States Grand Prix Formula One race each September.

The famed Indy 500 race is held on the Sunday of Memorial Day
weekend, with parties, parades, and other events occupying the
entire month of May. Inaugurated in 1994, the Brickyard 400 was
the first major racing event other than the 500 to be held at the
Speedway since 1911. This NASCAR Winston Cup stock car race is
now held annually and is becoming nearly as big an event as the Indianapolis 500. For both weekends, you can expect huge crowds,
traffic jams, and scarce accommodations at premium prices within
50-60 miles of the track, which holds upward of 400,000 spectators.
The US Grand Prix inaugural event held in September 2000 brought
Formula One racing back to the United States.

The rest of the year, travelers can visit the **Hall of Fame
Museum** on the speedway grounds and take a spin around the 2.5
mile track in a minibus that visits the pits and other areas of
interest. The museum has a collection of antique and classic passenger cars, some of them built in Indiana, and more than fifty
racing cars, many of them previous winners of the 500. Car buffs
from all over the United States come here to visit the mecca of
speed and the birthplace of many automotive innovations. The
museum is open 9:00 A.M. to 5:00 P.M. daily except Christmas.
Admission fee. For speedway information call (317) 484-6747. For
500 Festival information call (317) 237-3400.

Conner Prairie. 13400 Allisonville Road, Fishers 46038. Six miles
north of Indianapolis on Interstate 465 via exit 35. This living-history
museum re-creates an Indiana frontier village where it is always 1836
and where the past becomes the present as you watch village residents (skilled actors) explain how to build a bed, dye wool for spinning, or butcher a hog. The schoolmaster puts visitors through their
ABCs and is strong on discipline. Named one of the best living-history museums in the United States, Conner Prairie is not to be missed.
In the summer the Indianapolis Symphony Orchestra presents special
concerts on the Prairie. A beautiful interpretive museum center with
gift shop, exhibitions, classes, and a restaurant, plus a real archaeological dig, completes the activities. Many special events. Admission

fee. For hours call (317) 776-6006 or (800) 866-1836.

Indianapolis Department of Parks and Recreation. 200 East Washington Street, Indianapolis 46204. Prepare to discover or develop the outdoor lover within through an incredible variety of leisure and fitness activities offered. There are more than one hundred public parks in the Indianapolis area—from neighborhood parks to the magnificent Eagle Creek Park—and the recreation selection includes golfing, swimming, hiking, soccer, and biking. For a free seasonal guide, call (317) 327-PARK.

Eagle Creek Park. 7840 West 56th Street, Indianapolis 46254. This is a beautiful and outstanding park—and one of the largest municipal parks in the country, with 4,000 acres of wooded terrain and a 1,300-acre reservoir. It is perfect for sailing, swimming at the beach, canoeing, and kayaking. It is also popular for hayrides in season. Open dawn to dusk. Admission fee. Call (317) 327-7110.

Fort Harrison State Park & Golf Resort. 6002 North Post Road, Indianapolis 46216. Since 1903, Fort Harrison has played an important role in Indiana history. Although the fort was slated for closure in 1991, the U.S. Department of the Interior approved the state of Indiana's request to convert 1,700 acres into a state park and nature preserve. Today, Fort Harrison State Park includes one of the region's largest tracts of unbroken hardwood forest, an eighteen-hole golf course designed by Pete Dye, several small lakes, miles of creek and tributaries, trails, a nature center, and picnic areas. Open 7:00 A.M. to dusk. Call (317) 591-0904.

WHERE TO SHOP

Indianapolis, like all big cities, is full of places to shop, from boutiques to specialty malls. The city's two largest retailers—L. S. Ayres and Lazarus—are fun places to shop, but here are several special places.

The Fashion Mall at Keystone at the Crossing. Keystone Avenue (Ind. 431) at 86th Street, half a mile south of the Interstate 465 interchange with Ind. 431. This is 2 miles east of Meridian Street (U.S. 31) on the extreme north edge of the city.

Keystone is a different sort of shopping center, if one can call it that. It offers more than one hundred shops with a wide range of goods, such as bar supplies, handcrafted furniture, gifts, and leather goods. Restaurant operations range from a pizzeria to a steakhouse.

The mall is open 10:00 A.M. to 9:00 P.M. Monday–Friday, 10:00 A.M. to 6:00 P.M. Saturday, and noon to 5:00 P.M. Sunday. Larger restaurants remain open later. For information call (317) 574-4001.

Circle Centre. 49 West Maryland Street, Indianapolis 46204. Circle Centre has been integral to the startling revitalization downtown Indianapolis has undergone over the last ten years. This 800,000-square-foot retail and entertainment complex includes major department stores as well as nearly one hundred specialty shops, restaurants, nightclubs, a nine-screen movie theater, Steven Spielberg's GameWorks Studio virtual reality theme park, and the Indianapolis Artsgarden, an eight-story glass dome showcasing the local arts scene. Open 10:00 A.M. to 9:00 P.M. Monday through Saturday, and noon to 6:00 P.M. Sunday. The fourth floor entertainment area is open later. Call (317) 681-8000.

Indianapolis Downtown Antique Mall. 1044 Virginia Avenue, Indianapolis 46203, in the historic Fountain Square area 11 blocks southeast of Monument Circle. Forty shops feature a wide variety of antiques and collectibles. Open 10:00 A.M. to 5:00 P.M. Monday–Saturday and noon to 5:00 P.M. Sunday. Call (317) 635-5336.

WHERE TO EAT

Shapiro's Delicatessen. 808 South Meridian, Indianapolis 46225. This cafeteria-style Jewish deli is renowned for dishing up generous portions of corned beef and cabbage, stuffed peppers, heaping deli sandwiches, and luscious strawberry cheesecake. Rye lovers should not miss the crusty, fresh-baked rye bread. $. Open daily and serving breakfast, lunch, and dinner 6:30 A.M. to 8:30 P.M. Call (317) 631-4041.

Slippery Noodle Inn. 372 South Meridian, Indianapolis 46225. This is Indiana's oldest tavern (1850) and one of the city's liveliest night spots. There is live music nightly, including an open stage blues jam on Wednesday. Fare runs the gamut from bar snacks to burgers and full dinners. Open 11:00 to 3:00 A.M., Monday–Saturday, and 4:00 P.M. to 12:30 A.M. Sunday. $$. ❑. Call (317) 631-6974.

Peppy Grill. 1004 Virginia Avenue, Indianapolis 46203. Breakfast is served twenty-four hours a day and biscuits and gravy are just $2.95 and are served 8:00 P.M. to 11:00 A.M. Luncheon specials include meat, potatoes, and vegetable for a low price. Peppy's is one of the few "Yankee" spots where you can get an authentic glass of

Southern-style sweet iced tea. Open all day, every day except Thanksgiving and Christmas. $. Call (317) 637-1158.

Plump's Last Shot. 6416 Cornell Avenue, Indianapolis 46220. This casual pub offers an impressive menu of burgers, including a venison Plumpburger and a black Angus burger. Chicken wings are another favorite at Plump's. The full bar serves a number of beers on tap. Open 11:30 to 3:00 A.M. daily, and 11:30 A.M. to midnight Sunday. $. ❑. Call (317) 257-5867.

Buca di Beppo. 35 North Illinois Street, Indianapolis 46204. Enjoy the warmth and passion of this "immigrant" southern Italian restaurant, where real family recipes combine with a fun, bawdy setting that's reminiscent of the Italian supper clubs of the 1940s and '50s. Spaghetti and meatballs, chicken cacciatore, and rigatoni positano are specialties, served in giant helpings meant to be shared. $$. ❑. Serving dinner 5:00 to 10:00 P.M. Monday–Thursday, 5:00 to 11:00 P.M. Friday, 4:00 to 11:00 P.M. Saturday, and 12:00 to 9:00 P.M. Sunday. Call (317) 632-2822.

Palomino Euro Bistro. 49 West Maryland Street, Indianapolis 46204. This upscale, romantic European bistro offers trendy house signatures such as wood-oven pizza, fire-roasted garlic chicken, and Pacific fresh salmon. $$. ❑. For reservations call (317) 974-0400.

WHERE TO STAY

The Canterbury Hotel. 123 South Illinois Street, Indianapolis 46225. This ninety-nine-room hotel was recently restored and is a lovely retreat for many notables who visit Indy. A restaurant, lounge, and private entrance to Circle Centre are available. Call (317) 634-3000.

Crowne Plaza Hotel at Union Station. 123 West Louisiana Street, Indianapolis 46225. This 276-room, full-service hotel plays on the facility's railroad heritage with twenty-six authentic Pullman train rooms. A restaurant and nightclub are on-site. Call (317) 631-2221.

The Westin Hotel. 50 South Capitol Street, Indianapolis 46204. This big, beautiful hotel located across from the Indiana Convention Center offers fine dining and a lounge. Call (317) 262-8100.

Omni Severin Hotel. 40 West Jackson Place, Indianapolis 46225. Also close to the Convention Center and Pan Am Plaza, this facility was recently restored and expanded to its early 1900s grandeur. Marble, brass, glass, and mirrors add luxury to a gracious atrium lobby. The Severin Bar and Grill is a European cafe. Call (317) 634-6664.

The Hyatt Regency Indianapolis. One South Capitol Street, Indianapolis 46204. 1 block south and 2 blocks west of Monument Circle, across from the state capitol. It's worthwhile dropping by just to see the spectacular 20-story atrium and to ride the glass-enclosed elevator to the top, where the hotel has its Eagle's Nest Restaurant. Two other restaurants are also available. Call (317) 632–1234.

Adam's Mark Hotel & Suites Downtown. 120 West Market, Indianapolis 46204. Newly opened, 332-room, full-service hotel located one block west of the city's center. Call (317) 972–0600.

Indianapolis Marriott Downtown. 350 West Maryland Street, Indianapolis 46225. The city's newest hotel is now the state's largest, with 615 rooms. Connected via skywalk to the Indiana Convention Center, RCA Dome, and Circle Center. Call (317) 822–3500.

Stone Soup Inn and The Looking Glass Inn. 1304 North Central Avenue, Indianapolis 46202. Located 13 blocks north of the city's center, these charming "sister" bed and breakfasts offer guests old-world charm with modern amenities. Call (317) 639–9550 or visit www.stonesoupinn.com.

MORRISTOWN, INDIANA

From downtown Indianapolis follow Meridian Street south from Monument Circle to South Street. Turn left and follow South Street across the Interstate 65/70 overpass, then turn left onto Cedar Street, which will lead you to U.S. 52 eastbound.

WHERE TO EAT

The Kopper Kettle. U.S. 52, Morristown 46161, 23 miles west of downtown Indianapolis on the way back to Cincinnati. This is an old stone tavern on the roadside with a pleasant dining room and a garden. Its family-style country dinners have made the Kopper Kettle well-known in Indiana. Favorites include pan-fried chicken, filet mignon, and seafood dishes served with their signature heaping bowls of vegetables. "No one ever left hungry," the owner says. $$. □. Closed Monday and on holidays. For hours call (765) 763–6767.

To return to Cincinnati from here, take U.S. 52 west (back toward Indianapolis) for 4 miles; then drive south on Ind. 9 for 10 miles to Interstate 74. Eastbound 74 will take you directly to downtown Cincinnati. U.S. 52 also leads directly to Cincinnati but takes forty-five minutes to an hour longer.

Day Trip 1 North

0   10   20   30 miles

NORTH DAY TRIP 1

Dayton, Ohio
Wright-Patterson Air Force Base

The trip from Cincinnati to Dayton takes about an hour, leaving plenty of time to explore the city or drive out to Wright-Patterson Air Force Base on the northeast side of town to see the finest aviation museum in the world.

Take Interstate 75 north. From downtown Cincinnati to downtown Dayton is 55 miles.

DAYTON, OHIO

Originally teeming with Native Americans, Dayton was settled in 1796 at the confluence of the Stillwater, the Mad, and the Great Miami Rivers as a center for farming and trading. Today, this youthful, well-run city is also a rich confluence of culture, history, and industry. A visit to Dayton offers the opportunity to trace the birth of aviation, explore a prehistoric Indian village, and enjoy unique shopping and dining in a renovated historic district.

Dayton's history is one of innovation. In 1901 James Ritty invented the mechanical cash drawer, a contraption people found amusing at first. Ritty's invention was sold by Dayton's National Cash Register Company, now known as the NCR Corporation, and its computerized office equipment is in use around the world. In 1911 Charles Kettering invented the automotive self-starter here, both ending forever the chore of cranking up the old Model T and bringing the automobile industry to Dayton.

But of all the local innovators, none are more revered than two brothers, inveterate tinkerers, who hammered out their dreams in a Dayton bicycle shop and gave the world flight. Orville and Wilbur

Wright tested the world's first successful "aeroplane" in 1903 at Kitty Hawk, North Carolina, near Cape Hatteras, and managed a flight of 120 feet, not quite the wingspan of the modern Boeing 747. With that single flight the Wright Brothers forever changed the course of history and launched their hometown of Dayton on a course to become the center of all that is aviation. Today Dayton is home to Wright-Patterson Air Force Base—the USAF's foremost aerospace research and development center—hundreds of private businesses related to aviation, and the U.S. Air Force Museum, the world's premier museum devoted to flight.

The downtown area encompasses, within a few blocks, the confluence of the Mad River, the Stillwater River, and Wolf Creek into the Great Miami River. Some two dozen downtown bridges spanning these meandering waterways contribute a picturesque element to the city. Below these bridges, paralleling the Great Miami, is the Dayton River Corridor Bikeway, a 24-mile biking and jogging path. Work is underway to link the path to similar bikeways in Middletown and Hamilton all the way to the Ohio River. Call (937) 463–2707 for maps.

WHAT TO SEE

Aviation Trail. The Wright Brothers' heritage of flight marks Dayton as the "Birthplace of Aviation" and is memorialized by the Aviation Trail. This history-steeped trail is a self-guided driving tour marked by blue-and-white WRIGHT FLYER signs. Maps of the trail are available at the Wright Cycle Company, listed on the National Register of Historic Places, 22 South Williams Street, located in the Aviation Heritage National Historical Park. For hours call (937) 225–7705.

Paul Laurence Dunbar House. 219 North Paul Laurence Dunbar Street, Dayton 45407. Now a state memorial, this Victorian residence was the home of one of America's most illustrious black authors and poets, born in Dayton of former slaves in 1872. Dunbar's verses of melancholy and unrequited love captured the heart of turn-of-the-century America and seemed even more poignant upon Dunbar's untimely death in 1906 at the age of thirty-three. The house contains Dunbar's library, personal effects, and manuscripts. Open 9:30 A.M. to 4:30 P.M. Wednesday–Saturday and noon to 4:30 P.M. Sunday, Memorial Day to Labor Day. (Call for fall and winter hours.) Admission fee. Call (937) 224-7061.

Oregon Historic District. A 12-square-block neighborhood that begins 2 blocks east of Fifth and Main Streets downtown, this is Dayton's "Old Town," with some 175 private homes reflecting the spectrum of architecture between 1820 and 1915. The brick streets, detailed restoration, and charming restaurants and shops, plus an active night life, make this a fun place to visit. Call (937) 223-0538.

Carillon Historical Park. 2001 South Patterson Boulevard, 2 miles south of the city. Here you can get a good cross section of history in just one stop. Centering on an old lock that was part of the original Miami & Erie Canal, this sixty-five-acre park is the collecting ground for all manner of historical exhibits. The city's oldest building, Newcom Tavern, was relocated here, along with a one-room schoolhouse, an old gristmill, and a covered bridge. Among transportation exhibits are an 1894 railroad station and a vintage 1912 steam locomotive, an antique fire engine, and a streetcar. A Wright Brothers display features a replica of their bicycle shop and the Wright Flyer III, a plane the brothers built in 1905, two years after their first flight.

The entrance to the park is dominated by the landmark Deeds Carillon, Ohio's largest. Carillon concerts are held every Sunday afternoon. The park is open May–October, 9:30 A.M. to 5:00 P.M. Tuesday–Saturday and 1:00 to 6:00 P.M. on Sunday. Closed Monday, except holidays. Admission fee. Call (937) 293-2841.

Boonshoft Museum of Discovery. 2600 DeWeese Parkway, Dayton 45414. After merging with the Children's Museum of Dayton in 1996, it is emerging as one of the region's premier science museums. The "Wild Ohio" live animal exhibit is a treat. An astronomy section features a computer-controlled planetarium, laser light shows every Friday and Saturday evening, and a space theater with shows throughout the day. The museum has long been noted for its scientific programs for children, who help in managing some of the exhibits.

The museum is open 9:00 A.M. to 5:00 P.M. Monday–Saturday and noon to 5:00 P.M. Sunday and holidays. Laser shows are held Friday and Saturday every hour, on the hour 8:00 P.M. to midnight. Closed

Thanksgiving, Christmas Eve, Christmas Day, New Year's Eve, and New Year's Day. Admission fee. Call (937) 275-7431 or visit www.boonshoftmuseum.org.

Dayton Art Institute. 456 Belmonte Park North at Forest and Riverview Avenues, Dayton 45405. From downtown drive north on Riverview to just across the Great Miami River Bridge. After being closed for major renovations until June 1997, the institute reopened with three new wings, double the gallery space, and a host of new acquisitions. This Italian Renaissance building houses a wide range of art from ancient to modern times, but it is especially noted for its collection of East Asian art and paintings of the Baroque era (seventeenth and eighteenth centuries) and its collection of contemporary American art. The institute pioneered the concept of the Experiencenter, a participatory gallery that hosts themed exhibitions. The museum is open daily 10:00 A.M. to 5:00 P.M. and Thursday to 9:00 P.M. Call (937) 223-5277.

SunWatch Prehistoric Indian Village. 2301 West River Road, Dayton 45418. Operated by the Dayton Society of Natural History, SunWatch was opened in 1988 as a reconstructed prehistoric American Indian village of the thirteenth century. An audiovisual presentation in the crescent-shaped visitors center explains the history of the seventeen-year excavation and how archaeologists work. A self-guided tour through the village takes you into a cavernous thatched roof council house, a typical family dwelling, and displays of artifacts and replicas of Indian clothing. A scale model of the village demonstrates how SunWatch worked as a sun calendar for its inhabitants. Officials have added a summer house (made of tree bark) to the village, as well as an heirloom garden, which produces corn, beans, squash, and native tobacco. Open 9:00 A.M. to 5:00 P.M. Tuesday–Saturday and noon to 5:00 P.M. Sunday March 16–November 30. Admission fee. Call (937) 268-8199.

Cox Arboretum. 6733 Springboro Pike, Miamisburg 45342. This beautiful arboretum features 160 acres of cultivated gardens, mature woodlands, and trails. The Edible Landscape Garden is nationally recognized and is also delightful to look at. Fifteen garden areas, plus a visitors center housing classroom and exhibit space, gift shop, and an excellent reference library, make this an educational resource as well. Open daily 8:00 A.M. to dusk, except Christmas and New Year's Day. Free. Call (937) 434-9005.

WHERE TO EAT

Jay's Restaurant. 225 East Sixth Street, Dayton 45402. Just a mile from downtown in the historic Oregon District, Jay's is a must for seafood lovers. Fish is flown in fresh daily from Alaska and the coasts, and the award-winning wine list is a pleasant surprise. Fresh swordfish is the specialty, although pan-fried walleye drenched in pecan honey butter is a seasonal favorite. The hundred-year-old mahogany bar adds to the ambience of this historic building, which originally opened as a mill in 1852. Open nightly for dinner. Reservations recommended weeknights but not accepted Saturdays. $$$. ☐. Call (937) 222-2892.

L'Auberge. 4120 Far Hills Avenue, Dayton 45429. Drive 2 miles south on O-48 to Far Hills Avenue in Kettering. One of Ohio's finer restaurants, L'Auberge is modeled after a French country inn and features provincial specialties as well as the waistline-conscious "nouvelle cuisine" of France. Food is served by a mostly European staff. The menu boasts fine pâtés, a salad of duck and truffles, and cream of escargot soup, among other dishes. Beef, veal, and poultry dishes are delicately prepared, as is the fish, which is flown in fresh daily. Pastries and breads are baked in-house. The restaurant also includes an outdoor cafe with nightly entertainment. Closed Sunday and holidays. Reservations recommended. $$$. ☐. For hours call (937) 299-5536.

The Pine Club. 1926 South Brown Street, Dayton 45409. This pine-paneled intimate restaurant offers some of the best steaks and prime rib in the Miami Valley. Open for dinner Monday–Saturday. No reservations. For hours call (937) 228-7463.

Elinor's & Amber Rose. 1400 Valley Street, Dayton 45404. Housed in a renovated ninety-year-old general store, Elinor's serves a variety of American and European cuisine, with German and Russian dishes being specialties. The menu offers twenty different sandwiches, or you can try a popular sampler platter. Open for lunch 11:00 A.M. to 2:00 P.M. Monday–Saturday and for dinner 5:00 to 9:00 P.M. Tuesday–Sunday. $$. ☐. Call (937) 228-2511.

Thomato's. 110 North Main Street, Dayton 45403. Thomato's cozy dining spot is warmed with live piano music for both lunch and dinner. Known for its Mediterranean offerings, Thomato's includes sea bass and duck among its featured offerings. For something a little more traditional, steaks and salmon are also popular. Open for lunch 11:00 A.M. to 2:00 P.M. Monday–Friday, and dinner 5:00 to 9:00 P.M. on Monday, 5:00 to 10:00 P.M. Tuesday–Thursday, and 5:00 to 11:00 P.M. Friday –Sunday. $$$. ☐. Call (937) 228-3333.

Carver's. 1535 Miamisburg-Centerville Road, Centerville 45459. Carver's selectively hand-cuts steaks and chops right on the premises. The menu also includes a few seafood items. A spacious dining room and quick service make this a great place for business meetings. For a relaxing social evening, Carver's unique live jazz and cigar lounge is open Thursday through Saturday. Open 5:00 to 10:00 P.M. Monday–Thursday, 5:00 to 10:30 P.M. Friday and Saturday, and 4:00 to 9:00 P.M Sunday. $$$. ☐. Call (937) 433-7099.

IN THE AREA

Peerless Mill Inn. 319 South Second Street, Miamisburg 45342. Drive 8 miles south from Dayton on Interstate 75 to the Miamisburg exit and 3 miles west. This old inn, established in 1828 on the banks of the Miami & Erie Canal, is noted for its roast Long Island duckling. Whichever of the numerous entrees you order, you are automatically served homemade corn fritters fresh from the griddle. The inn bakes its own breads and pastries. $$. ☐. Enjoy Sunday brunch buffet 10:00 A.M. to 2:00 P.M. Dinner is served Tuesday–Sunday. For hours call (937) 866-5968.

LaComedia Dinner Theatre. About two-thirds of the way between Cincinnati and Dayton on Interstate 75. The dinner theater is on O-73 at the Franklin-Springboro exit. This bountiful buffet has a changing menu but always features appetizers, salad, several entrees, potatoes and other vegetables, and dessert. A live Broadway musical or comedy follows dinner, and the comfortable dining room is terraced so there is an unobstructed view from all 600 seats. Hours vary, but usually the dinner seating is at 5:30 P.M., with showtime at 8:00 P.M. Wednesday–Sunday. A discount luncheon matinee starts at 10:00 A.M. Wednesday, Thursday, and Sunday. Prices range from moderate to expensive for the dinner-show package. For program and reservations, call (937) 746-4554 or (800) 677-9505.

WRIGHT-PATTERSON AIR FORCE BASE

From downtown Dayton follow Third Street (Airway Road) 6 miles east; then follow the signs to the base. If heading north from Cincinnati on Interstate 75, pick up merging O-4 east, follow it 3 miles to the Harshman Road exit, and then follow the signs south to Springfield Pike.

Please note that the air base itself is off-limits to civilians at all times, but visitors are welcome in the museum area, which comprises several large hangars and a field area.

WHAT TO SEE

U.S. Air Force Museum. The world's oldest, largest, and most comprehensive military aviation museum, the U.S. Air Force Museum sprawls across more than ten acres packed with nearly 300 aircraft and missiles. Here you can trace the history of aviation from the earliest models built by the Wright Brothers to cutting-edge experimental planes, missiles, and spacecraft.

Peer into the 1909 Wright Military Flyer. What contrast that 100-mile-an-hour early flying machine creates with the supersonic experimental XB-70 Valkyrie, flown in the 1960s for research missions! With its rapierlike fuselage and six huge jet engines, the Valkyrie flew at three times the speed of sound and at altitudes up to 70,000 feet. This is the only one remaining of the two that were built. The other Valkyrie crashed in 1966, and the line was discontinued because of cost.

Humanity's fledgling efforts to fly are represented in displays of primitive flight instruments, early engines, and flying togs, as well as the curious old planes themselves: the Curtiss Jenny, the Spad, the Sopwith Camel, and the Thomas Morse Scout among them.

World War II buffs and veterans will remember with nostalgia the great planes of that era, among them the B-29 Superfortress, biggest bomber of the war. One of those Superfortresses on display, *Bockscar,* dropped the atom bomb on Nagasaki in 1945 three days after the first A-bomb destroyed Hiroshima.

Other aircraft of interest include the fork-tailed P-38 Lightning, the British Spitfire, the German Junker and Heinkel bombers, and a German V-2 rocket fished from the North Sea, where it fell short of its target during the blitzkrieg on Britain.

Old presidential airplanes also wind up here, including President John F. Kennedy's Air Force One and the first plane ever christened to exclusive presidential use. This was Franklin D. Roosevelt's *Sacred Cow,* a DC-4 used from 1944 to 1947. Visitors may board and inspect it, along with *Columbine III,* a Lockheed Constellation ("Connie") used by President Eisenhower from 1954 to 1961, and President Truman's *Independence,* used from 1947 to 1954.

Bring comfortable shoes for what could be an all-day hike through the big hangars and surrounding tarmac. Besides the continuous films shown at various points along the way, the complex includes an auditorium where three films about flying alternate throughout the day. There also are a gift shop, a cafe, a bookstore, and an aviation library, with a staff versed in everything from the U-2 spy plane to the famous Red Baron, and research facilities available to the serious researcher.

The museum also boasts an IMAX theater, which gives viewers many of the sensations of an actual space flight through its uniquely designed stereo sound system and six-story screen. Admission fee. Call (937) 253–IMAX.

The museum is open 9:00 A.M. to 5:00 P.M. daily except Thanksgiving, Christmas, and New Year's Day. The annex, where about thirty-five other planes are being restored and displayed, is open daily at reduced hours. No admission fee. Call (937) 255–3284.

VANDALIA, OHIO

Ten miles north of Dayton on Interstate 75, the peaceful farming community of Vandalia lies at the interstate's juncture with the old National Road (U.S. 40)—the country's oldest federal highway, and one of its most historic, running from the East Coast into the great continental interior.

Beginning in the original colonies at Baltimore, Maryland, the National Road passed north of Washington, through the Maryland panhandle, across the Alleghenies near Cumberland, Maryland, and headed northeast toward Pittsburgh and the Ohio River.

To this point it was roughly the route followed by George Washington on early surveying trips and later by General Edward Braddock on his ill-fated march to liberate Fort Pitt at Pittsburgh from the French during the French and Indian War. Somewhere, probably as they neared the banks of the northward-flowing Monongahela River, the road builders changed their minds.

The road veered west from the old trail and carved a more direct route to the Ohio River at what is now Wheeling, West Virginia (then Virginia), lopping 90 miles of river travel off the journey west.

The National Road joined the Ohio River as a major highway westward to St. Louis, Missouri, where, years later, pioneers would organize and provision wagon trains for their trek across the great western prairies. The highway eventually was extended to Kansas City, Denver, and Salt Lake City.

Vandalia, settled in 1838, was one of many towns to spring up along this well-traveled route, and it is now the world headquarters of the Amateur Trapshooting Association.

51

Day Trip 2 North

0   10   20   30 miles

WHAT TO SEE

Trapshooting Hall of Fame & Museum. 601 West National Road, Vandalia 45377. One of the largest collections of target-shooting memorabilia and artifacts housed anywhere is featured. It is also the only known museum devoted to this sport. The exhibits trace trap-shooting history and memorialize famous sharpshooters such as Annie Oakley. Open 9:00 A.M. to 4:00 P.M. Monday–Friday. Closed holidays. No admission fee. Call the Amateur Trapshooting Association at (937) 898-1945.

SPECIAL EVENTS

U.S. Air & Trade Show. Held every July at Dayton International Airport, which is located in Vandalia, the event, started in 1975, is quickly becoming one of the largest and most important air and trade shows in the world. Certified by the U.S. government, the Dayton show welcomes more than 250,000 visitors to displays and demonstrations of military, historic, and commercial airplanes and air-related activities. The four-day event also showcases new aerospace technology to international governments, businesses, and trade associations. Call (937) 898-5901.

Amateur Trapshooting Association Grand American World Trapshooting Tournament. Held every August, the tournament attracts 20,000 shooters who compete during the ten-day event. The competition trap line is a full 1.5 miles long and attracts entrants from more than fifteen countries. Call (937) 898-1945.

SPRINGFIELD, OHIO

You can hurry east to Springfield along Interstate 70 or take a slower pace along the old National Road (U.S. 40) from Vandalia, a distance of 28 miles. Both roads cross the broad, central Ohio flatlands in a fairly direct way, except the old road has 2-mile-long kink in it as it loops to pass downstream of a dam on the Great Miami River, one of two dams that control floodwaters north of Dayton.

On the western approach to Springfield, Interstate 70 intersects with O-4, a multilane, divided highway heading north. Follow O-4

7 miles to its intersection with the National Road (U.S. 40) and northbound U.S. 68. This is the western entrance to Springfield and the point to which you must return to continue this trip.

Springfield was founded in 1801 by James Demiut. When the National Road arrived three decades later, the city was already a thriving agricultural center. For a few years it had the distinction of being the road's western terminus. International Harvester (now Navistar) helped Springfield become a leading farm machinery center in the Midwest.

The Springfield Area Convention and Visitors Bureau at 333 North Limestone Street, Springfield 45503 has tours, maps, and information. Call (937) 325-7621.

WHAT TO SEE

Pennsylvania House Museum. 1311 West Main Street, Springfield 45504. Built in the 1820s, this restored stagecoach stop and inn along the National Road was the boyhood home of Dr. Isaac Funk, founder of Funk & Wagnalls. The house boasts a great collection of period memorabilia, including a doll collection and the Grace Porter button collection, one of the largest in the country. This remarkable Federal structure is open March through December by appointment. Admission fee. Call (937) 322-7668.

John Foos Manor Antique Gallery and Bed and Breakfast. 810 East High Street, Springfield 45505. This spectacular Italianate home was built in 1870 by Springfield industrialist John Foos. Foos Manor is perched atop a ridge overlooking Springfield. A striking 3-story, hand-carved winding staircase, burled walnut woodwork, and original Italian mosaic tile make a grand statement when you enter the main hall, where you're greeted by "Scrappy," the house dog. Overnight guests receive the royal treatment with a bubbling hot spa under the stars, a goodnight fruit-and-cheese platter, and a gourmet breakfast. This forty-five-room mansion, with its 16-foot ceilings and elegantly arched doorways, is filled with museum-quality antiques, with every piece available for purchase. As innkeeper and gallery owner Jackie Gross puts it: "If our guest likes the bed he slept in, he can take it with him." Free tours offered daily, 10:00 A.M. to 2:00 P.M. ☐. Call (937) 323-3444.

Springfield Museum of Art. 107 Cliff Park Road, Springfield 45501. This museum offers a nice collection of nineteenth- and twentieth-century American and European art, as well as a gift shop featuring original and unusual artwork. For hours call (937) 325–4673.

Buck Creek State Park. 1901 Buck Creek Lane, Springfield 45502. With more than 4,000 acres—including a 2,120-acre lake—Buck Creek offers scenery, solitude, and swimming. The park has twenty-six fully equipped family cabins for rent. Winter activities include snowmobiling, cross-country sledding, and hiking. Call (937) 322–5284.

David Crabill House. In Buck Creek State Park, on Clarence Brown Reservoir, 4 miles east on O-4. Now restored, this was the home of a pioneer settler and was built in 1826. It is maintained by the Clark County Historical Society and gives an interesting impression of the early days along the National Road. Elsewhere the park has picnic facilities, lake swimming, and hiking trails. No admission fee. For hours call (937) 324–0657.

Clark County Heritage Center. 117 South Fountain Avenue, Springfield 45502. Housed in the original city hall built in 1890, this exciting new interpretive center chronicles the events of Clark County. History comes to life with more than 1,000 artifacts, including the only surviving Union officers' tent, a Civil War battle flag, a rare Conestoga wagon, and much more. Galleries include The Early National Road Gallery, America's first public works project; The Clash of Cultures and the Opening of Ohio Gallery, which depicts the story of a frontier battle of the Revolutionary War with the Shawnee Indians; and The Agriculture and Industry Gallery and the Service to the Nation Gallery, dedicated to servicemen and women. No admission fee. For hours call The Clark County Historical Society at (937) 324–0657.

Clark County Historical Society Museum. 818 North Fountain Avenue, Springfield 45502. This small museum has an interesting display of historical items, including a fascinating collection of newspapers dating back to 1829. The museum offers various exhibits on occasion and provides extensive archives for researchers. No admission fee. For hours call (937) 324–0657.

WHERE TO EAT

Klosterman's Derr Road Inn. 4343 Derr Road, Springfield 45503. Springfield's only manor, overlooking the rolling hills that Simon Kenton once called home. Guests often request a table by the window to see the deer that freely roam the grounds. The sautéed salmon in shrimp cream sauce and homemade tiramisu always get rave reviews. Open 11:00 A.M.–2:00 P.M. and 4:00–9:00 P.M. Monday–Friday, 5:00–10:00 P.M. Friday and Saturday, and 4:00–8:00 P.M Sunday. $$. ☐. Call (937) 399–0822.

Tapestry & Tales. 14 East Main Street, Springfield 45502. Vintage hats, tapestries, and sewing memorabilia decorate the walls and tables of this Victorian tearoom, located in an historic home goods store. Take a midday break and try their famous English lemon curd tarts, chicken salad, quiche, and, of course, tea. Lunch is served 11:00 A.M.–2:30 P.M. Monday–Friday. $. ☐. Call (937) 322–8961.

SPECIAL EVENTS

Fair at New Boston. Each Labor Day weekend in George Rogers Clark Park, hundreds of authentically costumed aficionados of pioneer days create an enchanting, entertaining, and sometimes-raucous pioneer town festival complete with blacksmiths, weavers, gunsmiths—and at least one quack doctor. This is a lively family event; whole families dress the part, and people address each other with colonial-era expressions. Admission fee. For information write George Rogers Clark Heritage Association, P.O. Box 1251, Springfield, OH 45501.

Note for theater lovers: The Springfield Arts Council sponsors a series of exceptional programs at Cliff Park Amphitheater each summer, generally from mid-June through mid-July. For information call (937) 324–2712.

CEDAR BOG

Cedar Bog State Nature Preserve (called "Cedar Bog" by most) is truly a natural wonder—a geologic freak that has no equal in North America. Left behind by a receding glacier, the bog has managed to maintain its own "miniclimate" ever since. While other glacial areas aged in response to vast changes in temperature, the bog did not and has remained forever young.

In this time warp exists plant and animal life found nowhere else in such variety, including more than 100 rare or endangered species that could not survive without the bog's peculiar climate. Amid more than 1,700 species of plants are rare orchids that thrive in the bog's clammy atmosphere. Among other wonders are two types of spiders that were found here many years after 1925, when they were declared extinct.

Although the bog is now a state nature preserve and a national landmark, it remains doubtful that it can be saved indefinitely from humankind's intrusions. The highway itself is a dramatic example of how close the bog has come to extermination.

From Springfield's west side take U.S. 68 north from U.S. 40. This is a fine, multilane highway—going nowhere. Nine miles north of the junction, new U.S. 68 abruptly stops, halted by a public outcry to save the bog. An exit ramp winds apologetically eastward to old U.S. 68. Had construction continued, the highway would have cut a swath through the fringe of the bog, ruining the delicate ecological balance.

Proceed about a mile north on old U.S. 68, watching for Dallas Road as a reference point. One hundred yards past this intersection, to the left, is Woodburn Road, with a sign announcing CEDAR BOG. Turn left. Woodburn Road crosses a railroad track, then heads down a gradual hill and deadends at the edge of the bog at a parking lot and a farmhouse. This is the home and headquarters of the resident naturalist and the starting point for tours.

The bog covers about one hundred acres in a natural, dish-shaped depression and is fed by cold, alkaline springwater. This produces a chilly dampness, which is held in by the flow of warm air currents overhead that act much like a bell jar, or an invisible bubble, to contain this world where time has stopped. An improved 1-mile boardwalk, opened in 1987, carries visitors back eons in time. Near the center of the bog, one can gaze upon an eerie scene—Ohio as it appeared 18,000 years ago. Without the boardwalk one might sink to the knees in what is officially called "muck," a wet, slimy, black mud from which grow clumps of sedges, a tall grass whose blades are shaped like toothpicks.

This area is rimmed by a small cedar forest. Higher up the sides of the "dish" begins the modern forest, whose tall trees block out sunlight and eventually prevail over the smaller cedars. Among these three basic areas are fringes and pockets of vegetation that fill in a full panorama of development from the age of the glaciers to the present.

Although there were many bogs in the state, this one, originally comprising some 7,000 acres, was unique because of its constant water table and the unusually cool temperatures of its springs.

The wildlife here is incredible. Cedar Run holds eighteen species of fish and is the only stream in Ohio cold enough to support the brook trout. Owls, mice, possums, raccoons, fox, and deer abound, and this is the only known home in the Midwest of the massasauga, a short, stumpy rattlesnake. Spiders come in seventy-four varieties, biting flies in eighty-four, and mosquitoes in sixty-three.

In March call the bog to be placed on the "toad trilling list." You'll receive a call from naturalist Terry Jaworski in April or May, when the toads at Cedar Bog are about to begin "trilling." Trilling is a haunting, melodic—often incredibly loud—song the toad sings each spring to attract a mate. Once Terry calls, you'll have less than twenty-four hours to reach Cedar Bog in time to experience a true wonder of nature. Hundreds and hundreds of toads swarm down to the bog to mate. Cedar Bog is often challenged, but never beaten, by other preserves that claim to have louder and more prolific toad trilling. Bring a picnic meal and a flash camera.

Among flora are 546 kinds of vascular plants and flowers, forty-nine types of lichens, 195 species of mushrooms, and long lists of mosses and ferns. Each time of year presents visitors with a different floral display.

Two-hour tours are conducted by appointment. April–September, the bog is open from 9:00 A.M. to 4:30 P.M. Wednesday–Sunday. During the rest of the year or if you are going to visit on a different date, you can phone to arrange a tour at a mutually agreeable time. Please note that the bog has one staff member; patience is appreciated. Admission fee. Call (800) 860-0147.

YELLOW SPRINGS, OHIO

About 12 miles south of Springfield on U.S. 68 lies the village of Yellow Springs. Visiting this tiny, progressive community is like taking a trip back into the 1960s. Yellow Springs is a community that is fertile with artistic, spiritual, and intellectual freedom. Psychics, artists, musicians, and teachers find that Yellow Springs offers a friendly climate and a number of resources for studying and practicing alternative beliefs and sciences. The commercial district is lined with unique shops offering artifacts, books, New Age therapies, and items like crystals, pyramids, incense, and candles. The history of Yellow Springs has long fostered alternative healing and spirituality. The village owes its name to a yellow mineral spring that first attracted the prehistoric Hopewell Indians, who built a burial mound near it. Later the Shawnee Indians and their great chief Tecumseh bathed in its soothing waters. In the early and middle 1800s, the springs began to attract fashionable parties from Cincinnati, who arrived by stagecoach to stay in the resort hotels and take the water-cure treatments that flourished in the area.

In 1856 Judge William Mills, whose father owned the springs, decided to erect a planned community, complete with parks, schools, churches, and streets. About the same time an early mayor of Cincinnati, Aaron Harlan, built the stately Whitehall mansion at the northern edge of the village as a copy of the White House. Whitehall is claimed as the founding place of the Republican party, no matter what those upstarts in Ripon, Wisconsin believe.

Judge Mills also persuaded the Little Miami Railroad to run its tracks through the village, a development that contributed to its

growth. But perhaps Mills's most-lasting and -famous legacy is Antioch College. He gave the fledgling school twenty acres and $20,000 to locate in Yellow Springs in 1852, and the college has been an important part of the community ever since. Founded by pioneer educator Horace Mann, Antioch established innovative cooperative work-study programs and a tradition of passionate commitment to social change that have made it a leading liberal institution. One of the first coeducational and nonsectarian colleges in the country, Antioch was a hotbed of antiwar and counterculture sentiment in the 1960s and 1970s. Today Antioch still pushes the boundaries of higher education, with students from all over the world on its Yellow Springs campus and a network of learning centers on both U.S. coasts and in Europe.

The fertile atmosphere of the small campus permeates the town and has resulted in excellent town-gown relations, which have spawned performing arts programs, lecture series, workshops, seminars, and groups dedicated to myriad social programs. For information on college-related activities, call (937) 767-7331 or 767-2686.

WHAT TO SEE AND DO

A walking-tour brochure of the compact historic district of Yellow Springs is available from the Chamber of Commerce offices, located in a replica of the 1880s Yellow Springs Train Station on the bike path between Xenia Avenue and Dayton Street (937-767-2686). Nearly all of the forty-three buildings are included on the National Register of Historic Places and reflect a diversity of mid-nineteenth-century architectural styles. Several of the buildings are reportedly bedeviled by ghosts—friendly ones.

Caboose Bike and Skate Company. Corry Street Cabooses. Located right next to the biking/running path connecting Yellow Springs and Xenia and nestled in a pair of yellow cabooses once used on the Chesapeake & Ohio Railroad, the shop rents bikes and in-line skates. The Caboose Bike and Skate can outfit an entire family to participate in two of the most popular pastimes in the village. Open daily during the summer and on weekends the rest of the year, weekdays in the fall, weather permitting. For hours call (937) 767-2288.

Glen Helen Nature Preserve. 405 Corry Street, Yellow Springs 45387. In 1929 a former Antioch student, Hugh Taylor Birch, donated

1,000 acres of wooded forest and meadow to Antioch in memory of his daughter, Helen Birch Bartlett. Adjacent to the campus and virtually across the road from downtown Yellow Springs, Glen Helen is Antioch's beautiful retreat into nature. The famed Yellow Spring is visible along its 26 miles of trails, in addition to the glacier-carved Yellow Springs Creek gorge and Little Miami River. A Trailside Museum, Raptor Center, gift shop, library, and riding center offer numerous activities. Open daily during daylight hours. No fee. Call (937) 767–7375 or 767–7798.

Morgan House Bed & Breakfast. 120 West Limestone Street, Yellow Springs 45387. Situated in the heart of the town's historic district, Morgan House is within walking distance of many shops and restaurants. Call (937) 767–7509.

B&B Carriage Service. 3725 Cortsville Road, South Charleston 45368. Usually in Yellow Springs on Sunday afternoons, driver Bob Peterson and his Percheron geldings, Dan and Zack, offer carriage rides, hayrides, and sleigh rides. Call (937) 265–5125.

John Bryan State Park. 3790 O–370, 2 miles east of Yellow Springs. Adjacent to Glen Helen, the 750-acre park is the most scenic in the western half of Ohio. Its steep limestone gorge, cut by the Little Miami River, is a remarkable contrast to the area's flat farmlands. A large section of the gorge is designated as a state nature preserve—Clifton Gorge—and offers spectacular hiking, rappelling, and rock climbing. Naturalists and astronomers offer a variety of nature and observatory programs each weekend. A campground, a lovely picnic area, towering hardwoods, and abundant springs make this a popular spot. Open all year during daylight hours. No admission fee. Call (937) 767–1274.

Young's Jersey Dairy. 6880 Springfield-Xenia Road, Yellow Springs 45387. Save room for ice cream before heading out of Yellow Springs. Just 1 mile north on U.S. 68, Young's Jersey Dairy is home to fifty flavors of some of the freshest-tasting ice cream you'll ever sample. For milkshake lovers, the five-scoop "Bull Shake" weighs in at a full twenty-four ounces. This working dairy farm gives visitors a real taste of how ice cream is produced—from cow to cone. Take the wagon ride or walking tour to visit the farm animals. And don't miss Udders & Putters, with its driving range, batting cage, and farm-themed miniature-golf course where a cow moos on the eighteenth hole. Open daily except Christmas. Call (937) 325–0629.

The Golden Jersey Inn. The latest addition to Young's Jersey Dairy, this full-service restaurant complements the dairy complex, making it more than just a stop for ice cream and family fun. Great care was taken in constructing the building—it closely resembles the original barn built in 1869, with oak timber frames, wood pegs, and a 30-foot-high ceiling. Open for breakfast, lunch, and dinner, the restaurant features a variety of fresh home-cooked meals, desserts, and, of course, ice cream. Open 11:00 A.M. to 9:00 P.M. Monday–Friday and 7:00 A.M. to 9:00 P.M Saturday and Sunday. $. ☐. Call (937) 324-2050.

WHERE TO SHOP

Folks come from miles around to shop in Yellow Springs's unique shops, many of which reflect their proprietors' artistic abilities, literary interests, or eclectic tastes. Imported clothing, handmade jewelry, handcrafted pottery and furniture, gourmet kitchenware, spices, unusual foods, paintings, sculptures, toys, and dozens of other items are available. Many of the handcrafted items are locally produced. Most of the shops are clustered along Xenia Avenue.

Kings Yard. In the 200 block of Xenia Avenue. A cluster of stores strung along a brick pathway shaded by large trees, the yard offers pleasant surprises. **No Common Scents** is a purveyor of spices, scents, teas, crystal, and gifts. **Yellow Springs Pottery** sells handmade porcelain, stoneware, and raku ceramics of eleven area artists.

WHERE TO EAT

Ha Ha Pizza. 108 Xenia Avenue, Yellow Springs 45387. This funky pizza shop has been popular with students and locals alike for years. Catering to vegetarians as well as meat lovers, Ha Ha offers fresh-made crust in white or whole wheat with a variety of toppings, from standard favorites to more exotic additions like eggplant, falafel, and oysters. Open 11:30 A.M. to 10:00 P.M. Monday–Saturday and 1:00 to 9:00 P.M. Sunday. $. Call (937) 767-2131.

The Winds Cafe. 215 Xenia Avenue, Yellow Springs 45387. An elegant, comfortable atmosphere urges patrons to relax in the owner's very capable hands. Specialties are seafood, chicken, and vegetarian dishes from around the world. The Winds serves pasta specials

Monday–Thursday. A real adventure in eating. Open lunch and dinner, Monday–Saturday, brunch on Sunday. $. ◻. Call (937) 767–1144.

Ye Old Trail Tavern. 228 Xenia Avenue, Yellow Springs 45387. More than 2,500 autographed dollar bills line the walls of this old landmark, built from rough-hewn logs in 1827. Thursdays and Saturdays Ye Old Trail offers psychic readings in the back sunroom. Pizza and burgers are typical fare, although baskets of wings and fried shrimp are favorites. A hefty list of imported and domestic beers and wine is available, but no other alcoholic beverages. Open 2:00 P.M. to midnight Monday and Tuesday, 11:00 A.M. to midnight Wednesday–Saturday, and 2:00 to 8:00 P.M. Sunday. $. ◻. Call (937) 767–7448.

CLIFTON, OHIO

Clifton is a tiny town located on O–343 about 4 miles east of Yellow Springs, bordering the eastern edge of John Bryan State Park. A handful of antiques shops and the Clifton Opera House are just about all you will find downtown. Clifton is the site of a historic mill whose wheel is turned by the Little Miami before it plunges into Clifton Gorge.

Clifton Mill. 75 Water Street (O–72), Clifton 45316. The historic Clifton Mill is the largest operating gristmill in the country and sports an 18-foot waterwheel. Built originally in 1802, the mill was six stories high—or 55 feet tall. During a succession of owners, including John Patterson, founder of Dayton's National Cash Register Company, the mill provided cornmeal and flour to Union troops during the Civil War.

The gristmill burned down and was replaced twice, but the current mill was built in 1869. In the later 1960s the Satariano family purchased the site and established the Millrace Restaurant, which serves breakfast and lunch daily. There is a lovely deck on which to sit while you watch the mill operate and sample pancakes made from flour ground at the mill and sausage "grown" just 3 blocks away.

Tours of the mill take you through a maze of wheels, elevators, sifters, and grinders and demonstrate how the water's energy is harnessed to grind corn and wheat into flour. The gift shop offers bags of meal, flour, and pancake mix to take home.

During the holiday season, from Thanksgiving through New Year's, the mill strings thousands of lights down the waterfall below the waterwheel for a spectacular sight. A life-size nativity scene, a huge display of more than 3,000 Santa Clauses, and a miniature village add to the charm. The mill is open every day. Tours are offered daily except Tuesday and Thursday, 9:30 A.M. to 3:00 P.M. The restaurant is open 9:00 A.M. to 3:00 P.M. weekdays and 8:00 A.M. to 4:00 P.M. weekends. The store and mill are open 9:00 A.M. to 6:00 P.M. weekdays and 8:00 A.M. to 5:00 P.M. weekends. Hours vary in the winter. Closed Thanksgiving, Christmas, and New Year's Day. Admission fee. Call (937) 767-5501.

The Fish Decoy Company. O–72 and Dayton Street. Artist Steve Robbins has this tiny studio packed with his hand-carved, hardwood fish decoys. Patrons use his pieces as both lures and art. An impressive collection of vintage fishing lures and decoys will wow most anglers. Robbins makes and sells lures, decoys, and traps. Open daily 11:00 A.M. to 5:00 P.M. Call first (937) 767-8151. Many days a sign reading GONE FISHING hangs on the door.

Clifton Antique Mall. 301 North Main Street (O–72), Clifton 45316. Spectacular stained-glass windows, a garden gate of old relics, and pots of fresh flowers greet visitors to this 1878 Presbyterian church. Three stories jammed with attic finds and twenty dealers offering good prices await antiques aficionados. Dealers also buy, repair, and restore antiques. Owners Dee Ann and Bob Wright hail from Idaho and are probably the only folks in the Midwest carrying Idaho's gooey Farr candy bars. Try the nougatty, chocolate-covered "Idaho Spud." Open daily 11:00 A.M. to 5:00 P.M. and noon to 5:00 P.M. Sunday. Closed Tuesdays and Wednesdays in January and February. Call (937) 767-2277.

WILBERFORCE, OHIO

Take O–72 south from Clifton about 5 miles to U.S. 42. Turn right and travel southwest another 5 miles on U.S. 42 to Wilberforce, home of Wilberforce University. Wilberforce was a famous stop on the Underground Railroad, and its small educational institution, founded in 1856, became a symbol of freedom for the slaves who stopped here on their journey north. Wilberforce, the community and its university, became a center of black education and achievements and proudly carries on that tradition today.

In the mid-1900s, the state of Ohio established Central State University as the only historically black, publicly supported institution of higher education in the state. Together Wilberforce and Central State have become a national center for black education and cultural studies. In recognition of that prominence, the U.S. Congress established the National Afro-American Museum and Cultural Center at Wilberforce in the late 1960s.

National Afro-American Museum and Cultural Center. 1350 Brush Row Road, Wilberforce 45384, just off U.S. 42. Adjacent to Central State and located on the campus of the old Wilberforce University, which built a strikingly modern new campus across U.S. 42 in the 1960s, the National Afro-American Museum opened its doors in April 1988, with the completion of the first of four phases. The museum is a fascinating attempt to collect, preserve, and interpret the Afro-American experience. A permanent exhibit details the black experience during the turbulent 1950s and early 1960s. Temporary exhibits and displays complement the collections. The museum maintains an expanding collection of artifacts, manuscripts, and library materials and draws researchers from throughout the United States. Admission fee. Open 9:00 A.M. to 5:00 P.M. Tuesday–Saturday and 1:00 to 5:00 P.M. Sunday. Closed Monday and major holidays except Martin Luther King Jr. Day. Call (937) 376-4944 for more information and a schedule of events.

XENIA, OHIO

From Wilberforce it's a short 3-mile drive into Xenia on U.S. 42. Xenia is the county seat of Greene County and has a beautiful courthouse that withstood the ravages of the April 1974 tornado that destroyed much of the town. Today the scars of the violent event are barely visible as Xenia has rebuilt itself into a thriving community.

Once Old Town, located just north of Xenia, was the site of the Shawnee Indian Nation's largest settlement, and Shawnee Chief Tecumseh was born at what's now the Ohio State Fish Hatchery on the outskirts of Xenia. Tecumseh, his brother, The Prophet, and his adopted half-brother, Blue Jacket, all lived in the settlement, where frontiersmen Daniel Boone and Simon Kenton were once held captive.

Tecumseh strove to create a pan-Indian alliance to protect these tribal lands in the 1790s and early 1800s but failed to stem the encroachment of white civilization. Tecumseh's story is told in an outdoor drama in Chillicothe, Ohio, every summer (see Northeast Day Trip 4), while Blue Jacket's life is the subject of a similar outdoor drama just outside Xenia.

OUTDOOR DRAMA

Blue Jacket. Caesar's Ford Park Amphitheater, 5 miles east of Xenia, off Jasper Pike on Stringtown Road. From Dayton take U.S. 35 for 16 miles east to downtown Xenia and follow the signs to the park.

Historians may argue about the tale of Blue Jacket as shown in this drama. With some artistic license, the drama hinges on the story of Marmaduke van Swearingen, a white boy who is allegedly captured, then adopted, by the Shawnee at age seventeen and rose to be War Chief. Despite arguments over Blue Jacket's skin color and bloodline, all historians agree he was a brilliant strategist, unsurpassed by other Indian leaders. Among his many military achievements, Blue Jacket was victorious over General Arthur St. Clair in a battle in northern Indiana.

The drama unfolds on a three-acre stage, which includes part of Caesar Creek. It involves fifty actors, horses, flaming arrows, and even a cannon.

Blue Jacket is performed at 8:00 P.M. daily except Monday, June to September. Admission fee. Dinner and backstage tours are available before the show for an extra fee. In season, tickets can be ordered by writing P.O. Box C, Xenia, OH 45385-0692, by calling (937) 376-4318, or visiting www.bluejacketdrama.com. For information the rest of the year, call (937) 376-4358.

To return to Cincinnati from Xenia, follow U.S. 42 southwest to Cincinnati or take U.S. 68 south for 13 miles to Interstate 71 south. Both routes take about an hour.

Greene County Historical Society. 74 West Church Street, Xenia 45385. Established in 1929, the society is housed in four buildings, including a log cabin (circa 1799) built by settler James Galloway and a two-story Queen Anne (circa 1876) furnished to its original era. The historical society is open 9:00 A.M. to noon and 1:00 to 3:30 P.M. Tuesday–Friday, with tours at 1:30 P.M. and 4:30 P.M. daily June through August, or by appointment. Extended summer hours. Closed from Christmas through New Year's Day. Admission fee. Group rates available. Call (937) 372-4606.

Urbana, Ohio · West Liberty, Ohio

The trip from Cincinnati to Urbana takes about two hours, but it is an ideal overnight getaway if combined with the Dayton, Yellow Springs, or Springfield trip. To reach Urbana, take Interstate 75 north to Interstate 675 north. Just northeast of Dayton, pick up Interstate 70 east. Then take U.S. 68 north to Urbana.

URBANA, OHIO

Urbana, Ohio, is the picture of small-town America. In Urbana, complete strangers smile and wave as if they know you. The town square, built around a monument, is encircled by unique, locally owned shops and boutiques. **Carmazzi's** corner store, which hasn't changed much since it opened one hundred years ago, is packed with newspapers, toys, and old-time penny candy that's still under a nickel. **Sweet Annie's** for ladies and the home offers elegant dresses, dolls, and unique collectibles. **Kaleidoscope** is a one-of-a-kind shop stuffed with antiques and collectible flea market finds. Most stores are open Monday through Saturday, but Sunday is still a day of rest.

Champaign County gave Ohio one of the first governors (Joseph Brand in 1836) and one of the last lynchings (a deplorable event in 1897 that drew fire from nearly every newspaper editor in the state). It gave the nation William Saxbe, a feisty U.S. attorney general who refused to back down to Richard Nixon in the president's final days in office; A. B. Graham, an educator and farmer who improved rural life throughout America; and a West Point commander, Brigadier General Robert Eichelberger.

To the world this county provided John Quincy Adams Ward, father of modern American sculpture; Brand Whitlock, the first ambassador to Belgium; and international vaudevillian Billy Clifford. Other famous people who have lived in this county include Simon Kenton, the great frontiersman, and Richard Stanhope, George Washington's personal valet, who received his freedom and hundreds of acres in Champaign County when our nation's first president died.

The town of Urbana is located 6 miles north of Cedar Bog and 12 miles north of Springfield on U.S. 68. In downtown Urbana—in the heart of rural, Republican Champaign County—stands *The Man on the Monument*, a bronze statue honoring the county's contribution to the Union Army. Ohio Governor and future President Rutherford B. Hayes dedicated the solemn, thought-provoking figure in December 1871, amid a thirty-six-gun salute, the music of Vance's Silver Cornet Band, and the cheers and tears of 5,000 onlookers.

Several presidents have visited Urbana throughout the decades. Besides Hayes, William Henry Harrison and Teddy Roosevelt both spoke in the town square. Woodrow Wilson made a whistle stop at the depot in 1919, and—on a sadder note—the body of Abraham Lincoln passed through Urbana on its way to Springfield, Illinois, for burial in 1865.

WHAT TO SEE

Champaign County Historical Society Museum. 809 East Lawn Avenue, Urbana 43078. This museum offers an extensive Brand Whitlock collection, a Victorian parlor, and a country schoolhouse setting. Donations accepted. Open 10:00 A.M. to 4:00 P.M. Tuesday, other days by appointment. Call (937) 653-6721.

Scioto Street. Just head east from Monument Square and prepare to feast on architectural bravado. Included on this street are several remarkable Queen Annes (in the 500 block) and a genuine Andrew Jackson Downing located at 400 Scioto Street. With its chimney clusters and elaborate bargeboards characteristic of Downing's designs, this home reflects with textbook perfection the purist style of an architect who understood the country setting. For walking-tour maps stop at Main Graphics, 113 North Main Street, or call (937) 653-3334.

Robert Rothchild Berry Farm. 3143 East U.S. 36, Urbana 43078 (1.5 miles west of Urbana on U.S. 36). Rothchild's is a mecca for "foodies." Its fancy green-and-gold labels are spotted in the finest gourmet shops and upscale groceries around the United States. In 1976 a couple from San Francisco started the farm as a simple corn-and-beans operation. It has since grown to 170 acres with a 35,000-square-foot, award-winning gourmet food manufacturing facility. Today, Rothchild's makes everything from basic fruit preserves to unique blends of berries and herbs into raspberry vinegars, salsas, and mustards. In early summer, herb and raspberry plants are available. Gourmet items are sold in the retail shop. Don't miss the discounts in the back room. Walking through the acres of herbs, berries, and perennial flowers is relaxing, and the picnic shelter makes a nice lunch spot. In season (August and September), Rothchild's offers pick-your-own raspberries, and ice cream is served as an excuse to break into those berries before you even leave the farm. Tours available to groups only. Open 9:00 A.M. to 5:00 P.M. Monday–Friday and 10:00 A.M. to 2:00 P.M. Saturday. Call (800) 356-8933.

WHERE TO SHOP

Main Street Clothing and Collections for Men. 237 North Main Street, Urbana 43078. Top-quality women's clothes and rugged wear for men. Always a nice sales rack. Unique men's gifts guaranteed. Open 9:30 A.M. to 5:30 P.M. Monday–Saturday. Call (937) 653-7697.

Guild Galleries. 118 North Main Street, Urbana 43078. The shop reflects elegance and grace, and it offers classic gifts for a variety of prices. From pottery and bath items to one-of-a-kind prints, this store gets the job done. Check out the clearance room. Open 9:30 A.M. to 5:30 P.M. Monday–Saturday. Call (937) 653-6126.

WHERE TO EAT

Restaurant on the Square. 13 Monument Square, Urbana 43078. Every Ohio burg worthy of a stoplight has a diner where the locals go for an early-morning ritual that requires only fresh coffee, friendly advice, and an open seat at the counter. This ritual is as predictable as the sunrise; humanity meets before work to discuss life, love, and last night's activity at the firehouse. In downtown Urbana the Restaurant on the Square fills the bill. $. Open 5:30 A.M. to 1:45 P.M. Monday–Saturday and 8:00 A.M. to noon Sunday. Call (937) 653-9500.

Mayflowers Chinese Restaurant. 222 North Main Street, Urbana 43078. Casual dining in an intimate restaurant that offers the best Szechwan and Hunan cooking in the region. Owner Dale Tai and his wife, Carol, draw regulars from throughout the Miami Valley, especially those who love shrimp and scallops. The atmosphere is so cozy that guests typically invite the proprietors to join them for dessert. Open for lunch and dinner Monday–Saturday. $$. ☐. Call (937) 652-1050.

Millner's Cafeteria. 1629 East O-29, Urbana 43078. A place built by a fourth-generation restaurateur. Millner's is especially good for families—offering a wide selection of food, ample seating, and a spacious dining room. Regulars rave about Millner's real mashed potatoes, Swiss steak, and pineapple cake. Open for lunch and dinner daily. For hours call (937) 653-4411.

SPECIAL EVENTS

Marketplace Days. Typically held the third weekend in July, this event includes all the fixin's for a great downtown festival: street vendors, sidewalk sales, a 5K run sponsored by the Optimists, and a Main Street parade. For information call the Urbana Area Chamber of Commerce at (937) 653-5764.

Oktoberfest. Held the first Sunday in October on the lawn of the Champaign County Historical Society, this event draws crafts specialists from throughout the region. Bring your Christmas list. For information call (937) 653-6721.

Annual Candlelight Tour of Homes. Usually held the first weekend in December, this local Cancer Association fund-raiser offers a tour of unique or historic homes in the Urbana area. For information call (937) 653-7207.

WEST LIBERTY, OHIO

Head north out of Urbana on U.S. 68 toward West Liberty, Ohio. A picturesque, friendly little town in the gently rolling hills of Logan County, West Liberty was originally platted in 1817. Visitor centers welcome you at the Chamber of Commerce, 100 South Main Street, (888) LOGANCO, and the Shell station at the junction of O–245 and U.S. 68. West Liberty is a stop on the Simon Kenton Historic Corridor and is home to a number of historic buildings, including the Town Hall and Mt. Tabor Church. This old country church was the site of a camp meeting in 1816 at which frontiersman Simon Kenton joined the Methodist Church. Here, along with Christian Indians from nearby Mingo, Ohio, Kenton would come to worship.

WHAT TO SEE AND DO

Freshwater Farms of Ohio. 2624 North U.S. 68, 1 mile north of Urbana on the way to West Liberty, this former chicken farm is answering today's need for fresh farm-raised fish. The old chicken house is now home to six freshwater raceways teeming with aquatic life. Trout and perch are raised for eating, and bass, catfish, amur, crawfish, and bluegill are raised to stock ponds and lakes. Fancy koi and fantail goldfish are produced for decorating the garden pond. Even minnows for bait and feeder fish are available here.

Freshwater Farms started in 1986 when Dr. David Smith, a marine biologist, heard the call from the region's fine restaurants for top-quality fresh fish. Freshwater Farms now also sells live and dressed fish to individuals and upscale grocery stores. The growing popularity of outdoor fish ponds has prompted the farm to carry pumps, water plants, and other pond necessities.

"Dr. Dave's" mom is just one of the casual tour guides who seem to know their stuff when it comes to meeting the demand for fresh fish and helping the farmer and the homeowner maintain a healthy, ecologically balanced pond. Kids love Freshwater Farms, especially the invitation to feed the fish. Smoked trout (ask to taste a sample), fresh-dressed trout, vacuum-frozen trout patties and fillets (marinated or straight-up), and accompanying sauces are available to take home or have shipped anywhere in the world. Open 1:00 to 6:00 P.M. Monday through Friday and 10:00 A.M. to 6:00 P.M. Saturday. Drop in for a free tour of this one-of-a-kind aquaculture operation. Call (937) 652-3701.

Ohio Caverns. Continue north on U.S. 68, then head east on O–507, and follow the signs to what is billed as "An Underground Fairyland Carved by Nature." Ohio's largest underground caverns, these are also known as America's most colorful, offering some of the finest specimens of stalactites and stalagmites. Bring your camera and flash to capture the beauty of Devil's Tea Table, Palace of the Gods, Crystal Sea, and many other spectacular, nicknamed formations. At nearly 5 feet tall, the Crystal King is the largest, most perfectly formed pure white stalactite found anywhere.

Formed as calcium carbonate builds up over thousands of years, the many crystal-white formations of Ohio Caverns are particularly exquisite, thanks to a subtle new lighting system. When light passes through many of the stalactites, stalagmites, and helactites (hollow soda-straw formations), they give the caverns a soft, eerie glow.

The caverns' well-earned reputation for color comes from its variety of formations. The only dual formations in North America are found here. These combine spikes of milky-white calcium with pitted, honeycomb-shaped, red-brown, iron-manganese formations.

The caverns were discovered in 1897 when a seventeen-year-old farm worker wondered about the disappearance of water into a low spot in his field. Robert Nofsinger grabbed his shovel and dug down just a few feet before he discovered this subterranean wonder. The caverns were opened to the public that same year. In 1922, a horse-drawn elevator pulled up the muck that filled additional areas of the caverns. After these pathways were cleared, the first electric lights were added and public tours began.

The basic tour lasts forty-five minutes and takes visitors a full 103 feet underground. A longer historical tour is also available for groups of twenty or more. No matter what the above-ground temperature, Ohio Caverns are always fifty-two degrees, so you may want to bring a jacket. Comfortable shoes and a camera are a must. The tour is a comfortable one, over fairly smooth surfaces, but to leave the cavern, you'll climb sixty stairs as the music from the state song, "Beautiful Ohio," plays on an underground sound system.

Situated just above the caverns, a thirty-five-acre park, flower gardens, and a picnic pavilion offer a picture-postcard view of nearby hilly farm fields. Soft drinks are sold, but no food is served. An expansive gift shop offers cavern and geology souvenirs, plus some Indian artifacts. You can also see the state's largest amethyst geode—a 6.5 foot, 693-pounder. Open April through October 9:00 A.M. to 5:00 P.M. and November through March 9:00 A.M. to 4:00 P.M. Closed Thanksgiving and Christmas. Admission fee. Call (937) 465-4017.

Pioneer House. 10245 Township Road 47, West Liberty 43357. Built in 1828, this historic log house was an important stop on the Underground Railroad and was the home of Judge Benjamin Piatt and his wife, Elizabeth. As an elected official, Judge Piatt was not supposed to be involved in helping to free runaway slaves. Whenever he was away, therefore, a light in the doorway would let runaways know that Pioneer House was a safe haven. Elizabeth would hide them in a secret passage above the home's eleven rooms. Before returning home, Judge Piatt would send a runner ahead to warn Elizabeth to move the people along to their next stop on the Underground Railroad.

Pioneer House is now fully restored and functions as a charming country gift and antiques shop. Current owners proudly display restoration photos, including snapshots of a time when this important log structure was covered with rotting clapboard siding. Open daily May through December 11:00 A.M. to 5:00 P.M. and Sunday 1:00 to 5:00 P.M. January through April, by appointment only. The $1.00 admission fee includes a history-filled tour and a peek at the one-time hiding place for runaway slaves. Call (937) 465-4801.

Piatt Castles. O-245 at O-287, 1 mile east of West Liberty 43357. Two of Benjamin and Elizabeth Piatt's sons built spectacular homesteads known today as the Piatt Castles. Because of their love of the region's pastoral farmland, both sons settled very near Pioneer House. Their homes are listed on the National Register of Historic Places and are open for tours. Unheard-of amounts of elaborate woodwork, rich furnishings, and shelves of rare books seem to go on forever in these mansions. Forty-five-minute tours are offered for each "castle," with knowledgeable guides telling rich tales of regional, period, and family history.

Mac-A-Cheek, the home of Civil War general and gentleman farmer Abram Sanders Piatt, was completed in 1871. Abram started constructing Mac-A-Cheek, named for a local Shawnee Indian encampment, in 1860 on the top of a hill with a breathtaking view of Mad River Valley. Built from limestone carved on-site and finished in glowing hardwoods from the valley, this Norman French-style mansion is decorated with elaborate frescoed ceilings and stenciled walls. Mac-A-Cheek is still completely furnished with original Piatt family belongings.

Mac-O-Chee (also to honor another Native American camp), the creation of writer and social critic Donn Piatt, was started in the 1860s as a Gothic-style retreat. Its second stage, a Flemish limestone section that wraps around the original structure, was completed in 1881. After the home was completed, the family was renowned for regularly hosting elaborate parties. Area newspapers frequently carried stories of the revelry that took place at Mac-O-Chee. You can still see the sweeping path created long ago by horse-drawn carriages delivering partygoers to the door of the Mac-O-Chee castle.

An impressive collection of war relics, Native American artifacts, and European and Asian antiques fills the mansions. Both are available for special events and weddings. Open daily 11:00 A.M. to 5:00 P.M. for guided tours May through September, and noon to 4:00 P.M. April and October. Separate admission fee for each home. Call (937) 465–2821.

Marie's Candies. 311 Zanesville Road, West Liberty 43357. Rich, fresh-tasting chocolates, complemented by the rich history of how Marie King started creating candies, make a visit to this confectionery worthwhile. In 1941, Marie's husband, a hardworking farmer named Winfred, was stricken with polio and confined to a wheelchair. Marie thanked friends and neighbors for their outpouring of support and favors with gifts of handmade candy. The couple then turned that expression of thanks into the family livelihood, and Marie's Candies opened for business in 1956. In 1977, after his father's death, son Jay took over the operation, which now occupies the old West Liberty train depot.

If Marie's is making candy—and if the crew isn't too busy—you'll be allowed into the kitchen to watch as these delicious chocolates are made in much the same way Marie made them fifty years ago. Marie's still uses pure chocolate, 40 percent fresh cream, and real butter. There are always free samples, which are not to be missed, and Marie's will ship chocolates anywhere. Open 8:00 A.M. to 6:00 P.M. Monday–Saturday. Call (937) 465-3061.

WHERE TO SHOP

Liberty General Store. 102 North Detroit Street, West Liberty 43357. This is one of the last of a dying breed of general stores still found in America's small towns. Friendly owners Fred and Iris Latimer proudly proclaim: "We have everything. Or we can order it for you." Bulk garden seeds are sold by the scoop, and the store is packed with unique dry goods, notions, an array of clay pottery, hardware, and more. A working old-time penny scale still sits by the door. Fred's pride and joy, four model railroad trains, circle the store overhead on track laid just below the ceiling. Open 8:00 A.M. to 6:00 P.M. Monday–Friday and 9:00 A.M. to 5:00 P.M. Saturday. Call (937) 465-7911.

Global Crafts. 106 North Detroit Street, West Liberty 43357. A wide selection of decorative accessories, jewelry, and ethnic crafts imported from all around the world makes this a fun place to browse. Proceeds from Global Crafts benefit charity. Open 10:00 A.M. to 5:00 P.M. Monday–Friday, 10:00 A.M. to 4:00 P.M. Wednesday and Saturday. Call (937) 465-3077.

The Trumpet Vine. 108 North Detroit Street, West Liberty 43357. Scented candles, sachets, and potpourri permeate your senses when you enter the door. The Trumpet Vine is filled with traditional and upscale country boutique items. This gift shop has a hefty collection of primitives and charmingly dressed teddy bears. Open 10:00 A.M. to 5:00 P.M. Monday–Saturday. (937) 465-1270.

Liberty Antiques. 111 East Baird, West Liberty 43357. Roomy and dark, Liberty Antiques offers a small but interesting collection of antiques and period collectibles. Open 10:00 A.M. to 5:00 P.M. Monday–Saturday. Call (937) 465-0800.

WHERE TO EAT

Liberty Gathering Place. 111 North Detroit Street, West Liberty 43357. A typical small-town diner, Liberty Gathering Place offers a varied menu of hearty breakfasts, sandwiches, and family-style meals. Lumpy, real mashed potatoes and the fried-pork tenderloin sandwich are recommended favorites. $. ☐. Open 5:30 A.M. to 7:30 P.M. Monday–Friday, 6:00 A.M. to 7:30 P.M. Saturday, and 8:00 A.M. to 2:30 P.M. Sunday. Call (937) 465–3081.

Ice Cream Parlor. 100 North Detroit Street, West Liberty 43357. The Ice Cream Parlor has been scooping up creamy treats for residents of West Liberty for more than forty years. Giant scoops are just over $1.00. The Strapp family is proud to serve Nafziger's Ice Cream, made in nearby Archbold, Ohio. Nafziger's is the real thing. Try the Chocolate Caramel Royale—rich chocolate ice cream, gooey swirls of caramel, and huge chunks of real caramel-filled chocolates. Shakes, malts, sodas, and chips are also served. Open noon to 10:00 P.M. Monday–Saturday, and 2:00 to 10:00 P.M. Sunday. Call (937) 465–5950.

Kings Island

Just 20 miles northeast of Cincinnati on northbound Interstate 71 is the Kings Island recreation area, including and centering upon Paramount's Kings Island itself. This amusement park rivals the Disney operations in Florida and California.

If Kings Island were traced to its origins, it could claim to be the oldest of all the amusement giants, having been born not here but on the banks of the Ohio River well before the Civil War.

There was a piece of prime bottomland east of the city that had never been cleared for farming, as had most other property at the river's edge. It had enormous shade trees and a small orchard, and it was known as Parker's Grove. Nineteenth-century city folk enjoyed loading the family into the buggy and heading out there for a picnic and perhaps a wade in the river. Farmer Parker was happy to let them use this quiet spot, and later, in fact, he even built a shelter house for them. Then he began selling food there and added a bandstand and other attractions over the years.

Known in this century as Coney Island, the park grew to include one of the nation's earliest roller coasters and many other rides and attractions. A ferryboat operation started to bring people across the river from Kentucky, and steamboats regularly brought people up in summer from Cincinnati's Public Landing. That service ended when the last of these boats, a beautiful white sidewheeler called the *Island Queen*, exploded and burned during a winter overhaul in Pittsburgh in 1947. Many Cincinnatians over fifty remember that event with sadness, for the *Queen*'s excursions, her evening calliope concerts, and the lovely image of her, ablaze with lights, sailing the river at night were so very much a part of this city. Old Coney's Moonlight

Day Trip 1 Northeast

0   10   20   30 miles

Gardens was a popular dance hall, especially from the 1920s through the 1940s, and gave rise to many stars, including singers Rosemary and Betty Clooney.

But by the 1960s Old Coney suffered from overuse. There were many new things to add but not an inch of ground available for expansion. So its owners moved, like everyone else was doing, from the urban crowd to the broad, flat farmlands north of the city in 1971. Old Coney, on U.S. 52 next to River Downs Race Track and Riverbend, Cincinnati's summer concert venue, is popular today chiefly for Sunlight Pool, a mecca for swimmers.

KINGS ISLAND

You know you're almost there when you see in the distance the park's one-third scale version of the Eiffel Tower rising 330 feet above the plain. The Interstate 71 exit to Kings Mills Road is well-marked.

Today the 1,600-acre complex consists of several major parts. A left on Kings Mills Road takes you first to The Beach, a thirty-five-acre water park, and then to the Golf Center at Kings Island, a championship golf center. A right onto Kings Mills Road takes you to Kings Island Drive, then another right turn takes you to Kings Island Resort and Conference Center, the Paramount's Kings Island Campground, and finally the sprawling, 350-acre amusement park itself.

PARAMOUNT'S KINGS ISLAND THEME PARK

The Kings Island area is home to one of the largest thrill parks in the Midwest. Paramount's Kings Island specializes in family fun with more than 200 rides, attractions, and live shows. Explore a variety of themed areas, including Hanna-Barbera Land and Nick-elodeon Central. New family fun includes The Wild Thornberry's River Adventure; Nick Jr.'s huggable, lovable Blue; and Rugrats Runaway Reptar, a one-of-a-kind suspended kids' coaster. Son of Beast, the tallest, fastest, only-wooden roller coaster in the world, has joined its father, The Beast, at the park. The Beast held the world title as the longest wooden roller coaster for an astonishing twenty-two years.

The thirty-acre WaterWorks, free with park admission, offers a cool-down dunk from a lazy river float, including cool water slides and the WipeOut Beach body board surfing challenge, and more than thirty other water attractions.

The park has plenty of other entertainment options, with live Broadway shows, a variety of gift shops, and, of course, many restaurants and eateries.

In the fall the park transforms itself into a horrifying expanse of shock, dread, and terror for Fearfest. Five haunted walk-through experiences bring you face to face with mummies, ghouls, and skeletons. Fearfest is deemed too intense for the faint of heart and those under twelve, so Paramount's Kings Island also offers Kids' Howl-O-Fest on weekends in October. The park transforms its Hanna-Barbera Land into a fall festival with family activities.

One-price admission covers most park activities except food and gift purchases. Admission ranges from about $21 for seniors and children three to six years old to about $40 for adults. The state tourism office, (800) BUCKEYE, will send you discount coupons to this and other attractions. Children two and under are admitted free. Multiple-day and season passes are available at lower rates. Fee for parking. Prices change almost every year.

Paramount's Kings Island is open daily from Memorial Day through late August, on weekends from mid-April to Memorial Day, and on selected weekends from Labor Day through mid-October. The park opens at 9:00 A.M., with rides starting at 10:00 A.M. Closing time varies and is posted at the Main Gate daily but usually is between 9:00 and 11:00 P.M. A fireworks display winds up the day. Patrons are not permitted to bring food into the park. Picnickers must use tables near but outside the main gate.

For information write Paramount's Kings Island Theme Park, Kings Island 45034, or call (800) 288–0808.

WHERE TO STAY

Kings Island Resort and Conference Center. Across Kings Island Drive from the theme park. This large, modern hostelry offers indoor and outdoor swimming pools, a playground, Cassidy's Lounge, and free shuttle service to the theme park. Open all year. Call (513) 398–0115 or (800) 727–3050. Several other hotels, many newly opened, are also near the theme park at the Kings Mills exit off Interstate 71. For details, call (800) 791-4FUN or stop at the Kings Island Drive information booth.

THE GOLF CENTER AT KINGS ISLAND

Located off Kings Mills Road on the opposite side of Interstate 71 from the rest of the Kings Island complex, this center has hosted the Kroger Senior Classic, a PGA Tour event, and Tennis Masters Series–Cincinnati championship tournaments. At the former Jack Nicklaus Sports Center, you'll find the famous 27-hole "Grizzly," a championship course, and the 18-hole "Bruin," an executive course— both designed by Nicklaus. Overlooking eight championship tennis courts is a 10,500-seat stadium.

The Golf Center offers a driving range, a practice putting green, locker rooms, a resident golf pro, a pro shop, and a clubhouse and restaurant. The Course View Pavilion seats 350 people. It is open daily for public use—primarily meetings and banquets—on a fee basis March–December. For information call (513) 398-5200. For tee times call (513) 398-7700.

THE BEACH WATERPARK

Located off Kings Mills Road, across from the Golf Center, The Beach Waterpark complex is thirty-five acres of water fun nestled in a beautiful, wooded valley. With more than thirty-two rides and activities for all ages, the park is a popular attraction. One of the most thrilling rides is The Cliff, a five-story waterslide, partially free-fall, which ends in a tunnel chute to the landing pool. Thunder Beach Wave Pool makes ocean-size waves for body surfing, while the Lazy Miami, an inner-tube meander throughout the park, is very relaxing. And the water coaster, Aztec Adventure, sends riders up and down a water slide.

Open-air restaurants serve pizza, traditional picnic fare, barbecue, and ice cream. KoKoMo Kove is a beer-and-wine area with a stage featuring reggae bands and other entertainment. The complex includes sand volleyball, a basketball court, plenty of sand for castles, and live palm trees.

Patrons may not bring food or beverages into the park, but a picnic area is available on the east side of the parking lot. The Beach is open daily Memorial Day weekend through Labor Day weekend and selected weekends in May and September. Hours vary during the season but generally are 10:00 A.M. to 9:00 P.M.

General admission is $20.00 for adults, $6.00 for children, and free for children age two and under. Season passes are available.

There is a parking charge. Tube and locker rentals are also available. Call (800) 886-SWIM for information.

Vineyards again are blooming in the Ohio Valley, as they did in the early nineteenth century, and wineries have emerged to produce very creditable varieties of wines. Two such wineries are clustered around Lebanon, Ohio, just an hour's drive northeast of Cincinnati via Interstate 71. You may have time to visit the earthworks built by prehistoric Indians at Fort Ancient or watch the trotters at Lebanon Raceway, but the highlight of the trip is a meal at the Golden Lamb in Lebanon, Ohio's oldest continuously operating inn.

LEBANON, OHIO

Take Interstate 71 north from Cincinnati, past Kings Island, to the Lebanon (O–48) exit and follow O–48 north into town. This picturesque town is the county seat of Warren County and is full of lovely turn-of-the-century buildings. Rich in history, Lebanon offers two museums and more than fifty fine antiques and specialty shops in which to while away the day.

Lebanon was established as a farming community in 1796. That many of the early farmers were Shakers, a branch of the Quaker (Society of Friends) religion, contributed a note of orderliness and austerity to the city's early development. Today, however, little remains of the Shaker heritage, except for Union Village, former center of the Shaker community, which was sold in the 1920s and now serves as a retirement home.

Day Trip 2 Northeast

0   10   20   30 miles

WHERE TO EAT AND STAY

The Golden Lamb. 27 South Broadway, Lebanon 45036. This hand-some brick building in the center of town began as a log tavern in 1803 and has been in continuous operation ever since. As Ohio's oldest inn, it has served generations of travelers, including such illustrious ones as Charles Dickens, Mark Twain, and ten U.S. presidents. In memory of their visits, the inn displays their names on brass plaques attached to the doors of the rooms in which they stayed.

Widely known for fine dining, the Golden Lamb is most beautiful at night, when chandeliers sparkle through its antique windows and coach lamps spread a warm glow across its entrance, an inviting sight indeed. Dining here is a most rewarding experience. Be sure to make reservations before you leave Cincinnati.

Well-appointed tables, gracious service, and moderate prices distinguish this restaurant, which is owned by the internationally known Comisar family, proprietors of the five-star Maisonette restaurant in downtown Cincinnati. But there is no French menu at the Golden Lamb. Traditional American dishes include roast loin of pork, duckling in orange sauce, generous slices of prime rib, broiled trout, fried chicken with biscuits and gravy, and roast tom turkey from a Warren County farm. Baked goods are made in-house, and the celery seed house dressing for salads is so popular that it is sold by the jar at the front desk. Cocktails are also generous, and there is, of course, a Comisar wine list if you're in the mood to compare Ohio Valley wines with those of California, New York, France, Germany, or Italy.

The Golden Lamb has 18 guestrooms, and while they lack many modern comforts, the Golden Lamb is a unique overnight spot. Don't miss the extensive gift shop. $$$. ☐. Reservations are strongly recommended. Open for lunch and dinner every day. Closed on Christmas. For hours call (513) 932-5065.

Houston Inn. 4026 US 42, Lebanon 45036. Boasts Cincinnati's greatest salad selections and the house specialty, deep-fried frog legs. A wide selection of entrees. Open evenings only. Closed Mondays. $$$ ☐. For hours and reservations, call (513) 398-7377.

Best Cafe. 17 East Mulberry, Lebanon 45036. Unique sandwich and salad offerings and the prime rib brunch buffet are popular for lunch, with nightly dinner specials featuring unusually creative American and Continental cuisine. All are served up in a cozy cafe atmosphere. $$. ☐. Open 11:00 A.M. to 8:30 P.M. Monday–Thursday, 11:00 A.M. to 9:30 P.M. Friday and Saturday, and 10:00 A.M. to 4:00 P.M. Sunday. Call (513) 932–4400.

The Gourmet on Broadway. 20 North Broadway, Lebanon 45036. Gourmet desserts and coffees. Soups and salads. Fresh breads and Mediterranean specialties. Coffees by the pound. Lunch only, Monday–Saturday. $$. ☐. Call (513) 933–8377.

The Sycamore Tree Tea Room. 3 South Sycamore Street, Lebanon 45036. Soups, sandwiches, salads, desserts, and a full lunch menu served in a quaint Victorian setting. A great escape venue for quiet dining. $$. ☐. Call (513) 932–4567.

Shaker Run Golf Clubhouse and Grille. 4361 Greentree Road, Lebanon 45036. A public golf and dining facility with country club amenities. Open for lunch and dinner, offering a wide array of tantalizing menu alternatives to please every palate. Enjoy the scenery in a relaxed atmosphere. $$. ☐. Call (513) 727–0007.

The Village Ice Cream Parlor. 22 South Broadway, Lebanon 45036. A visit to Lebanon is not complete without a stop for a shake or a cone at this quaint parlor, with its old-time soda fountain, wrought-iron tables and chairs, and great sandwich menu. It's so picturesque that it has been used as a movie set, including scenes in *Milk Money,* starring Melanie Griffith. Open for lunch and dinner every day. $. Call (513) 932–6918.

WHAT TO DO

Warren County Historical Society Museum. 105 South Broadway, Lebanon 45036. Just down the street from the Golden Lamb, this museum contains an outstanding collection of Shaker furniture and artifacts. A reconstructed nineteenth-century village green, surrounded by turn-of-the-century shops, gives a real feel of what Lebanon was like one hundred years ago. Open 9:00 A.M. to 4:00 P.M. Tuesday–Saturday and noon to 4:00 P.M. Sunday. Closed Monday and major holidays. Admission is $3.00 for adults and $1.00 for students. Call (513) 932–1817.

Golden Turtle Chocolate Factory. 120 South Broadway, Lebanon 45036, half a block from the Golden Lamb in downtown Lebanon. Home of the Texas Tortoise and the Deluxe Almond Toffee, this is a tough shop to pass by. It ships its candy, too. Open 10:00 A.M. to 5:15 P.M. Monday–Saturday and noon to 5:00 P.M. Sunday. Call (513) 932-1990 or (800) 345-1994.

The Workshops of David T. Smith. 3600 Shawhan Road, Lebanon 45036. See museum-quality reproductions and American Redware pottery. Browse and shop in the showroom. Open 10:00 A.M. to 5:00 P.M. Tuesday–Saturday. Call (513) 932-2472.

Glendower State Memorial. 105 Cincinnati Avenue (U.S. 42), Lebanon 45036. This stately Greek Revival mansion, built around 1840, is furnished with period pieces and artifacts important to Warren County's history. In early December the mansion features candlelit tours of decorated rooms spiced with the aroma of hot cider, homemade Christmas cakes, and the fragrance of fresh greens. Open the first Wednesday of June through the last Sunday of October, noon to 4:00 P.M. Wednesday–Saturday, and 1:00 to 4:00 P.M. Sunday. Closed Monday, Tuesday, and major holidays. Open only weekends after Labor Day. Open in early December for Christmas tours. Admission fee. Special admission combination available with Warren County Historical Society Museum. Call (513) 932-1817.

Lebanon Raceway. 665 North Broadway, Lebanon 45036. Harness-racing fans love the action at Lebanon Raceway on the Warren County Fairgrounds. The racing season runs from October through May. Post time is 7:00 P.M., Tuesday, Thursday, Friday, and Saturday. Races are simulcast noon to midnight, Monday–Saturday. Closed in July. For exact dates and times, call (513) 932-4936.

Turtle Creek Valley Railway. 198 South Broadway, Lebanon 45036. The scenic Turtle Creek offers round-trip service from Lebanon Station on Saturday, Sunday, and holidays April through December, as well as Wednesdays and Fridays during the summer season. In autumn two-hour farm trips and hayrides offer leaf peepers a colorful excursion. Train Rides with Santa are a hit with children from late November to late December. Mystery Dinner Tours also are available. Call (513) 398-8584 for times and dates. Advance registration is required. Admission fee.

THE VINEYARDS

The art of wine-making was brought to the Ohio Valley by Swiss and German immigrants well before the Civil War. Cincinnati was a wine-producing center, where Nicholas Longworth's vineyards covered Mt. Adams, just to the east of downtown. Longworth made "the first American champagne" and cultivated the native American Catawba grape. Catawba wine moved a Longworth guest, poet Henry Wadsworth Longfellow, to pen one of his worst poems, but it ended with a famous verse that gave Cincinnati its title: "The Queen City." Wrote Longfellow:

> *The song of mine is the song of the vine,*
> *Which the winds and the birds shall deliver*
> *To the Queen of the West in her garlands dress'd*
> *By the banks of the beautiful river.*

Alas, the "song of the vine" was a short one. The Civil War pulled men from the fields for military service and the once-great vineyards deteriorated from lack of care. Soon after the war a blight known as the "Black Rot" swept the valley, ruining the industry. The oldest and largest Ohio Valley winery, Meier's in the Cincinnati suburb of Silverton, was able to survive only by moving its vineyards to the Isle of St. George and elsewhere along Lake Erie.

Blight conditions remain today, but thanks to research and experimental farms operated by Ohio State University, seasonal spraying of the vines protects the plants and produces healthy, juicy grapes. Now nearly a dozen wineries have sprung up in southern Ohio and southeastern Indiana.

The two wineries on this tour both offer sampling trays at a nominal cost, with small cups that hold barely an ounce each of the various labels. It is interesting to compare them. Some exhibit a "foxiness," or a very "grapey" taste that is peculiar to native American wild grapes. The term derives from the fox grape. Varying degrees of foxiness occur in the Aurora, Catawba, and Concord grapes, while French hybrids such as chenin blanc, Marshal Foch, and pinot noir are mellower, with richer overtones. Whites, reds, rosés—they're all here, and if you find one that pleases your palate, you can buy the modestly priced wines by the bottle or at a discount by the case.

Colonial Vineyards. 6222 North O-48, Lebanon 45036. From Lebanon take O-48 6 miles north. Look sharp for the sign to the right of the highway just before a left bend that takes you into Ridgeville.

The Norman Greene family farmhouse and a large remodeled barn are located just off the highway. The barn serves as both winery and tasting room.

Wines are bottled and labeled in the roadside barn. Colonial is open daily except 11:00 A.M. to 6:00 P.M. Sunday. Bottles to go and tasting trays are available, but food is not. Call (513) 932-3842.

Valley Vineyards. 2276 East U.S. 22, Morrow 45152. With forty acres at peak growth and 25,000 gallons of annual wine production, this is the second-largest vineyard in southern Ohio and one that has claimed several international awards. The winery, operated by the Ken Schuchter family, occupies a Swiss chalet-style building, with tasting and dining rooms on the main level, including a covered patio. Wine tasting can be accompanied by cheese and pizza, or you can try the popular Friday- and Saturday-night steak-and-wine dinners (reservations suggested). Tours of the wineworks on the lower level are available, and wine is for sale as samplers or by the bottle.

A large variety of grapes allows the Schuchters to produce fourteen labels, each with its own character and degree of sweetness. Additionally, the Schuchters blend their own sangria and also produce mead, an Old English specialty made of honey. If drunk daily for a month, the legend goes, mead will bring good fortune to newlyweds—hence the term *honeymoon.*

An interesting red wine is Schuchter's "Blue Eye" label. Once common from Pennsylvania to Missouri, the blue-eye grape was a favorite for making jellies but only on a small scale. The grapes, you see, ripened only on the side facing the sun and had to be hand-picked one by one. The blue eye eventually was abandoned for less troublesome varieties and, by 1950, was believed extinct. Then an Ohio State University oenologist spotted some of the vines growing along a suburban fence, and, with permission of the owner, took cuttings and established a vineyard. He then induced the Schuchters to do the same. Now Valley is the only known vineyard to produce a wine from the blue-eye grape. It is a delicious, robust, dry wine with only a slight foxy (grapey) overtone and is excellent with ham or rare beef.

The winery has imported Italian crushing machines and five antique oaken vats that hold 15,000 gallons each. Valley Vineyards is the focal point each September for a wine festival that draws 100,000 people in a single weekend. Open 11:00 A.M. to 8:00 P.M. Monday –Thursday, 11:00 A.M. to 11:00 P.M. Friday and Saturday, and 1:00 to 6:00 P.M. Sunday. Closed Thanksgiving, Christmas, and New Year's Day. Call (513) 899-2485.

FORT ANCIENT STATE MEMORIAL

Fort Ancient's earthworks, just off O–350 and 4 miles west of U.S. 22, are similar to many found in southern Ohio and Indiana but are older and are the second-largest in the nation after Ohio's Serpent Mound. (See Northeast Day Trip 4.) These fortlike walls of stone and clay were constructed between 300 B.C. and A.D. 600 by the Hopewell people.

The ramparts command a view from a bluff over the Little Miami River valley and enclose a one-hundred-acre field where graves and many artifacts were unearthed. Finds are now displayed in a museum on the grounds, along with relics taken from a nearby Indian village site. Despite extensive study, relatively little is known about these people or their origins, and the cause of their sudden disappearance remains a mystery.

The newly expanded fort now serves as the Ohio Historical Society's "Gateway Site" for Ohio American Indian history. New interactive exhibits lead visitors from 13,000 B.C., when the Ohio valley was first inhabited, to the present day. Indian artifacts from around the state are housed here, as well as a research library and classrooms.

The park, which also has a picnic area, is open daily from March 1 through late November starting at 10:00 A.M. with varying seasonal hours for the park site and museum. Admission is $5.00 for adults, $1.25 for children 6–12, and free for younger kids. Fees include admission to the park and museum. Call (800) 283-8904 or (513) 932-4421.

WHAT TO DO

Morgans' Canoe Livery. 5701 O–350, Oregonia 45054 (at the Little Miami River, at the foot of Fort Ancient State Memorial). The Morgans rent canoes, tubes, rafts, and kayaks and guide float trips for groups along the Little Miami, which has been designated a National Wild and Scenic River and is one of the top ten scenic rivers in the country. Trips vary from 6 to 16 miles in length. There is also a two-day trip. Except for experts, canoeing on this river is not recommended during the spring or after heavy rains. Rates vary. Picnic grove and snacks available. The livery is open daily April–October. Call (513) 932–7658 or (800) WE–CANOE.

The Dude Ranch. 3205 Waynesville Road, Cincinnati 45152. Help bring the herd home at The Dude Ranch. Enjoy the fun as you ride horseback along heavily wooded trails and across gently rolling meadows. Horses are available for riders of all ability levels, including horses perfect for kids ages seven and up. City slickers can saddle up for a real cattle drive with authentic Texas Longhorns. Call (513) 956–8099 for rates and reservations.

Piatt Castles
West Liberty
287
Ohio Caverns
507
245
68
36
Urbana
Rothchild Berry Farm
Cedar Bog
75
SPRINGFIELD
COLUMBUS
40
70
Vandalia
Wright Patterson
AFB
Clifton
DAYTON
Yellow
Springs
John Bryan
State Park
Wilberforce
Xenia
42
68
Caesar Cr.
71
23
Waynesville
Ridgeville
73
Harveysburg
48
Wilmington
Chillicothe
Lebanon
75
50
Fort Ancient
22
OHIO
42
Kings
Island
Morrow
Hillsboro
Bainbridge
50
275
73
124
Fort Hill
CINCINNATI
41
275
23
Serpent Mound
Locust Grove
New Richmond
Point Pleasant
Moscow
Ferry
8
52
Portsmouth
Augusta
Ripley
Manchester
Maysville
OHIO RIVER
52
27
Washington
75

Day Trip 3 Northeast

0   10   20   30 miles

Cynthiana

68

Paris   **KENTUCKY**

Columbus is Ohio's capital and largest city, with a metropolitan area touching seven counties, covering 3,584 square miles, and including almost 1.4 million residents. Thanks to aggressive annexation in the 1960s, Columbus offers a diverse ethnic mix, with no one group dominating, as evidenced by its German Village area south of downtown and its Italian and Victorian Village areas just north of downtown.

Columbus is characterized by tree-lined boulevards, many fine parks, a riverside esplanade and amphitheater downtown along the Scioto River, excellent museums, numerous festivals, the statehouse and government buildings, and the huge Ohio State University.

COLUMBUS, OHIO

Columbus is Ohio's third capital. The first, Chillicothe, served in that role from statehood in 1803 until 1810, when the capital was moved to Zanesville in east-central Ohio. But the urge to have a centrally located seat of government quickly won out, and in 1812 a plot of level land across the Scioto River from the village of Franklinton was chosen as the site of a permanent statehouse. Another plot, south of Franklinton, was chosen for a state penitentiary. Those two structures thus became the new capital's first two buildings.

Chillicothe and Zanesville returned to rural tranquillity, while Columbus grew and grew, eventually swallowing little Franklinton and most of Franklin County, and it is still growing quickly into neighboring Delaware County. In a sense, government was the city's first and only important industry until 1831, when parts of the

Scioto River were incorporated into the old Ohio & Erie Canal system, linking upstate commerce with vital boat transportation on the Ohio River. Two years later, the National Road, now U.S. 40, reached Columbus from the east, and in 1850 the first railroad came through. Within thirty-eight years Columbus had become an important transportation hub for the state and a center for agriculture, commerce, and industry. In the 1960s the advent of interstate highways gave Columbus another boost. Its strategic location at the crossroads of the Midwest helped the city build an economy based on education, government services, information services, research, banking, insurance, science, and computer technologies.

Because its demographics were so typical, in the 1960s and 1970s Columbus became known as the perfect test market for all manner of products. But the 1980s brought a spurt of growth and sophistication that has catapulted this once-sleepy capital into national prominence as one of the nation's best places to live, work, and visit.

The influx of thousands of white-collar workers to major employers like The Ohio State University, The Limited, and banking, computer, and high-tech firms has fueled an arts renaissance in the city, in addition to major retail, education, and building booms.

GETTING AROUND

Downtown Columbus is divided into four almost-equal quadrants by Broad Street, which runs east and west, and High Street, which runs north and south. The state Capitol stands at their intersection. Incidentally, Broad Street is also U.S. 40, the National Road. All other downtown streets are labeled north or south, east or west from the intersection of Broad and High Streets.

The Scioto River runs from north to south through the western quadrants but makes a big loop eastward in the center of the downtown area, curving to within 1.5 blocks of the statehouse. The tongue of land it defines is Columbus's West Side and includes the former village of Franklinton.

Third Street runs behind the Capitol a block east of and parallel to High Street. It is one-way south and is the route that reaches German Village a few blocks south of the downtown area.

Columbus Visitors Centers. Located in the Columbus City Center on the second level near Marshall Fields and at Easton Town Center, 160 Easton Town Center, Columbus 43219, the visitors centers are an excellent place to start your tour. Maps, brochures, and tour information provide quick orientation. Open 10:00 A.M. to 9:00 P.M. Monday–Saturday and noon to 6:00 P.M. Sunday. Special holiday hours. Call (614) 221-CITY or (800) 345-4FUN.

WHAT TO SEE AND DO: DOWNTOWN

Ohio Statehouse. Broad and High Streets. Completed in 1996, a $113 million restoration project returned the Ohio Statehouse to its original grandeur, resulting in one of the most spectacular state capitols in the United States. Enter the rotunda and look up at the splendid stained glass Great Seal of Ohio skylight. The beauty includes a grand white-marble staircase and painstakingly restored frescoes, hand-applied gold leaf, brass fixtures, detailed mosaic tile, and a room-sized state map inlaid in the floor with each county carved from a different marble. Even the doorknobs are special— solid brass stamped with the Great Seal of Ohio. The original cornerstone was laid in 1839, and the grand and unusual Greek Doric structure was completed twenty-two years later. Outside on the east side of the State house, a dramatic Veteran's Plaza was added in 1998 to pay tribute to war vets. When most recent renovations began, the Ohio Statehouse had 327 rooms. It is now open to the public for self-guided tours daily 8:00 A.M. to 7:00 P.M. Several guided tours are offered, beginning at 9:00 A.M. weekdays and 11:15 A.M. on weekends. Information booths in the rotunda and at the Third Street entrance offer tour brochures. Call (888) OHIO-23 or (614) 752-6350.

Columbus Association for the Performing Arts (CAPA). 55 East State Street, Columbus 43215, in the downtown area. This organization owns and operates the stunning Ohio Palace and Southern Theatres and offers top international touring entertainment—pop, jazz, folk, and classical music; dance; comedy—as well as classic films and a children's series. Call (614) 469-0939.

Columbus Symphony Orchestra. 55 East State Street, fifth floor, Columbus 43215. The highly acclaimed CSO and its music director, Alessandro Siciliani, perform classical and pops concerts

September–June in the historic Ohio Theatre and offer a popular outdoor summer series, Picnic with the Pops. Call (614) 228-9600.

Columbus Museum of Art. 480 East Broad Street, Columbus 43215, 4 blocks east of the statehouse. The museum has a wide range of art, from twelfth-century stone statuary and several Old Masters through modern stainless-steel kinetic sculptures. European sculpture, painting, and decorative arts from the sixteenth to the twentieth centuries are well-represented. Exhibits of nineteenth- and twentieth-century American paintings include numerous works by George Bellows and Elijah Pierce. An outdoor sculpture garden, the Palette Restaurant, and a museum gift shop are also available. Open 11:00 A.M. to 4:00 P.M. Tuesday–Friday, 10:00 A.M. to 5:00 P.M. Saturday, and 11:00 A.M. to 5:00 P.M. Sunday. Closed Monday and major holidays. No admission fee. Call (614) 221-6801.

Topiary Garden. Old Deaf School Park, East Town Street behind the Main Columbus Metropolitan Library at 96 South Grant. This magnificent, one-of-a-kind topiary garden was started in 1988 and is wholly developed and maintained by volunteers. The garden is a complete reproduction of Georges Seurat's painting *A Sunday Afternoon on the Island of La Grande Jatte.* More than fifty life-size topiary sculptures of men, women, children—even the dogs, the cat, and the monkey depicted in Seurat's famous painting—are sculpted from yews and other foliage. Topiary boats float atop a real pond, with the largest figure standing 12 feet tall. The best time for viewing this living masterpiece is April–November. Bring your camera.

Ohio Theatre. 39 East State Street, Columbus 43215, 1 block south of the Capitol. This magnificent Baroque-style theater, restored in the 1970s, is the home of the Columbus Symphony Orchestra and Ballet Met. The stunningly modern Galbreath Pavilion was added in the 1980s for rehearsal and classroom space and for receptions. Under the aegis of the Columbus Association for the Performing Arts, programs of American dance, classical theater, international artists, organ concerts, and special films are often booked here. For information or tickets, call (614) 469-1045 or 469-0939.

***Santa Maria* Replica.** Battelle Riverfront Park, at Marconi Boulevard and Broad Street in downtown Columbus. Tour a museum-quality, full-scale replica of Christopher Columbus's flagship.

Visitors learn about life as a fifteenth-century seaman. Admission fee. Open 10:30 A.M. to 6:00 P.M. daily in the summer. Call (614) 645–8760 for fall and winter hours.

COSI Columbus. 333 West Broad Street, Columbus 43215. A Columbus landmark for more than thirty-five years, the Center of Science and Industry has recently found a new home on the west bank of the Scioto River in downtown Columbus. The Fascination Destination, as it is referred to now, is a 300,000-square-foot Science Center with immersive, highly interactive, hands-on learning experiences for all ages. COSI houses eight Learning Worlds filled with challenging and intriguing exhibits, three theaters, a retail store, a restaurant, an outdoor science park, exhibit galleries, and the world's only high-wire unicycle. Everything in each Learning World is related to the world's title in some form, with a multitude of discovery opportunities that include: Adventure, Gadgets, Life, Ocean, Progress, i|o, and Space. Open 10:00 A.M. to 5:00 P.M.; theater, restaurant, and retail shop open until 9:00 P.M. Friday and Saturday. Admission and parking fees. Call (877) 257–COSI or (614) 228–2674.

WHERE TO SHOP: DOWNTOWN

Columbus City Center. 111 South Third Street, Columbus 43215. Just across the way from the statehouse, Columbus's hottest shopping area, opened in 1989, is a glittering $200 million, three-level complex of more than 135 fancy shops, department stores, and places to eat. New York's Metropolitan Museum of Art store was impressed enough to open a branch here. Marshall Fields and Abercrombie and Fitch joined the flagship Lazarus store and Jacobson's to make this retail center one of the best in the United States. Open 10:00 A.M. to 9:00 P.M. Monday–Saturday and noon to 6:00 P.M. Sunday. Call (614) 221–4900.

WHERE TO EAT: DOWNTOWN

The "newest" area for nightlife and entertainment in Columbus is the Arena district. It features the Nationwide Arena, ice skating at the CoreComm Icehaus, and a variety of clubs and restaurants. One of the most interesting is the **Gordon Biersch Brewery Restaurant.** Located at 401 Front Street, this brewpub is a delight to all of the senses with its upscale and imaginative menu, fresh-brewed lagers, and interesting architecture. Call (614) 246-2900 for more information.

Tapatio. 491 North Park Street, Columbus 43215. Serving regional Mexican, Latin American, and Caribbean cuisine, Tapatio offers a memorable dining experience. Demand for zesty Tapatio bread, crusty sourdough with crushed peppers served with herb butter, has been so great that it's now available for take-out at the restaurant and across the street at the North Market. Reservations are recommended at this popular spot. ☐. $$. Call (614) 221-1085.

Mitchell's Steakhouse. 45 North Third Street, Columbus 43215. Making Columbus home to a pair of great—albeit pricey—downtown steakhouses, Mitchell's was opened in 1998 by one of Columbus's favorite restaurateurs, Cameron Mitchell. In just five years, Mitchell has launched eight incredibly successful restaurants, nearly all with different concepts. The steakhouse, with its soaring 25-foot tin ceilings and chic art deco decor, feels like it would be at home in the Big Apple. But it's big steaks with big flavor that are the big draw, like the 24-ounce, $30 porterhouse. Everything on the menu is a la carte, including the memorable mashed potatoes. $$$. ☐. Call (614) 621-2333.

SOUTH OF DOWNTOWN

German Village. Take Third Street south from downtown to just past its junction with Interstate 70. Perhaps the city's best-known attraction, German Village is a charming area of restored nineteenth-century homes and gardens that now houses a multitude of shops and restaurants and a grand expanse of green called Schiller Park, named for the German poet. The area, from Livingston Avenue on the north to Nursery Lane on the south, includes some 1,800 buildings. Many of them have been restored.

Your first stop should be at 588 South Third Street, the village's information headquarters, for a self-guided walking-tour map and other information. Open from 9:00 A.M. to 4:00 P.M. Monday–Friday and 10:00 A.M. to 2:00 P.M. Saturday. Call (614) 221-8888.

The neighborhood was settled by Germans in the early nineteenth century. Most of the buildings are brick, with slate roofs, and are about 160 years old. The original German community began to break up under the pressures of World War I, the Great Depression, Prohibition, and World War II and disappeared with the migrations to the suburbs. The neighborhood rapidly deteriorated until 1960, when the German Village Society was formed to acquire and restore the buildings to save them from being demolished in an urban renewal plan. The area is now a National Historic Site.

The restoration project was so successful, it fueled similar revitalizations in two other historic neighborhoods, Victorian Village and Italian Village, both just north of the downtown area. As a result, downtown Columbus is flanked by a trio of beautifully restored districts.

German Village has dozens of interesting shops and good restaurants and is the setting for many annual events, including the Village Valuables Sale in May and the Haus und Garten Tour in June.

WHERE TO SHOP

The Book Loft. 631 South Third Street, Columbus 43206. No visit to the village is complete without a one- or two-hour browse through the thirty-two rooms of this all-discount bookstore. Any book imaginable can be discounted as high as 95 percent. For hours call (614) 464-1774.

Hausfrau Haven. 769 South Third Street, Columbus 43206. Sort of a general store, Hausfrau's offers unusual gifts, cards, wine, wonderful candy, and other stuff. It's worth a visit. For hours call (614) 443-3680.

WHERE TO EAT

Lindey's. 169 East Beck Street, Columbus 43206. One of the most popular restaurants in Columbus, Lindey's (formerly known as the Lindenhof) is nestled in the heart of German Village. The progressive American menu features gourmet pizzas, pastas, and grilled and sauteed entrees. Open daily. $$. ☐. Reservations recommended. Call (614) 228-4343.

Schmidt's Sausage Haus. 240 East Kossuth Street, Columbus 43206. One of the oldest traditional German Village eateries, where the proprietors make their own sausage and desserts to die for.

Located in a restored brick building, Schmidt's has an Old World atmosphere and plenty of German bier. Open daily for lunch and dinner. German entertainment Tuesday–Saturday nights. $$. ◻. Call (614) 444-6808.

Katzinger's Delicatessen. 475 South Third Street, Columbus 43206. This New York–style deli offers an extensive overstuffed sandwich menu, soups, salads, and a large selection of imported foods. Open daily. $. ◻. Call (614) 228-3354.

NORTH OF DOWNTOWN

Short North Arts District. Just north of the downtown area and south of the Ohio State campus is a 5-block-long district along High Street called Short North. Born in the 1980s of a collaboration of local businesses, entrepreneurs, and artists, the area is an exciting mix of art galleries, trendy boutiques, bars, and restaurants with eclectic menus. The first Saturday of every month, Short North jumps with the Gallery Hop, an evening of openings, performances, spirits, and victuals in more than thirty of the district's emporia. North Market, a lively farmers' market open daily, offers the freshest produce, flowers, meats, and ethnic foods.

Adjacent to the successfully restored neighborhoods of Victorian Village and Italian Village, the Short North attracts their residents, students from the campus, downtown professionals, and serious art lovers from all over.

Ohio State University Campus. 30 West Fifteenth Avenue, Columbus 43201. Mimicking the sprawl of Columbus, OSU is really a city within a city. Spread over about 1,600 acres, the university has 53,000 students, 28,500 employees, and uncounted cows, which graze in the veterinary school fields within sight of the famous Ohio Stadium. With eight schools and eighteen colleges, OSU is a national leader in medicine, the arts, education, the sciences, and research. Tours are available at 10:00 A.M. and 2:00 P.M. Monday–Friday. Call (614) 292-3030.

Wexner Center for the Arts. North High Street at Fifteenth Avenue. This gleaming paean to the arts opened in November 1989 to rave reviews from artists, architects, alumni, and students. Boosted by a $25 million gift from alum Leslie Wexner, founder of The Limited, the $43 million Wexner Center is devoted to showcasing the cutting edge in the visual and performance arts. Free self-guided tours. Galleries are open 10:00 A.M. to 8:00 P.M. daily. Call (614) 292–0330 or (614) 292–2354.

Ohio Historical Center and Ohio Village. Interstate 71 at Seventeenth Avenue. The Ohio Historical Center is the core museum of the Ohio Historical Society, a private, nonprofit organization created in 1885 that operates fifty-nine historic sites throughout the state. Holding more than two million artifacts, the museum offers the following permanent exhibits: "The First Ohioans," "Ohio: Two Centuries of Change," and the most recent addition, "The Nature of Ohio," a renovated 14,000-square-foot exhibition showcasing Ohio's natural history from the Ice Age to the present. The center also features the Conway Mastodon, which lived in Ohio 12,000 years ago. Open year-round 9:00 A.M. to 5:00 P.M. Monday–Saturday and 10:00 A.M. to 5:00 P.M. Sunday and holidays. Closed Thanksgiving, Christmas, and New Year's Day. The center's library is open 9:00 A.M. to 5:00 P.M. Tuesday–Saturday. Closed on holidays. Call (614) 297–2439 or 297–2300.

Located next to the center is Ohio Village, a re-created Civil War–era town that represents a typical county seat during the 1860s, including town hall, print shop, general store, schoolhouse, and doctor's office. A rural community, the village features sixteen buildings, including a church, gardens, a sitting park, and a duck pond. The village is open 9:00 A.M. to 5:00 P.M. Wednesday–Saturday, January through November. Closed holidays and during the Ohio State Fair. Admission fee. Group rates available. Call (614) 297–2680.

Columbus Zoo. Follow the signs off the Sawmill Road exit of Interstate 270. Located along the Scioto River, the zoo's 400 acres include naturalistic wildlife habitats, gardens, picnic areas, and even a golf course. Known as one of North America's great zoos, the zoo that Jack Hannah made famous is now even better, thanks to a laundry list of major renovations. The elephant house now has an outdoor yard more than ten times its former size. The "gang room," which holds up to ten elephants, a 2,200-square-foot rhino exhibit, and the elephant maternity room are also new. The result is loads more space for the pachyderms and an improved experience for visitors. A new songbird aviary and prairie dog exhibit offer excellent up-close viewing. And the manatee exhibit is sure to become a favorite. The large glass viewing area features a 190,000-

gallon pool simulating a waterway between two islands that guides visitors along the edge of a beach. Discovery Reef gives you a scuba diver's view of ocean life around a coral reef. Inside a 65-foot-long aquarium, 100,000 gallons of salt water, thousands of pieces of human-made coral, and special wave-producing equipment create a lifelike home for some incredible sea creatures—including sharks and stingrays. In addition, the zoo has more than 700 species and 11,000 specimens, including the endangered cheetahs, black and white rhinos, white Bengal tigers, and bald eagles. The zoo is open every day of the year and is host to an outstanding concert series in the fall, as well as a stunning light display during the holiday season. Admission fee. For hours call (614) 645-4550.

Wyandot Lake and Amusement Park. Located next to the Columbus Zoo, Wyandot is a family park with wet and dry thrill rides, including thirteen waterslides, a wave pool, and a small wooden roller coaster. Admission fee. For hours call (614) 889-9283.

WHERE TO SHOP

Easton Town Center. 160 Easton Town Center, Easton Exit 33 off I-270, Columbus 43219. Easton Town Center isn't a mall. It's a combination of indoor and outdoor entertainment, dining and retail experiences. This pedestrian-friendly "shopping village," with green space and comfortable walkways, comprises 750,000 square feet of "best-of-class" restaurant, retail, and entertainment operators, including thirty that are new to Columbus. Open 10:00 A.M. to 9:00 P.M. Monday–Thursday, 10:00 A.M. to 10:00 P.M. Friday and Saturday, and 10:00 A.M. to 6:00 P.M. Sunday. Call (614) 337-2200.

The Mall at Tuttle Crossing. 5043 Tuttle Crossing Boulevard, Columbus 43016, near I-270. The mall features a unique combination of major stores and specialty shops, including Pottery Barn, Ann Taylor, Harold's, Talbots, Banana Republic, and Bath and Body Works at Home. An inviting food court, relaxing coffee/cappuccino areas, and a creative children's playscape are among the center's special family-oriented amenities. Call (614) 717-9604.

Dublin, Westerville, and Worthington. Once suburbs of Columbus, these areas, as a result of a growth spurt, now abut Columbus. They offer quaint antiques shops, and fascinating boutiques, and are worth a stop. Contact the Dublin Convention & Visitors Bureau at (614) 792-7666, the Westerville Chamber of Commerce at (614) 882-8917, and the Worthington Convention & Visitors Bureau at (614) 841-2545.

WHERE TO EAT

La Chatelaine. 1550 West Lane Avenue, Coumbus 43221, across from the Lane Avenue Shopping Center. Stan and Gigi Wielezynski came to Columbus from France and discovered a need for a good French bakery. They answered that need with La Chatelaine, offering hearth-baked Old World breads and elaborate French pastries available for dining in or take out. In summer months a lovely patio is the perfect place to enjoy a fresh salad, a bowl of authentic French onion soup, or the favorite, croque monsieur—crusty French bread stuffed with savory meats and cheese, dipped in béchamel sauce, and baked brown on the grill. Also, try the excellent French roast coffee and macaroons. $. ☐. A second restaurant is located just north of Columbus in Worthington at 627 North High Street. Call (614) 488-1911.

Buckeye Hall of Fame Cafe. 1421 Olentangy River Road, Columbus 43212. Ohio State University football is an addiction in Columbus, and the Buckeye Hall of Fame Cafe offers fans a fix. With an eye-popping collection of OSU sports memorabilia, the Buckeye Hall of Fame appears to be more of a shrine than a dining spot. But don't let case after case of Heisman trophies, basketball shoes, and Woody Hayes photos fool you. The menu is diverse and the food is excellent. The mammoth meatloaf sandwich, with its accompanying pesto mashed potatoes, fried onion straws, and demi-glaze, is tops. And no meal is complete without the legendary "Buckeyes" for dessert. Two perfectly round scoops of peanut butter ice cream are coated in hard chocolate, drizzled with fudge sauce and chopped nuts, and served with real whipped cream on the side. The huge arcade jammed with virtual reality, pinball, and a myriad of fun and games makes a visit to the Buckeye Hall of Fame Cafe a full afternoon or evening's entertainment. $$. ☐. Call (614) 291-2233.

Columbus Fish Market. 1245 Olentangy River Road, Columbus 43212. Another of Cameron Mitchell's culinary creations, the Columbus Fish Market gives Ohio's capital city a much-needed top-notch seafood restaurant. The varied menu features only fresh seafood and mixes old favorites with creative, New Age touches. For example, grouper is grilled and sweet-basted with a side of cheddar cheese grits and market veggies. The atmosphere is lively and casual. Save room for one of eight delicious deserts $$. ▢. Call (614) 291–3474.

SPECIAL EVENT

The Ohio State Fair. Ohio Exposition Center, 717 East Seventeenth Avenue, Columbus 43211-2698. Held for three weeks each August, the century-old Ohio State Fair is the most elaborate and best-attended of any in the area covered by this book. It is also one of the nation's largest. There are daily live entertainment shows by top-name performers, fireworks, harness racing, carnival booths and rides, and a wide variety of food concessions, plus extensive agricultural, livestock, and homemaking competitions. For information call (888) OHIO-EXPO, (614) 221–6623, 644–3247, or the visitors bureau, (800) 345-4FUN.

WHERE TO STAY

Being a state capital, Columbus has ample visitor lodging. Downtown hotels are well located for sightseeing but are more expensive than hotels on the outskirts of the city. The newest, most unusual hotel, The Lofts, opened in 1998 in a renovated plumbing supply warehouse that's listed on the National Register of Historic Places. None of The Lofts' forty-four huge rooms are alike. With 17-foot-high ceilings and floor-to-ceiling windows, interiors are individually designed and appointed with the finest Italian linens. Each guest is assigned a personal butler who will perform a multitude of tasks—from concierge services to shining shoes. Each morning, your butler delivers a cart loaded with an impressive European-style breakfast. Located at 55 Nationwide Boulevard, the hotel offers unique weekend getaway packages that include everything from a horse-drawn buggy ride through town to a Swedish massage. Call (800) 73-LOFTS.

Adjacent to The Lofts, the Crowne Plaza Hotel, 33 Nationwide Boulevard, was also recently refurbished and offers an indoor pool, a workout facility, and several restaurants. Call (614) 461-4100.

The Westin Great Southern Hotel, another historic building restored in the 1980s, is located at 310 South High Street. Its decor is Victorian, and it offers an English pub and restaurant. A historic theater on site was restored in 1998. The Great Southern Theater now offers live theatrical and musical performances as well as classic movies. Call (614) 228–3800.

There are two Hyatts, one at Capitol Square, 75 East State Street (614–228–1234) and another, the Hyatt Regency, attached to the Convention Center (614–463–1234).

Red Roof Inns are headquartered in Columbus and have no fewer than seven inns scattered around the city. Call (800) THE-ROOF. There are numerous Marriotts, Cross Country Inns, suite hotels, and bed-and-breakfasts throughout the city. Contact the Columbus Visitors Bureau for help.

If you're returning directly to Cincinnati, drive south on Third Street to the southern edge of the downtown area and follow the signs to Interstate 71 south.

If you are heading for Dayton, do the same, but follow the signs to Interstate 70 west.

If you plan to visit Chillicothe and the Indian mounds (see Northeast Day Trip 4), follow Third Street south and pick up U.S. 23 by following the signs. Follow U.S. 23 through Circleville to Chillicothe, a distance of 39 miles, all divided highway.

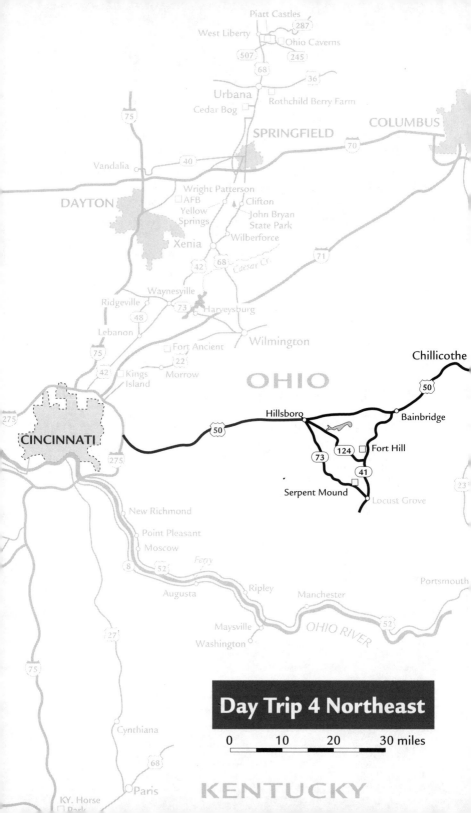

The gentle hills of south-central Ohio rise perceptibly as the traveler nears the Appalachian counties, cresting in such summits as Washburn Mountain, Rattlesnake Knob, and the peak that appears on the Great Seal of Ohio, Mount Logan. Two large human-made lakes, now the center of state parks, and a cave system lie along U.S. 50, the main route of this trip.

Chillicothe is deeply rooted in Ohio's early history. A pioneer settlement near Shawnee villages, it produced four Ohio governors and the state's constitution. Upon statehood in 1803 the village became Ohio's first capital.

But long before the Shawnee or the white settler, a mysterious race lived among these hills. They came here perhaps as long ago as 3,000 years and vanished about A.D. 1400, leaving few traces except for their earthen mounds. One, the effigy of a snake, is nearly a quarter-mile long.

As you travel east from Cincinnati on U.S. 50 on this trip, Ohio's past will begin to unfold, from the prehistory of the Hopewell Indians all the way through the establishment of the nation's first dental school in Bainbridge.

HILLSBORO, OHIO

A leisurely, 40-mile drive on U.S. 50 takes you to Hillsboro, Ohio, the county seat of Highland County. This fifty-minute drive goes through some of southwestern Ohio's best farm country. In summer you will see wide, rolling fields of corn, soybeans, and vegetables; numerous orchards; and frequent herds of grazing cattle. Farms here have a prosperous look about them. Barns are sturdy and freshly painted, and trim farmhouses stand in little groves of shade trees at the edge of the fields.

Hillsboro is an old, established community with many lovely, historic buildings, including the Highland County Courthouse, built in 1834. The brick edifice at Main and High Streets is the oldest courthouse in Ohio still being used for its original purpose.

The Highland County Convention & Visitors Bureau office at 1575 North High Street, Hillsboro 45133 is open 9:00 A.M. to 4:30 P.M. Monday–Friday and can help with information about the area. Call (937) 393-4883. The Highland House museum at 151 East Main Street is located in an 1842 house and is the home of the local historical society. Open Friday and Sunday afternoons, March through December. Call (937) 393-3392.

People from all over the county visit **McGees** at 129 West Main Street, Hillsboro 45133 to gobble the homemade pies. Thirty to fifty are made daily. Good home cooking makes this a popular lunch and dinner spot. Call (513) 393-2014.

Hillsboro's annual Festival of the Bells in early July commemorates the one-hundred-year heritage of the world's largest bell producer—C. S. Bell, headquartered in Hillsboro. Sadly, C. S. Bell went out of business in the mid-1970s, but its legacy still rings on farms, in schools, and in churches around the world.

WHAT TO SEE

Hillsboro forms the northwest point of the triangular area with Locust Grove to the southeast and Bainbridge to the east, within which are Indian mounds, lakes, and caves. The triangle is formed by O-73 from Hillsboro southeast to Locust Grove, O-41 northeast from Locust Grove to Bainbridge, and U.S. 50 on the north between Hillsboro and Bainbridge.

If you were in a helicopter, you would notice a definite craterlike formation 5 miles in diameter and nearly in the center of this triangle. Geologists do not agree on its origin. Some contend it was caused by a volcanic eruption. Others say the depression was gouged by a meteorite or is a sinkhole caused by the collapse of a cave or water basin deep underground. The human-made Serpent Mound is a mystery, too. It is easy to speculate that the two could somehow be related.

Serpent Mound State Memorial. On O-73, 18 miles southeast of Hillsboro (4 miles northwest of Locust Grove). This is by far the largest and the finest of any serpent effigy earthworks found in North America. It measures 1,348 feet from head to tail and is about fifteen feet high.

It is difficult to appreciate the mound fully without hiking up a 30-foot observation tower that looks out across its full length. The serpent's head is a stylized oval, cupped in a crescent. From here the body makes seven great back-and-forth loops and ends in a coil representing the tail. The mound and the area around it have been cleared of overgrowth and planted with grass to retard erosion. Archaeologists say it is not a burial mound but contains only rocks and yellow clay.

Because Serpent Mound contains no artifacts and was not constructed over burial grounds or remains of living areas, establishing which culture built it, and when, is difficult. Serpent Mound is believed to have been built by the Fort Ancient Indians, who settled in the area around 1,000 B.C. Nearby, a series of conical burial mounds were created by prehistoric Adena Indians sometime between 800 B.C. and A.D. 1. As a result of the discovery of these smaller mounds, archeologists originally associated the serpent effigy with the Adenas.

What little is known about these tribes is explained in displays at a small visitors center museum. There are hiking trails over the sixty-one-acre site, which includes a scenic gorge and picnic tables. There are three burial mounds on the grounds as well.

The park, established in 1889, is maintained by the Ohio Historical Society and is open 9:30 A.M. to 7:00 P.M. daily, Memorial Day–Labor Day. In April, May, September, and October, the park is open 10:00 A.M. to 5:00 P.M. Saturday and Sunday only. Museum hours vary. Parking fee. Call (937) 587-2796.

Fort Hill State Memorial. On O-41 just north of O-124. From Serpent Mound continue to Locust Grove, turn left (north) onto O-41, and proceed 7.5 miles north through Sinking Spring.

Fort Hill is an earthen rampart that encloses forty acres atop a bluff. Its use as a "fort" or defense of some kind is disputed, and it is considered that this, like Serpent Mound, probably was a ceremonial structure. The visitors center here also provides information on the prehistoric cultures and gives an interesting account of the unusual geography of the area. The center is open weekends 9:30 A.M. to 5:00 P.M. and during the week by appointment. The fort is open year-round during daylight hours. Call (937) 588–3221.

Rocky Fork Lake State Park. This can be reached from Fort Hill by returning half a mile to O–124, turning right (northeast), and proceeding 8 miles to the park entrance. You can also get to the park from Hillsboro on O–124, heading southeast from town 8 miles. Park roads circle a 2,000-acre lake popular for fishing and water-skiing. There are two swimming beaches, a bathhouse, and a restaurant on the south shore, and the park offers hiking and nature programs, including guided walks. At the north end of the lake is a wetlands area, and a bird-watching area is accessible from the campground. Open all year. Call (937) 393–4284.

Paint Creek State Park and Pioneer Farm. On U.S. 50, 5 miles west of Bainbridge or 17 miles east of Hillsboro. Also a state park, with a 1,200-acre lake and trails suitable in winter for cross-country skiing. There are picnic facilities, horse trails, very popular mountain-bike trails, boat rentals, a campground, and swimming areas. Opened in 1980, the Pioneer Farm includes several log buildings, livestock, gardens, and fields that represent a typical early-1800s farm. Living history programs are presented throughout the year. The park is open all year. Call (937) 365–1401.

Murphin Ridge Inn. 750 Murphin Ridge Road, Hillsboro 45133. Several Amish bakery and furniture stores are located on the road to Murphin Ridge. To reach the inn, continue south on O–41 to Dunkinsville. Turn right on Wheat Ridge Road. Drive 2.5 miles to Murphin Ridge and turn right to the Murphin Ridge Inn. Here, innkeepers Sherry and Darryl McKenney have raised hospitality to an art form. Murphin Ridge Inn is home to the **Adams County Art Gallery,** where local artists show and sell their work. Dining takes place at the heart of the inn, in an 1820s farmhouse perched atop scenic Murphin Ridge. Meals are often created using home-grown produce and herbs. 'Tater pie, potato crisp chicken, and marinated pork loin, as well as homemade soups and desserts such as apple streusel pie and Kentucky chocolate cake, are all delicious. A hearty country breakfast is included with overnight stays. Inn accommodations are as delightful as the dining. The ten-room lodge is furnished with Shaker repro-ductions. The swimming pool, tennis court, and hiking trails offer plenty of opportunity to work up an appetite. After dinner, guests can relax and take dessert by an outdoor campfire. Open for lunch and dinner 11:30 A.M. to 1:00 P.M. and 5:30 to 8:00 P.M. Wednesday–Saturday, and noon to 2:00 P.M. Sunday. Call (937) 544-2263.

BAINBRIDGE, OHIO

O–41 from Locust Grove to Bainbridge and U.S. 50 from Bainbridge to Chillicothe have been designated Scenic Routes by the state of Ohio because of the dramatic, hilly countryside. Bainbridge, at the east tip of our triangle, has several points of interest.

WHAT TO SEE

The Seven Caves. 7660 Cave Road, Bainbridge 45612. U.S. 50, near the entrance to Paint Creek State Park. This privately owned, one-hundred-acre park is a beautiful wilderness, featuring seven lime-stone caves linked by three nature trails. Each cave has paved walkways, handrails, and interior lighting of its unique formations. A gorge carved out over 400 million years offers waterfalls, cliffs, rapids, and canyons. There are more than 250 species of plants and sixty types of trees, many of them endangered or rare. One type of fern is thought to exist only in the gorge's chilly dampness. The Cliff House offers snacks, gifts, and a huge porch that gives a full view of the park's magnificent scenery. A picnic grove and shelter house are available. Open daily—unless the trail is icy—9:00 A.M. to dark. Admission fee. Call (937) 365-1283.

Dr. John Harris Memorial Dental Museum. U.S. 50 in town. Dr. Harris was a pioneer dentist who lived and worked in this house and, in 1827, founded the nation's first dental school here. The place has been restored to its original condition, and you may take comfort from the thought that the early tools of the trade that are on display here are no longer in common use. Open afternoons Friday–Sunday June 1–Labor Day or by appointment. Admission fee. Call (614) 634-3725.

Continue east on U.S. 50 to Chillicothe.

CHILLICOTHE, OHIO

Pioneers settled here in 1796. In 1800 Chillicothe became the capital of the Northwest Territory, which then included Ohio and most of Michigan. In 1803, when Ohio became the first state to be carved from this territory, Chillicothe became its capital. Most of the work in organizing Ohio's government was done here. The capital was moved to Zanesville in 1810 and back to Chillicothe in 1812 while state officials prepared Columbus as a permanent site. In 1816 the capital left Chillicothe forever and moved to Columbus.

Chillicothe is now an industrial center and home to a branch of Ohio University. It has many beautiful nineteenth-century restored homes and brick buildings.

WHAT TO SEE

Main Street. Chillicothe has a number of Greek Revival homes that date from 1803 to 1887 and were built as the homes of the state's founders and early statesmen.

A walking tour of Caldwell and East Fifth Streets, where some of Chillicothe's most-unique and -historic homes are located, is available at the Ross-Chillicothe Visitors Bureau, 14 South Paint Street, (740) 702-7677, or at the Pump House Art Gallery. Historic homes on the route are marked with signs. The tour brochure highlights architectural elements and unveils interesting cultural and personal details about the homes' original inhabitants.

Adena State Memorial. Off Adena Road, west of O-104. On a hilltop overlooking the Scioto River valley and its surrounding countryside is the handsome stone home and estate of Thomas Worthington, Ohio's first U.S. senator and its sixth governor. He named it Adena, associated with the Hebrew word for Eden.

Originally a large log house, this was the site of many political meetings. When the document framing the state constitution was completed, Worthington packed it into his saddlebag and took it to Washington by horseback.

After one all-night session at Worthington's home, so the story goes, he and associates stepped out on the porch for a breath of air and watched the sun rise over Mount Logan, turning the Scioto River into a band of gold across the fields. This scene was copied on the Great Seal of Ohio, with the addition of a sheaf of wheat and a sheaf of seventeen arrows, representing Ohio's rank as the seventeenth state.

In the twenty years before his death in 1827, Worthington entertained many notables here, including President James Monroe, statesman Henry Clay, Blue Jacket, and the Indian leader Tecumseh.

The present house, built in 1807, is furnished throughout with antiques. It is surrounded by gardens and the typical outbuildings of the day, including a barn, a smokehouse, and a washhouse. The house and grounds are open Memorial Day through Labor Day 9:30 A.M. to 5:00 P.M. Wednesday–Saturday and noon to 5:00 P.M. Sunday and holidays; hours in September and October are 9:30 A.M. to 5:00 P.M. Saturday and noon to 5:00 P.M. Sunday. Admission fee. Call (740) 772–1500.

The Chillicothe Gazette. 50 West Main Street, Chillicothe 45601. The city's daily newspaper is housed in a building that is a reproduction of the first statehouse. The newspaper is the oldest continuously published newspaper (1800) west of the Alleghenies. A lobby display has examples of printing through the ages dating to Babylonian times. *Gazette* offices are open 8:00 A.M. to 5:00 P.M. Monday–Friday. Closed weekends and holidays. Tours available by appointment. No admission fee. Call (740) 773–2111.

James M. Thomas Telephone Museum, 68 East Main Street, Chillicothe 45601, one block east of the *Gazette* office. Run by the Chillicothe Telephone Company, the museum shows the evolution of the telephone since its invention by Alexander Graham Bell with a display of early telephone sets. Open 8:30 A.M. to 5:00 P.M. Monday–Friday. No admission fee. Call (704) 772–8200.

Ross County Historical Society Museum. 45 West Fifth Street, Chillicothe 45601. This is one of the nicest local history museums in the state, and its collection includes the table upon which Ohio's constitution was signed and some excellent artifacts related to the Civil War. Tours here take you to the Franklin House, a women's museum featuring women's clothing, china, and quilts throughout the ages (children's items are also displayed) and to the Knoles Log House, a 2-story log house furnished to the period of 1800–25. The historical society museum also boasts an excellent library, which has early published books and materials related to a broad range of topics. The library is open 1:00 to 5:00 P.M. Tuesday–Sunday, April–November. The historical society museum is open 1:00 to 5:00

P.M. daily except Monday from April through August, 1:00 to 5:00 P.M. Saturday and Sunday from September through December, and January through March by appointment only. Admission fee. Call (740) 772-1936.

The Pump House Art Gallery. Enderlin Circle in Yoctangee Park. The old Chillicothe Water Company pumping station, circa 1833, was in danger of being bulldozed, but area preservationists were determined to save this unique piece of local history and turn it into an art gallery. Completely restored and beautifully landscaped, the Pump House now rotates six art exhibits yearly, many featuring local artists, and hosts a number of special and community events. Much of the work displayed here is for sale. Free. Open 11:00 A.M.to 4:00 P.M. Tuesday–Friday and 1:00 to 4:00 P.M. Saturday and Sunday. Call (740) 772-5783.

Hopewell Culture National Historical Park. Four miles north of town on O-104. This 120-acre site on the banks of the Scioto River contains some twenty-three burial mounds, an earthworks wall, and the excavated remains of what may have been a prehistoric dwelling or community house. A modern visitors center explains the site and exhibits many Hopewell Indian relics. Open daily 8:30 A.M. to 5:00 P.M. Labor Day to June and extended hours in the summer. Closed on major holidays as well as Mondays and Tuesdays December through February. Admission fee. Call (740) 774-1125.

Tecumseh Outdoor Drama at Sugarloaf Mountain Amphitheater. Five miles northeast of town on U.S. 23. Take the Delano Road exit and follow the signs reading OUTDOOR DRAMA. From mid-June through Labor Day weekend, this theater offers the outdoor drama *Tecumseh!* at 8:00 P.M. daily except Sunday. Tecumseh was the greatest of the Indian leaders at the dawn of the nineteenth century. He nearly succeeded at uniting the Indian nations in a war against the white man. This excellent drama reveals him as a savvy leader and a vulnerable man. A pleasant evening's entertainment can be had in this rocky, gorgelike setting where the Shawnee ride again. Backstage tours, open-air dining, a museum, and a gift shop are available. Admission fee. Call (740) 775-0700 after March 1.

There is much early Ohio history northeast of Cincinnati, in part because of Indian traces that paralleled the Little Miami River and pointed the way north for white pioneers. Early settlers in the area also used the Little Miami, now designated a National Scenic River, as a route into the wilderness. As civilization spread north from Cincinnati, a stagecoach route developed northeast up the same river valley toward Columbus, roughly parallel to what is today U.S. 42. A forty-minute drive north on U.S. 42 takes you through historic Lebanon and then into equally historic Waynesville, Ohio, which was settled in 1797, five years before Lebanon. Some of the earliest Waynesville settlers were Quakers, the gentle pacifists who also settled the other destination on this trip, Wilmington, 18 miles to the east.

WAYNESVILLE, OHIO

Antiques buffs from all over the world recognize the town of Waynesville as the "Antiques Capital of the Midwest." In the space of just two decades—the 1970s and 1980s—the tiny village of Waynesville transformed its historic Main Street into a 6-block-long mecca for antiques lovers. According to the locals, it all began when Violet Jones started selling glassware and china she had collected over the years, using several rooms in her sprawling frame house as sales areas.

Her success inspired others to start shops, and their businesses grew quickly. Now Mrs. Jones's home is full of shelves stocked with Depression glass, and she and her neighbors welcome shoppers, who increasingly come from out of state or from out of the country.

Piatt Castles

West Liberty · 287
Ohio Caverns
507 · 245
68 · 36
Urbana · Rothchild Berry Farm
Cedar Bog
SPRINGFIELD · COLUMBUS
75 · 70
Vandalia · 40
Wright Patterson
AFB · Clifton
DAYTON · Yellow · John Bryan
Springs · State Park
Xenia · Wilberforce
68 · 71
42 · Caesar Creek
State Park
Waynesville
Ridgeville · 73
48 · Harveysburg
Lebanon · Wilmington
75
42 · 22
Kings · Morrow · OHIO · Chillicoth
Island
CINCINNATI · 50
275 · Hillsboro · Bainbridge
275 · 73 · 124 · Fort Hill
41
New Richmond · Serpent Mound · Locust Grove
Point Pleasant
Moscow · Ferry
8 · 52 · Portsmou
Augusta · Ripley · Manchester
52
Maysville · Manchester · OHIO RIVER
Washington
27

Day Trip 5 Northeast

0   10   20   30 miles

Cynthiana

75

68
Paris · KENTUCKY

Part of Waynesville's attraction is the beautiful restoration of many of its earliest buildings into private homes, antiques emporia, and public buildings. Established in 1797 and named after General "Mad" Anthony Wayne, who engineered the treaty of Greenville, Waynesville was proposed as the capital of the Northwest Territory, the area that the Greenville Treaty ceded to the whites from the Indians. Waynesville quickly became a center of commerce, culture, and invention and an important stagecoach stop.

Many of the earliest settlers were Quakers, who built the first meetinghouse west of the Alleghenies, which is still in use. Much of the Quakers' architecture is still visible throughout the village, and some of their handsome buildings are now antiques shops. During the annual two-week Christmas in the Village festival, a walking tour of some of the Quaker buildings is available.

WHERE TO SHOP

Waynesville boasts more than three dozen antiques shops, plus many specialty craft shops, with more added yearly, and they are all located within a compact 6-block area that makes browsing or serious shopping easy. All shops are open weekends, noon to 5:00 P.M. Most are open during the week with varying hours. Some of our favorites follow:

Spencers' Antiques. 274 South Main Street, Waynesville 45068. George and Fay Spencer have more than thirty-five years in the antiques business and have a rambling frame house crammed full of furniture to prove it. Whether it's an oak table or a primitive pine dry sink, the Spencers are bound to have it. Walking through three floors of furniture, plus a huge warehouse (with space totaling 10,000 square feet), takes you past old carousel horses, white wrought-iron lawn furniture, and big brass church bells. Spencers' is easy to find—just look for the 30-foot-tall statue of Uncle Sam next to the house. Open daily 10:00 A.M. to 5:00 P.M. Call (513) 897-7775 or 897-5223.

Brass Lantern. 100 South Main, Waynesville 45068. Filled with beautifully restored furniture, glass and brass lamps, and one-of-a-kind pieces, the artfully arranged Brass Lantern is almost like a museum. Call (513) 897-9686.

Baker's Antiques. 98 South Main, Waynesville 45068. The quintessential antiques shop, crowded to overflowing with one fascinating piece of history after another, Baker's is one of the oldest shops in the village. A player piano is usually plinking away in this shop, which specializes in early Ohio furniture. Open Tuesday and Thursday–Sunday; other times by appointment. Call (513) 897-0746.

WHERE TO EAT

Hammel House Inn. 121 South Main, Waynesville 45068. Originally a busy stagecoach stop, the circa 1822 Hammel House is now both a restaurant open daily for lunch and a bed-and-breakfast. $$. ☐. Call (513) 897-2333 or 897-3779.

Village Restaurant. 144 South Main, Waynesville 45068. Downhome cooking is available here for breakfast, lunch, and dinner. Popular with the locals. $. ☐. For hours call (513) 897-8835.

Der Dutchman. Just east of Main Street on U.S. 42, Waynesville 45068. This establishment offers authentic Amish family-style dining and features homemade soups, breads, pan-fried chicken, real mashed potatoes, and milk pie. Open daily except Sunday 11:00 A.M. to 9:00 P.M. $. ☐. Call (513) 897-4716.

Cobblestone Café. 10 North Main Street, Waynesville 45068. This delightful restaurant features furniture by David T. Smith and artfully combines the best that Waynesville offers: good food and antiques shopping. $. ☐. Call (513) 897-0021.

SPECIAL EVENTS

Ohio Sauerkraut Festival. King Cabbage is celebrated annually on the second full weekend in October with more than 400 exhibitors and food booths lining Main Street. The event is known as one of the finest folk-art festivals in the Midwest; artisans come from all over the country to participate. Kraut is served in every imaginable form, often unbelievable but always tasty. These include sauerkraut chocolate fudge, sauerkraut pizza, and sauerkraut cookies. The sauerkraut doughnuts are worth waiting in line for. For details call the Waynes-ville Chamber of Commerce at (513) 897-8855.

Christmas in the Village. Waynesville celebrates its past each year on the first two weekends in December with a variety of activities. Horse-drawn carriage rides, historical walking tours, strolling carolers and musicians, storytelling, a town crier, and crafters demonstrating early customs set the stage for a memorable visit. Every shop is decorated and open longer hours for the holidays, while many offer punch and cookies. The candlelit Christmas Walk, featuring 1,300 luminarias, on the Friday evening of the festival is a real treat. For details call the chamber at (513) 897–8855.

CAESAR CREEK STATE PARK

Just 5 miles east of Waynesville on O–73 lies the 10,000-acre Caesar Creek State Park and Pioneer Village. Popular for waterskiing, pleasure boating, swimming, and fishing, Caesar Creek Lake offers a huge beach and four boat ramps. The lake was created when Caesar's Creek, which empties into the Little Miami River, was dammed by the Army Corps of Engineers for flood control and water resource management. Legend has it that the innocuous creek was named for a runaway slave named Cézar who camped on its banks and lived with a local Indian tribe.

Caesar Creek also offers campgrounds, hiking and bridle trails, picnic areas, and a nature preserve and wildlife area. The park is open daily year-round. Call (513) 897–3055.

WHAT TO SEE

Caesar Creek Lake Visitors Center. 4020 North Clarksville Road, Waynesville 45068. Just north of the dam, the visitors center is one of only seven Corps of Engineers Regional Visitors Centers in the country. The beautiful center contains three interpretive galleries, a nature display, a theater with a multimedia orientation program, nature trails, and a scenic overlook of the lake and dam. Open 8:30 A.M. to 4:00 P.M. daily, with extended summer and weekend hours. Free. Call (513) 897–1050.

Caesar's Creek Pioneer Village. Located in the southwest portion of the park, the Pioneer Village was created when several early nineteenth-century log structures were moved from the area to be covered by the new Caesar Creek Lake. The village consists of more than twenty restored buildings, including the 2.5-story log Luken's house, which is on its original site and has a full basement. Many of the buildings were built by Quakers, including the Caesar Creek Meeting House. A series of festivals highlights the life and times of the settlers who built these buildings. Call (513) 897-1120.

SPECIAL EVENT

Ohio Renaissance Festival. Just east of Caesar Creek State Park on O-73, near Harveysburg. The Ohio Renaissance Festival transports fair goers to a mid-sixteenth-century English village fair for a day. Hundreds of costumed performers entertain with feats of juggling, jousting, music making, and magic. Shakespearean performers and more than one hundred artisans welcome Queen Elizabeth I to the village for merriment and demonstrations of crafts and customs, and they include fair goers in their activities. Food and drink include authentic steak on a stake, turkey legs, and ale, in addition to more contemporary festival fare. But the most fun is to be had watching the outrageous mud beggars. Admission fee. Open 10:30 A.M. to 6:00 P.M. Saturday and Sunday for eight weekends from late-August through mid-October, including Labor Day. Call (513) 897-7000.

WILMINGTON, OHIO

About 18 miles east of Waynesville on O-73 lies Wilmington, a quiet, peaceful town that also reflects its Quaker heritage. Much of the countryside between the two communities was populated by Quakers, but these gentle folk chose Wilmington in which to establish Wilmington College, a well-respected private school, in the mid-1800s.

WHAT TO SEE

Rombach Place. 149 East Locust Street, Wilmington 45177. This was the home of General James W. Denver, a commander during the Mexican War (1846–48) and governor of the Kansas Territory before the Civil War. Part of that territory became Colorado in 1876, and the capital of the new state was named in his honor. His home here is named for his wife's family, the Rombachs, and is headquarters for the Clinton County Historical Society. Displays of early Indian photographs and sculptures by Quaker artist Eli Harvey are particularly interesting. Open 1:00 to 4:30 P.M. Wednesday–Friday. Call (937) 382-4684.

Historic District Walking Tour. Maps for a walking tour of the downtown area are available at the Clinton County Convention & Visitors Bureau. More than forty buildings are featured, several on the National Register of Historic Places. The old courthouse, the General Denver Hotel, and the restored Murphy Theater are highlights. Now a community arts center with a full series of performing arts programs throughout the year, the Murphy Theater is a huge Italianate old vaudeville theater restored to its original 1918 splendor. For information call the bureau at (937) 382-1965.

Cowan Lake State Park. Five miles south of Wilmington off U.S. 68 is 1,775-acre Cowan Lake State Park, with a 700-acre lake ideal for sailing, canoeing, fishing, and low-horsepower boating. Cabins and campgrounds border the peaceful lake, which is also ringed with hiking trails and several spots for fossil hunters. Open year-round. Call (937) 289-2105.

WHERE TO EAT AND STAY

The General Denver Hotel. 81 West Main Street, Wilmington 45177. Built in 1927, the half-timbered, Tudor-style hotel was a popular meeting spot until it closed in 1978. After a $1 million renovation, which restored its 1920s decor, the Denver was reopened in late 1988 as a very comfortable hotel with a dining room and English-style pub. The food in the Denver Hotel dining room is very good. Open for lunch and dinner daily. Weekend reservations recommended. $$. ☐. Call (937) 382-7139 for accommodations and (937) 382-3593 for dining reservations.

Cedar Hill Bed & Breakfast. 4003 O-73 West, Wilmington 45177. Located in an area with log houses and acres of woodland trails. Call (937) 383-2525.

To return to Cincinnati, take U.S. 22 southwest out of Wilmington for a scenic drive, or head north from Wilmington on U.S. 68 for 5 miles to Interstate 71 for the trip south.

Day Trip 1 Southwest

0   10   20   30 miles

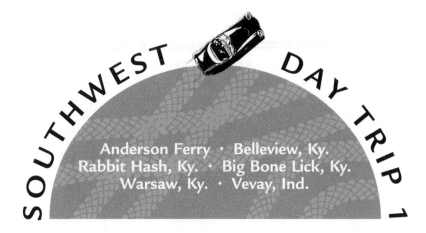

SOUTHWEST DAY TRIP 1

Anderson Ferry · Belleview, Ky.
Rabbit Hash, Ky. · Big Bone Lick, Ky.
Warsaw, Ky. · Vevay, Ind.

If you're in a hurry to get out of town, here's your ticket. Just about fifteen minutes west of downtown Cincinnati via River Road (U.S. 50) is Anderson Ferry—the beginning of an excursion that includes a boat ride, charming river towns, a salt lick with traces of the prehistoric past, and one of the mightiest dams on the Ohio River. This route, which also offers beautiful views of the Ohio winding among steep, wooded hills, is ideal for a leisurely day trip.

ANDERSON FERRY

River Road follows the Ohio shore. About 4 miles west of downtown Cincinnati, turn left at Anderson Ferry and proceed down the drive to the ferry landing—and to the threshold of the nineteenth century.

In the late 1860s a Mr. Kottmyer ran a ferryboat named *Boone* across the Ohio River at this spot. Until 1986 his great-grandson Richard ran a ferryboat named *Boone* at this spot; now *Boone No. 8* alternates with the *Little Boone,* and the operator is Paul Anderson, a longtime employee of Richard, who bought the business in 1986.

About the only change from the old days is that the present boats run on diesel fuel and the first Kottmyer boat ran on oats and hay.

Great-grandfather's ferry had stalls on either side of the deck where horses, walking on inclined treads, turned the port and starboard paddle wheels. When you wanted to go, you released the brakes on the treads and the horses had to begin walking to keep from falling down. To turn the boat you simply braked one horse and let the other keep going. A slap on the flank would improve speed, and you could count on the current to back you away from the landing when you were ready to head away from shore. It's still interesting to watch the pilot maneuver his boat against the current.

The atmosphere is much the same as ever: the clanking old boat, the cool breeze, the wide expanse of river winding around the next bend, and the richly wooded hills showing few traces of the city you just left behind. The river's ocher color is natural, the result of silt (tiny particles of clay and sandstone) washed away by its tributaries and held in suspension by the water's constant motion.

The one-way crossing between Ohio and Kentucky still costs less than $3.00 per vehicle. At the top of the Kentucky landing, there used to be an old stone tavern that served pig drovers while they waited for the ferry to take their hogs across the river to the Cincinnati market—back in the days when the city was nicknamed "Porkopolis" because of its many slaughterhouses. The ferry operates 6:00 A.M. to 9:30 P.M. Monday–Saturday and 7:00 A.M. to 9:30 P.M. Sunday and holidays. Call (859) 485-9210.

WHERE TO EAT

River Saloon & Eatery. 4333 River Road, Cincinnati 45204. This lively pub features a patio with a terrific view of the river, where you can watch the ferry, barges, and tugs travel the Ohio. A casual menu includes burgers, steaks, chicken wings, and salads. Live music, sand volleyball, boat dock, and a full-service bar make this a popular party spot. $. ☐. Open daily for dinner in the summer. Call (513) 451-0022 for hours.

BELLEVIEW, KENTUCKY

When you reach the top of the Kentucky landing, turn right onto K–8 and proceed half a mile to the junction of K–20. Follow K–20 west through Petersburg and south to K–18 just before Belleview. Turn left for the short drive to the Dinsmore Homestead.

Dinsmore Homestead. K–18, Burlington. This 1842 Greek Revival house is one of the few nineteenth-century homes in the United States that has stayed in the same family. The eighty-acre homestead nurtured five generations of Dinsmores, who were socially close to presidents from George Washington to FDR. Original furniture, books, clothing, and household implements lend authenticity to this rare historical continuum. Tours are offered on the hour 1:00 to 5:00 P.M. Wednesday, Saturday, and Sunday. Admission fee. Call (859) 586–6117.

RABBIT HASH, KENTUCKY

From Dinsmore Homestead take K-18 west into Belleview, then K-20 south several miles to K-338. Follow this road south and east into Rabbit Hash. This quaintly named village on the Ohio River is a regular stop for riverboats on their way to Madison, Indiana. When the boats dock during the summer, a village blacksmith usually appears to demonstrate his trade. **The Kentucky Huckster**—a local crafts store—and an antiques store are open varied hours throughout the year. No one seems to have the official story of how Rabbit Hash got its name, but locals have several versions, so be sure to ask them.

The General Store. Opened in 1831, this scenic stop on the banks of the Ohio River is the place to find a snack, Bybee pottery, natural foods, or some sarsaparilla. Open year-round 10:00 A.M. to 7:00 P.M. Sunday–Thursday and 10:00 A.M. to 9:00 P.M. Friday and Saturday. Call (859) 586–7744.

BIG BONE LICK, KENTUCKY

From Rabbit Hash proceed south and then east on K-338 to Big Bone Lick State Park.

Considered to be the greatest graveyard of Ice Age animals ever found, Big Bone Lick was named by the Shawnee. They came here to dig for the salt deposited around the sulphur springs, the natural "licks" that attracted migratory animals traveling their well-worn trail to the Carolinas each autumn and back to the northwestern prairies each spring. In the soft mud around the salt beds, the Indians found bones of animals the likes of which they had never seen: mammoths and mastodons and other creatures long vanished from the earth. White explorers found the site in 1729. In the 1830s a 16-foot tusk was removed from here, taken east on a steamboat, put on display, and subsequently lost or stolen. It was from here that the white captive Mary Ingles escaped the Shawnee and made an arduous, months-long trek along the Ohio and Kanawha Rivers back to her settlement in West Virginia.

The 525-acre park contains a nature center with dioramas of Ice Age scenes and animals. On display are many of the bones found at the site. It is theorized that the larger animals became mired in the mud in their search for salt and died there. Outside is a model dig, showing how archaeologists recovered the remains. A museum and gift shop are open 8:00 A.M. to 8:00 P.M. daily April–October and 9:00 A.M. to 5:00 P.M. Monday and Thursday November–March. Closed in January. Year-round camping, a pool, picnic shelters, and fishing are also available. Admission fee. Call (859) 384–3522 or (800) 255–PARK.

WARSAW, KENTUCKY

Take K-338 east 5 miles to U.S. 42 and turn southwest toward Louisville. Soon after the highway reaches the banks of the Ohio River, it enters Warsaw, Kentucky, a pretty, peaceful, drowsy little river town that has basked in enviable tranquillity here for more than a century—except for Christmas Day 1959, when the beer warehouse blew up and broke every window in town.

WHAT TO SEE

Markland Locks and Dam. Five miles west of Warsaw on U.S. 42. When opened in 1957 Markland was the first of a new breed of high-level dams on the Ohio, and today it remains the largest in terms of height and drop between the two pool levels. The high-level system has twelve dams along the Ohio's 981-mile course from Pittsburgh to the Mississippi, replacing all of the fifty-three original low-level dams that were dedicated by President Herbert Hoover in a ceremony at Cincinnati in 1929.

Ohio River dams are not for flood control but to ensure that commercial navigation will have at least 9 feet of water in the channel all year. The river usually averages about 25 feet in depth, but before 1929 summer droughts often left shipping stranded in port because of low water. The difference between upper and lower pools at Markland is 35 feet, and boats pass through locks to get from one pool to the other.

High-level dams cut lock-through time considerably, first because there are fewer dams and second because the lock chambers now are large enough (1,200 by 110 feet) to accommodate a towboat pushing fifteen barges, which is about as big as tows get on the Ohio River. They haul vital supplies of coal, petroleum products, chemicals, and grain, and their crews live on board thirty days at a time, followed by thirty days' leave. The larger boats carry a captain, a pilot, a cook, and up to a dozen crew members. Insurance companies classify their work as the second most dangerous in the United States, after coal mining.

Visitors are welcome to an observation room and deck overlooking the locks. Although it is not staffed, the room has displays explaining how dams work and how boats are locked through. The facility is open all year during daylight hours. Public parking is provided.

WHERE TO EAT

Dan's Restaurant. A roadside stop at the backwater marina, halfway between Warsaw and Markland Dam on U.S. 42. Not only can you enjoy a river view and good down-home cooking but you can also watch for downbound tows from here and beat them to the dam to watch them lock through. A tow's downbound speed is only 10–12 mph. The restaurant is open daily all year and is best known for its prime rib. $. ☐. For hours call (859) 567-8044.

VEVAY, INDIANA

A road across the top of Markland Dam serves as a bridge to Indiana. Crossing here puts you onto Ind. 156. Turn right from the exit and proceed west about 5 miles to Vevay, Indiana. If you pronounce it "VEE-vay," you're wrong. Locals pronounce it "VEE-vie" like "Stevie," in honor of its namesake, Vevey, Switzerland. Swiss settlers founded the town in 1802, and it flourished during the next century. More than 300 structures built before 1883 can be seen, including examples of Victorian, Gothic, Greek Revival, and folk architecture.

Many artifacts of the past can be seen at the Switzerland County Historical Society Museum at Main and Market Streets. Open May through October noon to 4:00 P.M. daily. Admission fee.

WHERE TO STAY

If you want to experience Vevay as it was during the river's heyday, an overnight stay at the **Rosemont Inn Bed and Breakfast** will help. This stately home overlooks the Ohio River, and is situated at 800 Market Street, Vevay 47043. Call (812) 427–3050 for reservations.

Belterra Casino Resort. 777 Belterra Drive, Belterra 47020. One mile east of the Markland Dam Bridge. This sixteen-story hotel with 308 deluxe rooms and luxury suites offers spectacular views of the Ohio River and surrounding countryside. Restaurants, lounges, entertainment, and casino. Call (888) BELTERRA or (812) 427–7777, or visit www.belterracasino.com.

MADISON, INDIANA

Just 15 miles west of Vevay on Ind. 56 lies Madison, Indiana, the Hoosier State's largest historic district, boasting more than 1,000 structures and two National Historic Landmarks. The road traverses the Ohio River bottoms—the flat, fertile farmland between the bottom of hills and the top of the riverbank. This is one of the most unspoiled stretches of the Ohio. No industries. No power plants. Just an occasional farmhouse, a barn, or a frame country church amid fields of corn and hay. This is America as it once was and soon may never be again.

Cradled between steep bluffs that rise well above the town, Madison lies on a sharp southward bend in the river. Its many lovely old homes and gardens are a legacy of the steamboat era, which by 1850 had made Madison Indiana's largest city. Having hoped to become the capital of the state in the 1850s, Madison drifted into a one-hundred-year Rip Van Winkle sleep when the newly completed Madison-to-Indianapolis railroad took the boom north to Indy.

WHAT TO SEE

James F. D. Lanier Home. Second Street between Elm and Vine Streets. This Greek Revival mansion with four massive columns and locally made wrought-iron work looks out over the Ohio River. Among the many stately homes here, this is the most sumptuous. It was built in 1844 by James Lanier, who made such a large fortune in

Day Trip 2 Southwest

| 0 | 10 | 20 | 30 miles |

banking that he kept Indiana financially afloat during the Civil War by lending it more than $1 million. Easily the most elegant home anywhere along the banks of the Ohio, the Lanier mansion has a long, rolling lawn and restored historic gardens, and it is furnished with handsome antiques, property of the original family. Donations accepted. Open 9:00 A.M. to 5:00 P.M. Tuesday–Saturday and 1:00 to 5:00 P.M. Sunday. Closed Monday and holidays. Call (812) 265-3526.

Sullivan House. Northwest corner of Second and Poplar Streets. Madison's first mansion, this Federal-style gem was home to Jeremiah Sullivan, an early Indiana Supreme Court justice, who also named Indianapolis. Open 10:00 A.M. to 4:30 P.M. Monday–Saturday and 1:00 to 4:30 P.M. Sunday April–October. Admission fee. Call (812) 265-2967.

WALKING TOURS

Madison Area Convention and Visitors Bureau. Jefferson and Main Streets, Madison 47250. The Visitors Bureau has pamphlets on two recommended walking tours. Attractions include the Shrewsbury–Windle House (1846–49), built by a steamboat captain in an effort to outdo the Lanier mansion; an 1857 doctor's office that also served as a hospital and displays early medical tools; the restored Talbot-Hyatt Pioneer Gardens (1810); the Madison Railroad Station, restored by the Jefferson County Historical Society and containing railroad memorabilia and changing exhibits; and several other noteworthy spots. The CVB offices are open 9:00 A.M. to 5:00 P.M. Monday–Friday, 9:00 A.M. to 3:00 P.M. Saturday, and 10:00 A.M. to 3:00 P.M. Sunday all year, except holidays. Call (812) 265-2956.

SPECIAL EVENTS

The Madison Regatta is a weeklong schedule of festivities, including a hot-air balloon race, a food court, a parade, and music on the riverfront. It culminates on the Fourth of July weekend with fireworks and unlimited hydroplane racing events on the river, seen by more than 60,000 spectators. Call (812) 265-2956 for information.

The Madison Chautaqua is held the fourth weekend in September. This outdoor art show covers an eight-block area and is considered one of the Midwest's premier art exhibitions.

Madison looks most beautiful during the **"Nights before Christmas"** on the two weekends following Thanksgiving. The town dresses its public buildings and private homes in Christmas finery for candlelight tours. Strolling carolers, carriage rides, and specialty shopping transport visitors to the 1850s.

WHERE TO SHOP

Madison is well-known for its antiques and specialty shops. Most are located along Main Street. Here are some of the better ones:

Margie's Country Store. 721 West Main Street, Madison 47250. Margie's specializes in "women's things," including dishware, ceramics, calicos, and gifts. Call (812) 265-4429.

The Attic. 631 West Main Street, Madison 47250. This shop offers original prints, an art gallery, and a coffee shop. Call (812) 265-5781.

Lumber Mill Antique Mall. 721 West First Street, Madison 47250. More than 100 dealers constantly replenish their booths in an old converted flour mill. Call (812) 265-6606.

The Birdhouse. 108 East Main Street, Madison 47250. Specializing in birdhouses, feeders, and nature-related gifts from clothing to garden sculptures.

WHERE TO EAT

The Wharf. A floating restaurant located at the end of Vaughn Drive, Madison 47250. Guess who has good seafood. $$. ❑. For hours call (812) 265-2688.

Historic Broadway Tavern & Hotel. 313 Broadway, Madison 47250. This venerable hostelry still has its original bar, vintage 1859. The hotel has been in continuous operation since then, except for Prohibition years. Today the dining room is best known for its barbecued ribs, served each Friday night. The regular menu features steaks and seafood. $$. Closed Sunday. Call (812) 265-2346.

Key West Shrimp House. 117 Ferry Street, Madison 47250. This atmospheric pub serves seafood, steaks, and chicken. Closed Monday. $$. ❑. Call (812) 265-2831.

The Pines. 2700 Michigan Road, Madison 47250. Take West Street up the hill from Main Street. At the top of the hill, proceed through the first traffic light (where West Street becomes Michigan Road) and continue 2 blocks to the restaurant. The Pines offers a fine buffet of roast beef, ham, chicken, and Icelandic cod, plus salads and desserts. $$. ☐. For hours call (812) 273-4645.

WHERE TO STAY

Best Western Motor Lodge & Lounge. 700 Clifty Drive, Madison 47250. Take Cragmont Street (Ind. 7) up Hanging Rock Hill. The road passes a rocky ledge which, if there have been recent rains, turns into a waterfall. (The old road used to pass behind the falls.) Continue through the flashing light at the top of the hill, turn left onto Clifty Drive (Ind. 62) and continue 2 blocks to the lodge. Open all year. Call (812) 273-5151.

   Hillside Inn. 831 East Main Street, Madison 47250. Clinging to the hillside, this hotel features rooms with balconies overlooking the town and river. Call (812) 265-3221.

   Clifty Falls State Park Inn. One mile west of Madison on Ind. 56. Also sits atop the bluff but commands a striking view of the Ohio River, punctuated by the soaring twin smokestacks of the Clifty Creek Power Plant. The newly renovated lodge offers meeting and banquet rooms with fireplaces, and the dining room is popular for business lunches and for family groups. The park itself has hiking trails into a gorge so deep that the sun reaches it only at high noon. The stunning rock walls expose 425-million-year-old shale and limestone beds laden with fossils. Through the gorge Clifty Creek, bordered by banks of ferns, tumbles over falls and rapids on its course toward the Ohio River. Call (812) 265-4135.

   Cliff House Bed & Breakfast. 122 Fairmont Drive, Madison 47250. You can stay in Victorian splendor high atop a limestone cliff overlooking Madison and the river. Call (812) 265-5272.

   Stonefield's Bed & Breakfast. 411 West First Street, Madison 47250. A Victorian next door to the Lanier mansion, this hundred-year-old home is furnished with a mixture of period furniture and handmade quilts. Call (812) 265-6856.

IN THE AREA

Hanover College. This beautiful, 600-acre Georgian campus perches high atop the cliffs overlooking the mighty Ohio River just 5 miles west of Madison on Ind. 56. The view of the river and surrounding hills from in front of the president's house is spectacular. Call (812) 866-7000 for information on campus activities.

CLARKSVILLE–JEFFERSONVILLE, INDIANA

From Madison take Ind. 62 west and south about 40 miles through some beautiful Indiana countryside until you reach Jeffersonville and its neighbor, Clarksville. These two Indiana river towns lie just off the north end (first exit) of the Kennedy Memorial Bridge (Interstate 65) across the Ohio River from downtown Louisville—Clarksville to the left of the bridge and Jeffersonville to the right.

WHAT TO SEE

The Falls of the Ohio State Park and Interpretive Center. 201 West Riverside Drive, Clarksville 47129. Now the "falls" are rocky, fossilized ledges left high and dry by diversion of the Ohio River. The area can be viewed from access points along South Clark Boulevard and Harrison Avenue.

In prehistoric times the falls provided a natural ford for migrating animals in late summer when the river was low. The falls prompted General George Rogers Clark to establish his stockaded village here on Corn Island. That village was the earliest Louisville settlement, and it grew mainly because of the falls. Many a boat was carried to its doom when the river crashed unimpeded through these chutes, although an expert pilot who knew the falls could navigate them safely. Many such pilots settled here and made their living taking flatboats through these perilous rapids for a fee. When the river was low for lack of rain, usually in late summer, boatmen, and frequently entire families heading west with all their worldly goods and livestock, would have to tie up at Louisville and wait for the water to rise.

Today dams keep the river at a navigable level all year, and here at the falls the Louisville & Portland Canal safely carries boat traffic around the Louisville side of the falls. Four-fifths of the river's width is now blocked off by a dam and a hydroelectric plant.

Although viewing points are in Indiana, the ledges—even those along the Indiana shoreline—are in Kentucky. After an age-old border dispute, only recently settled in court, Kentucky claims the entire river to the low-water mark on the opposite bank. Call (812) 280-9970.

Howard Steamboat Museum. 1101 East Market Street, Jeffersonville 47130. The bridge's first Indiana exit puts you on Court Avenue. Continue to the traffic light, turn right (toward the river), and proceed 3 blocks to Market Street on the riverfront. Turn left (east) and follow Market Street 15 blocks to the museum, which is housed in a twenty-two-room Victorian mansion directly across the street from Jeffboat, the largest boatyard on the Ohio River.

The mansion was built in 1890 by a boatbuilding family whose heirs continue that trade today. It contains the finest collection of steamboat memorabilia anywhere, including beautiful models of the *Natchez* and the *Robert E. Lee,* steamboats that won fame in a race from New Orleans to St. Louis in 1870. The *Lee* won with a time of three days, eighteen hours, and thirty minutes, a record that remains unbroken today. In 1949 the diesel towboat *Harry S Truman* tried it pushing fifteen barges and failed by sixty-one minutes to beat the *Lee's* record.

Incidentally, the *Robert E. Lee* was built 7 miles downstream from here at New Albany, Indiana, just after the Civil War. Because of lingering animosities, she was towed across the Ohio River to Kentucky (the South) to be christened in honor of the Confederate general.

Jeffboat's biggest trade is in building the huge barges—routinely 200 to 220 feet long—that carry coal, chemicals, ore, gravel, grain, and petroleum products on America's inland waterways. The Ohio River alone carries more than 170 million tons of cargo a year. The firm also builds towboats, the workhorse boats that push the barges and, in 1976, built the all-steel *Mississippi Queen,* the largest steamboat ever built. The *Queen,* owned and operated by the Delta Queen Steamboat Company of Cincinnati, runs overnight passenger excursions on the Mississippi River out of New Orleans.

The museum is open all year 10:00 A.M. to 3:00 P.M. Tuesday–Saturday and 1:00 to 3:00 P.M. Sunday. Closed holidays. Admission fee. Call (812) 283-3728.

DINNER THEATER

Derby Dinner Playhouse. 525 Marriott Drive, Clarksville 47129. Interstate 65, Stansifer Avenue exit, in Clarksville next to the Holiday Inn Lakeview. Musicals are performed in the round here daily except Monday and often feature top-name stars. Dinner seatings are at 6:00 P.M., with an 8:15 P.M. curtain time. Matinees are offered Wednesday with an 11:45 A.M. buffet and a 1:00 P.M. showtime and on Sunday with an 11:45 A.M. buffet and a 1:35 P.M. showtime. Admission fee. Call (812) 288-8281.

LOUISVILLE, KENTUCKY

Louisville, Kentucky's largest city and home of the Kentucky Derby, is easily reached by a brief drive south across the Ohio River on the Clark Memorial Bridge (Interstate 65) from Clarksville and Jeffersonville. Louisville is also easily reached by Interstate 71, 101 miles southwest of Cincinnati. Driving time is about an hour and fifty minutes.

Lying along the Ohio River, threshold of the South, Louisville is a curious blend of influences that is neither northern nor southern—an amalgam of Kentucky tradition, steamboat heritage, industrial growth, and bright modern development, giving the city a tone quite apart from what is found elsewhere in the state.

The city grew up from Corn Island, settled in 1778 as a Revolutionary War supply base and training camp by General George Rogers Clark before his march toward British outposts in Illinois and Indiana. The camp was strategically located just upstream from the Falls of the Ohio, a 3-mile series of rapids that posed the river's greatest hazard to boatmen and, at periods of low water, provided a natural fording place that had been used by Indians and migrating herds since prehistoric times. After his victories on the western frontier, Clark returned to make Louisville his home and is buried here. The river has been diverted through a canal and through McAlpine Locks and Dam, leaving the falls high and dry for exploration by fossil hunters.

Day Trip 3 Southwest

0   10   20   30 miles

Named in honor of Louis XVI of France because of his aid to the Colonies during the American Revolution, Louisville today is a thoroughly modern, cultural, historical, and industrial center presided over by numerous distilleries that produce more than half the world's bourbon whiskey.

The city's early settlers, Germans and Creoles from New Orleans, combined forces to develop the city into a sophisticated lady who puts on her best show during Derby Week.

The Kentucky Derby, on the first Saturday of May, climaxes more than two weeks of festivities and revelry, from glamorous balls to steamboat races. Tens of thousands of visitors descend upon Louisville on Derby Day, and unless you have made careful advance arrangements, you may not find a room within 50 miles of the track.

Downtown Louisville has undergone extensive redevelopment in the past decade, yet much of its architectural heritage has been preserved, as evidenced by the reflection of restored nineteenth-century facades in the soaring glass walls of the Kentucky Center for the Arts on Main Street.

Hometowners can spot each other easily because they pronounce the city's name "LOW-a-vul." Those who say "LOO-a-vul" are from elsewhere in the Ohio Valley, and the "LOOEY-ville" set are true aliens.

GETTING AROUND

Greater Louisville Convention & Visitors Bureau. After crossing into Louisville on the Clark Memorial Bridge, turn right onto Main Street and left onto Third Street. Located one block ahead in the lobby of the Kentucky International Convention Center. The center has complete tour information. You may want to inquire about the Kentucky Center for the Arts, which houses the Kentucky Opera, the Louisville Orchestra, the Louisville Ballet, the Broadway Series, and the Stage One Children's Theater. Also of interest are the Tony Award–winning Actors Theater (yes, one Tony a year is awarded to an outstanding local/regional theater company), Bach Society performances, Shakespeare in the Park, the rapidly growing Humana Festival of New American Plays, and other shows and expositions. Seasonal events are listed in this book's Directory.

The center is also one pickup point for three-hour tours of the city, which run daily. For information call Joe & Mike's Pretty Good Times at (502) 459-1247. The center is open 8:30 A.M. to 5:00 P.M. Monday–Friday, 9:00 A.M. to 4:00 P.M. Saturday, and 12:00 to 4:00 P.M. Sunday.

For more information write Greater Louisville Convention & Visitors Bureau, 400 South First Street, Louisville, KY 40201, or call (502) 582-3732 or (800) 792-5595.

WHAT TO SEE: OUTLYING ATTRACTIONS

Churchill Downs. 700 Central Avenue, Louisville 40208, 3 miles south of downtown via Third Street or Interstate 65. This famous track is the undisputed world capital of thoroughbred racing and is the site of the annual Kentucky Derby. The twin Edwardian spires of its clubhouse, built in 1885, are a city landmark.

Since Aristides beat Volcano by a length in the first derby in 1875, the "Run for the Roses" has drawn fans from around the globe. Of the 140,000 Derby-goers, the more-illustrious fans watch from the stylish "Millionaire's Row" section, while others fill the 45,000-seat grandstand or struggle for a view from the general admission infield. The entire city is riveted to the TV for this event, the climax of a month of mounting excitement. Crowds and traffic, however, can be discouraging.

You need not see the Derby to enjoy Churchill Downs, however. Racing meets are held there from late April through June and during November. For racing information call (502) 636-4400.

Derby Week. Actually, more than two full weeks of festivities lead up to the Derby, which is run the first Saturday in May. Programs are available at the Visitors Information Center. Events include the Great Steamboat Race, in which the *Delta Queen* of Cincinnati races the *Belle of Louisville* on the Ohio River; the Derby Festival Great Balloon Race; and the Pegasus Parade. There are art shows, sports events, regattas, music events, and house tours. Call (502) 584-6383.

The Kentucky Derby Museum. 704 Central Avenue, Louisville 40208, Gate 1 at Churchill Downs. This recently renovated museum offers a spectacular multimedia presentation about the Derby plus hands-on computerized exhibits that trace Derby history and underscore the importance of thoroughbred racing to the state's economy. You can test your handicapping skills in a computerized race and sit on a life-size horse in a real starting gate. Guided walking tours of the Downs are offered. Open daily 9:00 A.M. to 5:00 P.M. Closed Thanksgiving, Christmas, and Derby Day. Admission fee. Call (502) 637-1111.

Farmington Historic Home. 3033 Bardstown Road (U.S. 31 east), Louisville 40205, at the intersection of Watterson Expressway (Interstate 264), which circles the city's outskirts. This fine old mansion, with its fourteen acres of gardens, built in 1810 by John and Lucy Speed, is now restored to its former elegance. The Speed's son, Josh, once brought his friend young Abe Lincoln home for dinner. What is fascinating about the house, however, is that it was built from plans drawn by Thomas Jefferson, a master of inventiveness, and includes a concealed staircase and twin octagonal rooms. Also on the grounds are a barn, a blacksmith's shop, and the inevitable gift shop. Open all year, 10:00 A.M. to 4:30 P.M. Monday–Saturday and from 1:30 to 4:00 P.M. Sunday. Last tours begin at 3:45 P.M. Admission fee. Call (502) 452-9920.

The Speed Art Museum. 2035 South Third Street, Louisville 40208. Adjacent to the University of Louisville's campus, this exquisite museum is Kentucky's first and largest art museum and has recently completed a multi-million dollar restoration. Collections are distinguished by major medieval, Renaissance, and French works. Modern and contemporary art is also strongly represented, in addition to special exhibitions. Don't miss the contemporary sculpture court and the elaborate, oak-paneled seventeenth-century English room. Open 10:30 A.M. to 4:00 P.M. Tuesday, Wednesday, and Friday, 10:30 A.M. to 8:00 P.M. Thursday, 10:30 A.M. to 5:00 P.M. Saturday, noon to 5:00 P.M. Sunday, and closed Mondays and holidays. Call (502) 634-2700.

Locust Grove Historic Home. 561 Blankenbaker Lane, Louisville 40207, 5 miles east of downtown on River Road, then right 1.5 miles on Blankenbaker. When General George Rogers Clark first saw this property during the American Revolution, it was virgin forest. Twelve years later, this manor, surrounded by a fifty-five-acre plantation, was built. Clark moved here in 1809, and Locust Grove became his final home. This gracious old mansion was built for entertaining and includes an impressive ballroom—a far cry from the days of Clark's Corn Island stockade. The home is open 10:00 A.M. to 4:30 P.M. Monday–Saturday and 1:30 to 4:00 P.M. Sunday. Closed Christmas Eve, Christmas, Derby Day, Easter, Thanksgiving, and New Year's Day. Admission fee. Call (502) 897–9845.

Cave Hill Cemetery and Arboretum. 701 Baxter Avenue, Louisville 40204, at the east end of Broadway (U.S. 150) and Baxter. Here are 300 lush acres of rare shrubs, trees, flowers, and lakes. Both a botanical garden and a cemetery, Cave Hill is the final resting place of George Rogers Clark, who founded the city, and Colonel Harland Sanders of Kentucky Fried Chicken fame. Open daily 8:00 A.M. to 4:45 P.M. Call (502) 451–5630.

Louisville Ballet. 315 East Main Street, Louisville 40202. One of the top-rated ballet companies in the United States. Times for evening and matinee performances vary with production. Call (502) 583–3150.

WHERE TO SHOP

Louisville Antique Mall. 900 Goss Avenue, Louisville 40217. More than 50,000 square feet of Kentucky heritage. Open 10:00 A.M. to 6:00 P.M. Monday–Saturday and noon to 6:00 P.M. Sunday. No admission fee. Call (502) 635–2852.

WHAT TO SEE: RIVERFRONT
PLAZA/BELVEDERE/WATERFRONT PARK

The Belvedere, an 800-foot-long esplanade along the Ohio between Fourth and Sixth Streets, is an ideal place to begin a hike because it is next to a 1,600-car parking garage.

With higher water levels today, it is hard to visualize the riverfront as the long dirt embankment it was in the Flatboat Era (1780–1810), when the legendary flatboat rowdy Mike Fink came this way. Fink never displayed an accurate understanding of law and order, and there were several warrants out for his arrest. Few men, indeed, were willing to serve them. In Louisville a constable and several residents tried to pull Mike Fink—boat, crew, and all— out of the water with a team of oxen, but his men set their poles into the bank and dragged the oxen back to the river's edge three times before collapsing in a gale of laughter. At last overwhelmed, they were hauled up Third Street in their boat, hooting and waving to the crowd along the way to the courthouse. For the record, Fink was acquitted for lack of evidence and was escorted back to the river. After many escapades in the Ohio Valley, his trail finally ended somewhere in Missouri.

Today a more genteel riverfront features a promenade, a stained-glass wall, and a 12-foot bronze statue of General George Rogers Clark. Louisville's new $58 million Waterfront Park features The Great Lawn and Festival Plaza, both designed to host festivals and events. Linear Park and the Children's Play Area offer restful stops for watching the river and its barges roll by. The view from the path on the new 12-mile River Walk is popular with joggers, cyclists, skaters, and walkers alike.

The **Belle of Louisville** and the **Spirit of Jefferson,** a smaller replica of a paddlewheeler. Riverfront Plaza at Fourth and River Roads. Built in 1914, the *Belle* is the oldest operating Mississippi-style stern-wheel steamboat in existence. She was recently named a National Historic Landmark. Individual and group rates available. Call (502) 574–BELL.

WHERE TO EAT AND STAY: RIVERFRONT PLAZA

The Galt House. Foot of Fourth Street at Riverfront Plaza. This splendid hotel has 1,300 rooms and suites, many with river views. The Galt House has shops, a pool, and three restaurants, including a revolving one atop the building. Admirably located for sightseeing. $$$. ☐. For hours call (502) 589–5200.

WHAT TO SEE: DOWNTOWN

Historic Main Street. Just 2 blocks south of the river, the area between 100 and 900 West Main Street has largely been restored because of its handsome nineteenth-century brick architecture and New Orleans–style wrought-iron work. But most important and intriguing is the collection of cast-iron buildings restored to their original grandeur. Louisville's collection of such facades is second only to New York City's Soho district. A stroll along this pleasant street gives a true feeling of Steamboat Era charm.

Louisville Slugger Museum and Bat Factory. 800 West Main Street, Louisville 40202. With the 120-foot "Super Slugger" bat parked by the front door, you can't miss this new facility—the 68,000-pounder is visible from the river, the highway, and most of downtown Louisville. Makers of the famous Louisville Slugger bats and other sporting equipment, Hillerich & Bradsby opened the museum in 1996. Start your tour of the only museum and factory dedicated to baseball bats and hitting by watching the informational film in the museum's hundred-seat theater. You can walk through an underground locker room onto a playing field featuring rare memorabilia and photos. Check out the replica of a white ash forest and H&B's 1890s woodworking shop before beginning your tour of the actual bat factory. Open 9:00 A.M. to 5:00 P.M. Monday–Saturday and 12:00 to 5:00 P.M. Sunday. Admission fee. Call (502) 588-7228.

Louisville Science Center. 727 West Main Street, Louisville 40202. Besides occupying a historic building, this museum has much else to commend it, especially the Foucault pendulum suspended in a five-story atrium. It demonstrates the rotation of the Earth by appearing to follow a pattern on the floor and striking a different peg each nineteen minutes. The pendulum actually swings an unchanging path—it is the floor (and the Earth) that rotates. The museum features the exhibit "The World We Create," with interactive displays of just about everything we grow, invent, manufacture, or develop. The IMAX Theatre uses a 4-story screen and state-of-the-art sound system to create a roller coaster for your mind. Open 9:00 A.M. to 5:00 P.M. Monday–Thursday, 9:00 A.M. to 9:00 P.M. Friday and Saturday, and noon to 5:00 P.M. Sunday. Admission fee. Call (502) 561-6100.

American Printing House for the Blind. 1839 Frankfort Avenue, Louisville 40206. Tour a totally different world of publishing—including talking books and Braille—at the nation's oldest nonprofit agency for visually impaired people. Open 8:00 A.M. to 4:30 P.M. Monday–Friday. No admission fee. Call (502) 895-2405.

Kentucky Center for the Arts. 5 Riverfront Plaza, Louisville 40202, across Main Street from the Humana Building. The Kentucky Center for the Arts is the cultural center of the state and home to Louisville's opera, ballet, orchestra, children's theater, and theatrical association. Its premier performing facilities also host a world-class sculpture collection, galleries for changing exhibits, and a year-round series of performing artists. No admission fee. Tours available. Call (502) 584-7777, or 562-0100.

The Kentucky Opera. Performances take place at the Center for the Arts (above); the office is located at 101 South Eighth Street, Louisville 40202. Masterpieces of great music, drama, and dance, as well as beautiful set designs and remarkable costumes, work together for a spectacular experience. English translations projected above the stage. October– April. Group rates available. Call (502) 561-7928.

Actors Theater of Louisville. 316 West Main, Louisville 40202. A cultural innovator for thirty years, Actors Theater has achieved a worldwide reputation as one of America's leading theaters. Its Humana Festival of New American Plays has spawned Tony Awards and Pulitzer Prizes. The performance facilities include a National Historic Landmark 1837 complex of three theaters and a restaurant. Actors Theater underwent a $12 million expansion and renovation that added a nine-story parking garage and a 320-seat, arena-type theater. The season is January–June and September–December. Tours are available. Call (502) 584-1265.

Bunbury Theatre. 112 South Seventh Street, Louisville 40202. Located just 4 blocks west of the Actors Theater at Main and Seventh. Louisville's alternative theater offers a full season of off-Broadway-style hits, old favorites, and contemporary works. The season runs from August through May. Special performances and staged readings are available by group request. Call (502) 585-5306.

WHERE TO EAT AND STAY: DOWNTOWN

The Camberly Brown Hotel. 339 West Broadway, Louisville 40202. Restored and reopened in 1985, this Georgian Revival gem originally opened in 1923. It was once known as "the most elegant hotel south of Chicago." The Brown's beautiful lobby of stone, marble, and intricate plaster friezes welcomes guests to the English Grill for fine dining, and to J. Graham's for its famous "Hot Brown" sandwich. Call (502) 583-1234.

The Seelbach Hilton Hotel. 500 Fourth Avenue, Louisville 40202. Another restored success, the 1905 Seelbach was reopened in 1982 as a striking example of Beaux Arts architecture. Now listed on the National Register of Historic Places, the Seelbach inspired F. Scott Fitzgerald in writing *The Great Gatsby*. Its famous Rathskeller room is full of Rookwood pottery tiles. Two restaurants plus the legendary Oak Room restaurant offer opportunities to enjoy the ambience. Call (502) 585-3200 or (800) 528-0444.

WHERE TO SHOP: DOWNTOWN

Louisville Galleria. Fourth Avenue, Louisville 40204, between Liberty and Muhammad Ali. The Galleria has two levels of retail stores and specialty shops, a third-floor food court, and a seven-story glass-enclosed atrium. Adjacent to the Seelbach, it is open 10:00 A.M. to 6:00 P.M. Monday–Saturday, and noon to 5:00 P.M. Sunday. Call (502) 584-7170.

WHAT TO SEE: BUTCHERTOWN

The Bourbon Stockyards was the unlikely nucleus for this neighborhood, located off Grinstead Drive near Cherokee Park in the southeast quadrant of the city. Founded in 1834, primarily by Germans, Butchertown was—as the name implies—home to many families who walked to work at nearby meat-processing companies. An early suburb of Louisville, it includes many "shotgun" and "camelback" houses, affordable to the early-Victorian working class. Points of interest are noted below.

Thomas Edison House. 729 East Washington Street, Louisville 40202. Although the Ohio inventor lived and worked here only two years (1866–67), he made a lasting impression on the city when he returned in 1883 to throw the switch that lit up 4,600 light bulbs in the neighborhood—a world record at that time. The museum is open 10:00 A.M. to 2:00 P.M. Tuesday–Thursday and Saturday. Other days by appointment. Admission fee. Call (502) 585-5247.

Hadley Pottery. 1570 Story Avenue, Louisville 40206. This pottery studio was founded by Mary Alice Hadley, namesake of the foundation that continues to operate it. Workers still handpaint Mary Alice's original designs, which brought her national attention in the 1940s. Pottery tours are available. The sales area is open 8:30 A.M. to 4:30 P.M. Monday–Friday and 9:00 A.M. to 12:30 P.M. Saturday. No admission fee. Call (502) 584-2171.

Louisville Stoneware Company. 731 Brent Street off East Broadway, Louisville 40204. This company has been turning out fine, handcrafted dinnerware and stoneware since 1906. You can see the process from potter's wheel to the kiln. Showrooms offer seconds and overruns at good prices. Open 8:00 A.M. to 5:00 P.M. Monday–Friday. No admission fee. Call (502) 582-1900.

Baxter Avenue antiques stores. The old German neighborhood of Phoenix Hill lies immediately southeast of Butchertown, approximately from Story and Main Streets southeast to the east end of Broadway. Phoenix Hill's main street, Baxter Avenue, is noted for its many antiques stores. Singling out any of these places is too perilous, because the best buy could await you just next door. Many of the wares come from the breakup of old estates and family collections that could date to the early nineteenth century.

OLD LOUISVILLE

Louisville's first suburb, this restored area is located west of Interstate 65, near Third Street just south of the downtown area. The grandest, most elegant of all Louisville neighborhoods was the site of the 1883–87 Southern Exposition, an industrial fair that was a national attraction. You can see some of the most beautiful nineteenth-century Victorian residences in the country on a driving or walking tour. Stop at the Information Center at 1340 South Fourth Street in Central Park for directions. Open 12:30 to 4:30 P.M. Monday, Tuesday, and Thursday and 10:30 A.M. to 4:30 P.M. Wednesday. Call (502) 635-5244.

WHERE TO EAT

Kunz's. 115 Fourth Avenue, Louisville 40202. The oldest downtown restaurant, Kunz's specializes in steaks, seafood, and a renowned raw bar, in addition to German specialties. Here's a place to eat heartily after a day's touring. Reservations essential on theater nights. $$. ❑. For hours call (502) 585-5555.

Vincenzo's. Fifth and Market Streets. The Gabriele brothers are famous for their light "Europa Cuisine," as well as richer American fare. They are especially well known for Italian dishes. Open for lunch Monday–Friday and for dinner Monday–Saturday. Closed Sunday. Reservations essential on weekends. $$$. ❑. Call (502) 580-1350.

SPORTING EVENTS

The following highlights provide Louisville with a national reputation in sports arenas, in addition to its horse-racing "arena."

Louisville Motor Speedway. 1900 Outer Loop Road, Louisville 40219. Located several miles south of the city off Interstate 65, the speedway features NASCAR-sanctioned stock car racing. Call (502) 966–2277.

The Kentucky Fair and Exposition Center. Located in the southern region of the city near the point where Interstates 65 and 264 meet, this is the home of the Louisville Panthers American Hockey League team and the University of Louisville Cardinals basketball team.

Louisville Slugger Field. 401 East Main Street, Louisville 40233. Home of the Louisville Riverbats, a minor league team for the Cincinnati Reds. One of the country's best new minor league ballparks. Call (502) 212–2287.

FORT KNOX, KENTUCKY

The 109,362-acre Fort Knox military reservation is the U.S. Army's armor center and repository of the nation's gold reserve. It is 30 miles southwest of Louisville on U.S. 31/60 west. Many recruits from the Cincinnati area have taken basic training here.

WHAT TO SEE

U.S. Gold Depository. Gold Vault Road, Fort Knox 40121. In this two-story granite, concrete, and steel building is stored a large portion of the U.S. gold reserve in almost-pure mint bars and alloyed coin. Visitors are permitted to view the outside of the building only. Not too exciting, perhaps, but many are enthralled by the very thought of such wealth. Nowhere else on earth is there known to be such a treasure in one spot. Security includes everything from electronic sensing devices to the bulk of the army's Sherman tanks, stationed less than a mile away.

The Patton Museum of Cavalry and Armor. Off U.S. 31/60 west, Chaffee Avenue exit, in Keyes Park, Fort Knox. On display here are the personal belongings of the blustery, hell-for-leather General George S. Patton, who some people say could have won World War

II single-handedly had his superiors not held him back. The museum has his pearl-handled revolvers (made of bone, actually), his specially equipped combat jeep, and the army limousine he was in when a traffic crash ended his life in 1945.

Cavalry gear and armor from the Revolutionary War through the Vietnam conflict are displayed here, along with enemy armor captured by Patton's troops. A separate display traces the evolution of the helicopter. Each November 11, Armed Forces Day, the armored division at Fort Knox has an equipment display, and each July 4, it stages a mock tank battle on the grounds of this military reservation.

The museum is open 9:00 A.M. to 4:30 P.M. Monday–Friday and 10:00 A.M. to 4:30 P.M. Saturday and Sunday. In May–September weekend hours are extended to 6:00 P.M. Closed December 24, 25, 30, and January 1. Its Library of Military History is open museum hours on weekends and by appointment on weekdays. No admission fee. Call (502) 624-3812.

WHERE TO EAT AND STAY

Otter Creek Park. Two miles west of Fort Knox on K-1638. This 3,600-acre park is located along the Ohio River and is a Louisville public park. A lodge, cabins, a campground, and a restaurant are complemented by hiking trails, a nature center, a boat ramp, and scenic river views. Call (502) 583-3577.

Doe Run Inn. Ten miles west of Fort Knox on K-1638. Doe Run Inn is located in a tiny cove in a circa 1792 stone mill and features Kentucky ham, fried chicken, and lemon pie. Smorgasbord dinners on Friday and Sunday. Open daily 7:30 A.M. to 9:00 P.M. $. Call (270) 422-2982 or 422-2042.

Metamora
Greensburg
Oldenburg
Batesville
229
52
75
74
42

INDIANA

275

Anderson Ferry

CINCINNATI

275

Belleview

338

Big Bone
Lick

Rabbit
Hash

Columbus

65

156
Markland
Dam

Madison

Vevay

42

36
56

Warsaw

227

Carrollton

62

27

OHIO RIVER

71

KENTUCKY

75

Cynthiana

Jeffersonville

Clarksville

LOUISVILLE

Frankford

64

KY Horse
Park

31W

31E

60

4

LEXINGT

44

Bluegrass Pkwy.

68

75

Fort Knox

Shaker Village

Bardstown

Harrodsburg

150

68
127

31E

Springfield

Perryville

150

Danville

Knob Creek

55

52

84

Lebanon

954

21

Hodgenville

Day Trip 4 Southwest

0   10   20   30 miles

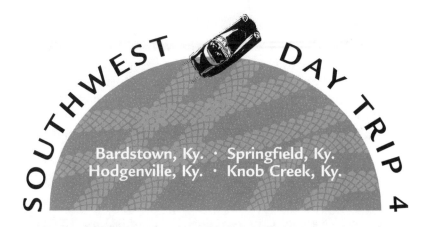

SOUTHWEST DAY TRIP 4

Bardstown, Ky. · Springfield, Ky.
Hodgenville, Ky. · Knob Creek, Ky.

BARDSTOWN, KENTUCKY

Bardstown, Kentucky, is a bit beyond our two-hour range, but its attractions and nearby spots associated with Abraham Lincoln are so unusual and interesting that the extra driving is worthwhile. It is often called "the place you don't miss when you visit Kentucky."

If you're visiting the Louisville area, Bardstown is only 45 miles southeast on Bardstown Road (U.S. 31 east). But it is quicker and easier to reach Bardstown from Cincinnati by taking Interstate 75 south to Lexington and U.S. 60 west 10 miles to the entrance of the Bluegrass Parkway, a fine, multilane road built by the state. Bardstown lies just 4 miles north of the Bardstown exit. Total driving time from Cincinnati is a little over two hours.

Bardstown missed, by just a few months, being Kentucky's oldest town. It was settled by trailblazing Virginian frontiersmen in 1775, some seventeen years before Kentucky became a state but after the settlement of Harrodsburg. It does, however, have the oldest inn and tavern in continuous operation west of the Alleghenies.

The city's chief claim to fame is Kentucky's anthem, "My Old Kentucky Home," written by Stephen Foster in fond recollection of his visit to the Federal Hill mansion here in 1852.

Another famous visitor who left his mark was the Duke of Orleans, later King Louis Philippe of France (1830–48), who came here during a period of exile to see an old friend, a Belgian priest who was pastor of St. Joseph Cathedral. Louis Philippe was the only European monarch to have had a taste of the American frontier.

Bardstown is nestled among the sudden, sugar-loaf hillocks of "Knob Country" that form a semicircle around Kentucky's central bluegrass area. It is the county seat of Nelson County, home of four bourbon whiskey distilleries, which represent the principal industry of the area. Check at the visitors center about which distilleries offer tours.

WHAT TO SEE AND DO

Bardstown–Nelson County Tourist Commission. 107 East Stephen Foster Avenue, Bardstown 40004. Brochures outlining walking tours of historic sites are available. Open daily 8:00 A.M. to 7:00 P.M. Memorial Day to Labor Day and 8:00 A.M. to 5:00 P.M. the rest of the year. Horse-drawn carriage rides and open-air bus tours are also available. Call (800) 638–4877 or (502) 348–4877.

My Old Kentucky Home State Park. 501 East Stephen Foster Avenue, Bardstown 40004, 1 mile east of downtown Bardstown on U.S. 150/62.

Stephen Foster, whose music captured the romantic spirit of the Steamboat Era, was a man of the river. Born in Pittsburgh, he came of age in his elder brother's shop on Cincinnati's waterfront, where 8,000 steamboat arrivals and departures a year gave life its pulse and prompted young Stephen to write "Oh, Susanna!" While there he was invited to visit Federal Hill, home of his cousin Judge John Rowan. Although the story is disputed by some historians, Foster made the trip by steamboat to Louisville and thence overland by coach.

Federal Hill is just as gracious today as it was then, a lovely Georgian colonial mansion of rustic brick, shaded by big trees and rimmed with flower beds. Costumed hostesses welcome visitors. "My Old Kentucky Home" is an emotional song, tinged with deep sadness, and true Kentuckians always stand up when they hear it. It is played at all public events and at many a funeral in the Bluegrass State.

Open every day 9:00 A.M. to 5:00 P.M. year-round. Admission fee. Call (502) 348–3502.

Stephen Foster: The Musical. 501 East Stephen Foster Avenue, Bardstown 40004. This outdoor musical drama is staged at the amphitheater of My Old Kentucky Home State Park adjacent to the

Federal Hill grounds. It is a rollicking production of more than fifty Foster tunes, with choruses and banjos. Frequently you'll hear the voices of young singers who take this as a summer job. Curtain time is 8:30 P.M. Tuesday–Sunday, with an additional 2:00 P.M. matinee Saturday. The season is early June to Labor Day. Admission fee. Call (502) 348-5971 or (800) 626-1563.

Old Talbott Tavern. 107 West Stephen Foster Avenue, Bardstown 40004. The Old Talbott has been an operating inn since 1779. A large room on the second floor is decorated with murals said to have been painted by a member of the Duke of Orleans's entourage. Bullet holes in it were added later by tenants whose artistic appreciation didn't extend much beyond marksmanship. There are no formal tours, but the owner does show people around if they're interested. The tavern has hosted Daniel Boone, Jesse James, Abraham Lincoln, and General George Patton. The tavern is known mostly as a restaurant. Open 11:00 A.M. to 9:00 P.M. Monday–Saturday; Sunday hours seasonal. Closed Christmas. For hours call (502) 348-3494.

St. Joseph's Proto-Cathedral. 310 West Stephen Foster Avenue, Bardstown 40004. Built in 1819, St. Joseph's is the oldest Catholic cathedral west of the Alleghenies. It is perhaps better known for the dozen or more large paintings given by King Francis I of Naples and Pope Leo XII. A National Landmark listed by the U.S. Library of Congress, the building is open year-round 9:00 A.M. to 5:00 P.M. Monday–Friday, 9:00 A.M. to 3:00 P.M. Saturday, and 1:00 to 5:00 P.M. Sunday. Donations accepted. Call (502) 348-3126.

Spalding Hall Museum. Fifth Street off West Stephen Foster Avenue, Bardstown 40004, around the corner from the cathedral. This historic building housed St. Joseph's College when it was built in 1839 to replace the first school building (1819), which was destroyed by fire. In the Civil War it became a Union hospital and later served as a seminary and an orphanage. In 1968 it closed as a boys' prep school after more than fifty years in that role. Today, as the Bardstown Historical Museum, it houses memorabilia of Stephen Foster and more than 200 years of area history.

Early in 1984 it became a full-time museum, taking over the Oscar Getz Museum of Whiskey History, formerly housed at the Old Barton Distillery. This whimsical collection of manuscripts, documents, bottles, posters, and photographs traces the history of whiskey in American life from precolonial days, including Prohibition. Moonshining, still-busting, and hatchet-wielding Carry Nation are all represented, and one treasured bottle, dated 1854, is marked with the name of Philadelphia distributor E. C. Booz, who gave his name to the term *booze*. Open 9:00 A.M. to 5:00 P.M. Monday–Saturday and 1:00 to 5:00 P.M. Sunday May–October; open 10:00 A.M. to 4:00 P.M. Tuesday–Saturday and 1:00 to 4:00 P.M. Sunday November–April. No admission fee. Call (502) 348-2999.

My Old Kentucky Dinner Train. 602 North Third Street, Bardstown 40004. You can enjoy an elegant lunch or dinner aboard the train in 1940s railroad cars as it travels from Bardstown to Limestone Springs and back. The train operates daily except Monday February–March. For hours and prices call (502) 348-7300.

Trappist Monastery of Gethsemani. Seven miles south of town on U.S. 31 east, then left on K-247 for 5 miles. This is the home of a community of Catholic monks, headed in the age-old tradition by an abbot. The order follows the austere Trappist philosophy of work, prayer, and silence.

The monks, who live in silence except when speech is necessary to accomplish their work, are noted far and wide for their robust cheeses, rich fruitcakes, and bourbon fudge, which are available by mail.

Visitors are welcome to the reception center and the church from 3:15 A.M. to 7:30 P.M. daily, all year. It is well worth the time to witness the concelebration of the Mass by the abbot and the entire community of monks in a ceremony that dates to the Middle Ages. You can watch daily at 6:20 A.M. and Sunday at 10:20 A.M. from the church's visitors gallery.

The chapel, once ornate, was stripped of its gingerbread and redone in a modern style with no ornamentation except for the tall, stained-glass windows in shades of gray and earth tones. The result is a striking atmosphere of simplicity, serenity, purity, even joy.

The internationally known ecumenist Thomas Merton was a member of this community and is buried in the monastery graveyard. Call (502) 549-3117.

John Fitch Monument. Courthouse Square. This memorial, with its miniature replica steamboat, is dedicated to a local man who ought to be famous but isn't. Fitch invented the steamboat in 1791, but it was Robert Fulton who gained the glory in 1807 by actually putting such a boat into a river and making it go. The *New Orleans* was the first Fulton boat to steam the Ohio and Mississippi Rivers. The Indians called it "Walk-on-Water" because it ran without sails or any visible human power. Others witnessing that voyage in 1811 called the steamboat the devil's work and blamed it for every calamity that ensued, including the 1811 earthquake at New Madrid, Missouri. Perhaps Fitch was lucky.

Old Bardstown Village Civil War Museum. 310 East Broadway, Bardstown 40004. This 7,000-square-foot museum is the culmination of thirty years of collecting and research by Hank and Rita Herr-mann. Once the Bardstown Waterworks and Ice House, the hundred-year-old structure now houses hundreds of authentic Civil War displays and artifacts representing both the North and the South. Costumed interpreters lead tours of the museum, where you'll find five original cannons, including a rare 1841 solid-bronze model. Battle flags, weapons, clothing and uniforms, an authentic campsite display, and a new museum highlighting the role of women in the Civil War round out this unique million-dollar collection. The gift shop features Civil War memorabilia and books. Admission fee. Open 10:00 A.M. to 5:00 P.M. Tuesday–Saturday and noon to 5:00 P.M. Sunday. (502) 328-0291.

Makers Mark Distillery. On K–52E, 20 miles south of Bardstown in Loretto via K–49 and 527. It is the distillery famous for its sour-mash whiskey. Tours are free Monday–Saturday every hour 10:30 A.M. to 3:30 P.M. Sunday tours offered at 1:30, 2:30, and 3:30 P.M. Call (502) 865-2099.

WHERE TO SHOP

Sutherland Gallery. 97 West Flaget Avenue, Bardstown 40004. More than seventy-five works of art by more than a dozen established regional artists fill this shop. You'll find watercolors, acrylics, oils, and sculptures. Call (502) 349-0139.

Bardstown Art Gallery and Thomas Merton Books. 310 Xavier Drive, Bardstown 40004, off Fifth Street. Books and original pottery and paintings by local artists are offered for sale. Closed Monday. For hours call (502) 348-6488.

WHERE TO EAT

Kurtz Restaurant. 418 East Stephen Foster Avenue, Bardstown 40004. Family owned and run since 1937, Kurtz's features home-made cooking, Southern-style. Open 10:00 A.M. to 9:00 P.M. week-days, 10:00 A.M. to 10:00 P.M. Saturday, and 7:00 A.M. to 9:00 P.M. Sunday. Closed Christmas. Reservations suggested. $. Call (502) 348-8964.

Old Talbott Tavern. 107 West Stephen Foster Avenue, Bard-stown 40004. Here is all the wonderful old atmosphere you expect of a 200-year-old tavern, and this one is widely known for its version of fried country ham. The menu also features fried chicken and other regional favorites. $$. ◻. Closed Christmas. For hours call (502) 348-3494.

Xavier's Restaurant. 112 Xavier Drive, Bardstown 40004. Located on the ground floor of what used to be a seminary college built in 1819 by Bishop Flaget, this restaurant shares the building with the Oscar Getz Museum of Whiskey History and the Bardstown Historical Museum. The owner is a Culinary Institute of America graduate and has received rave reviews for his New American cuisine. The restaurant also features a full bar with regional bourbons and a wine list. Serving dinner 5:00 to 10:00 P.M. Tuesday–Saturday. $$$. ◻. Call (502) 349-9464.

WHERE TO STAY

Jailer's Inn. 111 West Stephen Foster Avenue, Bardstown 40004. Located in the center of historic Bardstown, this inn offers five guest rooms decorated with heirlooms and antiques. Call (502) 348-5551.

The Mansion. 1003 North Third Street, Bardstown 40004. This National Register of Historic Places home features eight guest rooms brimming with period antiques. Built in 1851 by one of Kentucky's most powerful political families, The Mansion is a stately brick structure painted white. The grand 50-foot front hall leads to an unusual freestanding staircase, which sweeps to the right. The 18-foot Christmas tree is left up year-round to keep the holiday spirit flowing. A breakfast of country ham and biscuits with fruit is served on the finest of china and silver. Peace and quiet abound, especially in the private cottage out back. The Mansion's three acres are particularly lovely in spring, when spectacular pink and white dogwoods burst into bloom. Tours are offered by reservation. Call (502) 348-2586.

SPRINGFIELD, KENTUCKY

From Bardstown take U.S. 150 southeast 16 miles to Springfield. Turn left onto K–528 and proceed 5 miles to Lincoln Homestead State Park.

WHAT TO SEE

Lincoln Homestead State Park. A 150-acre park on land originally settled in 1782 by Abraham Lincoln, the president's grandfather. Thomas Lincoln, father of the president, grew up here.

Framed by split-rail fences, the site includes a replica of the Lincoln cabin and contains furnishings made by Tom Lincoln. Nearby is the original Berry house, home of Nancy Hanks when Tom was courting her. The picture of a pioneer Kentucky settlement is completed by replica blacksmith and carpentry shops.

This is the first of three points of interest in the Bardstown area associated with the early life of Abe Lincoln. They are presented here in chronological order to give a sense of continuity to Lincoln's local history. Museum tours are given 8:00 A.M. to 6:00 P.M. daily May–September 30 and October weekends. Call (606) 336-7461.

To continue on the route, return to Springfield, pick up K–55, and head south 8 miles to Lebanon, Kentucky. In Lebanon pick up westbound K–84 and continue 20 miles to the road's dead-end junction with U.S. 31 east; then turn left for the final 3 miles into Hodgenville.

HODGENVILLE, KENTUCKY

The road from Springfield takes visitors through some of the most scenic reaches of "Knob Country," winding among steep hills and following, much of the time, the meandering course of the Rolling Fork River.

WHAT TO SEE

Abraham Lincoln Birthplace National Historic Site. Three miles south of Hodgenville on U.S. 31 east. A columned, granite temple here enshrines what is almost certain to be the original log cabin in which the sixteenth president was born.

Each of the fifty-six steps leading to it represents a year of Lincoln's life. Since the memorial's completion in 1911, it has become one of the most visited shrines in the nation.

After their marriage Tom and Nancy Hanks Lincoln built that cabin here between a fresh limestone spring and a large oak tree that had been used as a surveying point. The spring still flows, but the tree finally succumbed.

It is thrilling to stroll these 116 acres and reflect upon the homey, woodland environment that gave this lad his start. A visitors center has an interesting audiovisual program dealing with the Lincoln family history. The site and visitors center are open 8:00 A.M. to 5:45 P.M. daily April, May, September, and October; 8:00 A.M. to 6:45 P.M. daily June–Labor Day; and 8:00 A.M. to 4:45 P.M. daily the rest of the year. Call (502) 358-3137.

KNOB CREEK, KENTUCKY

Lincoln Boyhood Home. U.S. 31 east, 7 miles northeast of Hodgenville on the way back to Bardstown. At Knob Creek the Lincoln family built its second cabin and remained here until Abe was seven years old. Then they moved to Indiana in 1816, the year Indiana became a state. A replica of the Lincoln cabin stands on the original site, close to Knob Creek, where Abe nearly drowned one day while playing. He was saved by a playmate. It was here that Abe first saw slave dealers herding slaves along the public road. The cabin and gift shop are privately owned. Open 9:00 A.M. to 5:00 P.M. April–October. Closed November–March. Admission fee. Call (502) 549-3741.

The very heart and soul of Kentucky is "The Bluegrass," a seven-county area centering upon Lexington in the north-central part of the state. This is the land of wide, rolling pastures framed with tidy, white-plank fences, where thoroughbreds graze and colts frolic in the sun. Up on the rise there is generally a handsome old home, headquarters of the estate.

Bluegrass country is the birthplace of bourbon and home to the mint julep and burgoo. Juleps are a mixture of bourbon, simple syrup, and crushed wild mint. Burgoo is a tasty stew of beef, poultry, vegetables, and sometimes wild game for extra zest. And the grass is not blue at all, unless allowed to "top out" in seedlings, which have a bluish tint. But the calcium-rich grass is prized for its role in developing the blueblood thoroughbreds so beloved of the horse-racing world.

From Cincinnati Interstate 75 makes a beeline straight south to Lexington, roughly following the route of the old "Dixie Highway" (U.S. 25). The 75-mile trip takes about an hour and fifteen minutes, passing through lovely, hilly countryside, where farms raise mostly corn, soybeans, tobacco, hogs, and a few head of cattle.

You will see the nation's only park devoted to the love of horses, the beautiful and aristocratic old city of Lexington, and Frankfort, capital of the commonwealth.

KENTUCKY HORSE PARK

Fine Thoroughbred horses are what the Bluegrass is all about, and it would be a shame to visit without seeing them. Thirty years ago you

Day Trip 1 South

0   10   20   30 miles

could have wandered up to the gates of any of the farms around Lexington and found a groom or a stable hand who would be happy to show you around. But times and manners change.

Mobs of tourists descended upon these hospitable folk, not only taking the farm staff away from its duties but also causing incredibly wanton damage, including pilferage and costly fires from careless smoking around stables, where there is a lot of hay. Sadly, many of the top farms—whose investment in horse breeding runs into millions of dollars—closed their gates to the public entirely. Some farms continue to conduct free tours, however. For a complete list, call the Lexington Convention and Visitors Bureau at (800) 845–3959.

In the 1970s the Commonwealth of Kentucky came to the rescue by establishing the Kentucky Horse Park. The state bought and restored a beautiful 1,032-acre estate that had been part of a well-known private standardbred farm for eighty years. At the park visitors can see the operations of a real working horse farm as it showcases more than forty breeds of horses.

GETTING THERE

The park is easily located at Exit 120 off Interstate 75, 6 miles north of downtown Lexington. The park is open daily 9:00 A.M. to 5:00 P.M. March 15 through October 31 and 9:00 A.M. to 5:00 P.M. Wednesday –Sunday, November 1 to March 14. Closed Thanksgiving, Christmas Eve and Day, and New Year's Eve and Day. A restaurant, campground, and gift shop are available. Admission fee. Call (859) 233–4303 or visit www.kyhorsepark.com.

WHAT TO SEE AND DO

Horse park officials want everyone who visits the complex to "touch a horse," and there are ample opportunities to stroke a sleek equine flank or pat a velvet nose.

Visitors Information Center. Near the park entrance. The center shows fine, wide-screen films, such as *Thou Shalt Fly without Wings,* an orientation to the exciting world of horses. Visitors can explore the park grounds and barns, and can take a narrated horse-drawn trolley tour.

International Museum of the Horse. On the park grounds. The equine kingdom and people's love of horses are the themes of this growing exhibit, which traces the history and development of the horse, its care and breeding, and racing, the "Sport of Kings." The museum also houses a carriage collection and the famous Calumet trophy collection.

Man o' War Memorial. On the park grounds. Herbert Haseltine's bronze statue of Kentucky's most famous thoroughbred, atop a granite base and surrounded by a moat, is the centerpiece of this small memorial garden, where Man o' War and several of his offspring are buried, including War Admiral, the 1937 Triple Crown winner.

Man o' War, considered by many to be the greatest racehorse ever, won twenty of his twenty-one races, including the Belmont Stakes and the Preakness in 1920. He also beat 1919 Triple Crown winner Sir Barton in a match (two-horse) race at Kenilworth Park in Canada. And he set new speed records in five track-distance categories, bringing him international acclaim.

His single defeat was the 1919 U.S. Hotel Stakes to a horse named, appropriately enough, Upset.

When he retired, in 1921, Man o' War's career earnings were $249,000, a world record at that time. Put out to pasture at Faraway Farms, north of Lexington, Man o' War set new records. He sired 296 foals, including 53 big-stakes winners and 96 other winning thoroughbreds that together ran 956 races and collected more than $2.6 million for their owners. Thus, Man o' War became the world's most productive stallion ever.

Because his owner thought it was cruel to run a growing three-year-old horse in such a long race, Man o' War was never entered in a Kentucky Derby and, in fact, never raced at all in Kentucky.

Horseback Riding. From mid-March through October, depending on the weather, Kentucky Horse Park offers 45-minute guided trail rides for an extra charge. There is also a fenced ring where children can take pony rides for a fee. Contact the visitors center for information. Private carriage rides are also available for a fee on a very limited basis.

Parade of Breeds. Staged twice daily at the Breeds Barn, mid-March through October, the colorful parade features fine examples of the park's forty-plus breeds performing in the show ring. The intimate show ring and interesting commentary make this a highlight. For a fee, guests may have their photos taken on horseback.

Hall of Champions. A special barn is reserved for the elite of the equine world. Champion horses from four different breeds are shown three times a day in the show pavilion behind the Hall of Champions. Thoroughbred racing legends John Henry and Cigar are joined by standardbreds Cam Fella and Staying Together, the American saddlebred CH Skywatch, and the American quarter horse racing great, Sergeant Pepper Feature.

Special Events. Everything from polo matches to Olympic equestrian qualifying events are held at the park throughout the season. Contact the visitors center in advance for information.

American Saddlebred Museum. On the grounds of the Kentucky Horse Park. A multi-image show and exhibits feature the American Saddlebred Horse, a native Kentucky breed. Call (859) 259-2746.

LEXINGTON, KENTUCKY

Lexington, with a population of more than 500,000, is Kentucky's second largest city, center of the Bluegrass country, and the world's largest burley tobacco market. Known as the Horse Capital of the World, the city has the largest and most famous horse farms on its periphery.

While Louisville is definitely a river city and blends the styles of North and South, Lexington has a totally Southern atmosphere, where voices are subdued, manners are gracious, and life proceeds at a more aristocratic pace. There is a tranquillity among the city's tree-shaded streets and elegant old homes that one might more readily expect in Savannah or New Orleans.

Lexington was named by a small band of frontiersmen who camped on this site in 1775 a few weeks after the first major battle of the American Revolution was fought at Lexington, Massachusetts. A permanent settlement was founded four years later and was organized as a city in 1781. The first college, Transylvania, and the first newspaper west of the Alleghenies were established here, and the most revered citizen came to be Henry Clay, orator, senator, and three-time unsuccessful candidate for president.

Although Kentucky was one of four "slave states" to remain loyal to the Union, Lexington's leanings were definitely toward the South. Many residents enlisted in the Confederate Army, including Gen.

John Hunt Morgan, and rebel troop movements were common south of Lexington in preparation for an assault northward to gain the Ohio River. This threat ended at the Battle of Perryville, 40 miles southwest of Lexington, in October 1862.

Even so, "Morgan's Raiders" struck repeatedly at Indiana and Ohio towns near the river throughout the war, mainly to loot county treasuries for the Southern cause. Eventually captured, Morgan escaped from the Ohio Penitentiary with the same slipperiness that marked his military sorties.

Hemp for rope making was Lexington's earliest industry. When smoking became popular after the Civil War, the city grew wealthy on its tobacco crops. Today it boasts the largest burley tobacco market in the world. The city also markets beef cattle, top-grade spring lambs, and sheep, and more than 125 industries have diversified the economy into oil, coal, service, and high-tech businesses.

Horse breeding is the city's labor of love. Early settlers brought fine horses with them from Virginia and improved them with blooded lines imported from overseas. Today the trend is reversed, with overseas buyers looking over the Kentucky stock. Keeneland races and sales bring English royalty, sheiks from the Middle East, and horse lovers the world over to Lexington. Keeneland Race Course continues a proud heritage of thoroughbred racing dating to 1787, while Lexington's famed Red Mile, a red-clay harness-racing track, has hosted standardbred racing for the past century.

The past few years have brought restoration and redevelopment of the downtown area into a vibrant, exciting complex. Triangle Park, in the heart of downtown, features a stepped wall of fountains and flowering pear trees. The park is bounded by the Rupp Arena and Convention Center, luxury hotels, and the shopping and entertainment attraction, Victorian Square.

At Victorian Square an elaborate restoration turned an entire block of late-nineteenth-century buildings into a modern shopping, entertainment, and office complex.

TOURS AND INFORMATION

Lexington Convention and Visitors Bureau. 301 East Vine Street, Lexington 40507. Information, maps, and tour arrangements of the area are all here. One of the best ways to see the surrounding horse country is on a guided tour. The Convention and Visitors Bureau works with tour operations that offer a variety of tours to area horse farms and can provide a self-guided scenic walking and driving tour map. Staff members will help you find the best tour for your interests. Open 8:30 A.M. to 5:00 P.M. Monday–Friday. The visitors center is open 10:00 A.M. to 5:00 P.M. Saturday year-round and noon to 5:00 P.M. Sunday, May through August. Call (859) 233-7299 or (800) 845-3959.

WHAT TO SEE

Gratz Park. Bounded by Second, Third, Market, and Mill Streets downtown. The park is fringed with a score of historic homes built between 1794 and 1901. One is an early Transylvania University building called "The Kitchen." Gratz Park captures the atmosphere of Lexington in the early 1800s when it was regarded as the cultural center of the United States west of the Alleghenies. It is said that the U.S. premiere of Beethoven's First Symphony was performed in Gratz Park in 1817.

The Aviation Museum of Kentucky. Bluegrass Airport on Versailles Road, Lexington 40544-40118. This facility has 12,000 square feet of hangar space for exhibits, a repair shop for aircraft restoration, a conference room, a gift shop, and a library. Admission fee. For hours call (859) 233-7299.

University of Kentucky Art Museum. Rose Street at Euclid Avenue. This museum features a permanent collection of more than 3,500 works in all media—Old Masters, nineteenth-century European and American paintings and sculpture, and art of Asia and Africa. Open year-round noon to 5:00 P.M. Tuesday–Sunday. Closed university holidays. No admission fee. Call (859) 257-5716.

The Thoroughbred Center. 3380 Paris Pike (U.S. 27), Lexington 40511, 1.5 miles northeast of the road's junction with Interstate 75. From the interstate take exit 113. Not to be confused with the Kentucky Horse Park north of the city, this establishment specializes in the training of horses. Visitors can tour the thoroughbred center to get a behind-the-scenes glimpse of the thoroughbred industry, including watching horses work out on two tracks. Open year-round April through October. Tours begin at 9:00 A.M., 10:00 A.M., and 1:00 P.M.

Monday–Friday, and at 9:00 A.M. and 10:30 A.M. Saturday. Tours by appointment November through March. Call (859) 293–1853.

Keeneland Race Course. Six miles west of downtown on Versailles Road (U.S. 60) and across the highway from Bluegrass Airport. Keeneland was built on property granted to the Keene family in 1783 by their cousin, Virginia Governor Patrick Henry. It is the top track in the Bluegrass and the setting each spring for the Toyota Bluegrass Stakes, an important preliminary for horses bound for the Kentucky Derby. This beautiful 1 1/16 mile oval track and accompanying clubhouse and grandstand are among the most modern in racing. They were built in 1936 and have been almost continuously remodeled ever since. The spring meet is in April, the fall meet in October. The track is closed Monday, Tuesday, and Easter Sunday. Post time is 1:00 P.M. (*Note:* Policies concerning admittance of children to parimutuel betting facilities vary. Phone ahead for information.) If you've never tried a mint julep or Kentucky burgoo, reasonable versions of both are available at the track. Call (859) 254–3412.

Transylvania University. 300 North Broadway, Lexington 40508. The university, enrolling about 1,000 students and the oldest west of the Alleghenies, has a collection of pioneer medical equipment of the early 1800s, displayed in the Old Morrison Building, itself a Greek Revival National Historic Landmark. Also on campus is the Patterson Cabin, which was built in 1778 and is Lexington's oldest building. It stands at Third Street and Broadway and is open by appointment only. Call (859) 233–8242.

Mary Todd Lincoln House. 578 West Main Street, Lexington 40508. Recently restored, this was the Todd family home in the early 1800s. One must wonder what this aristocratic family thought of the rangy young lawyer from the backwoods who came courting Mary Todd. Mary and Abe Lincoln were married in 1842. Although they eventually moved to the White House, their marriage was turbulent because of Mary's instability and her great sadness brought on by the loss of a son and a demoralizing war. Tours of the home feature numerous personal articles of the Lincoln and Todd families. Open 10:00 A.M. to 4:00 P.M. Monday–Saturday, mid-March through November. Admission fee. Call (859) 233–9999.

Ashland. 120 Sycamore Road on the 1400 block of Richmond Road (East Main Street), Lexington 40502. This stately, twenty-room home, now a National Historic Site, was the residence of former Secretary of State Henry Clay (until his death in 1852) and of four other generations of the Clay family. Esteemed as a statesman and an orator, Clay aspired to the presidency and entered his first campaign at the age of forty-seven. He was defeated by John Quincy Adams in 1824, Andrew Jackson in 1832, and James Knox Polk in 1844.

Ashland, built in 1806, is furnished with Clay family possessions, including the original French draperies and silver doorknobs and hinges. The twenty surrounding acres have gardens, outbuildings, and a lovely grove of ash trees, which not only gave the estate its name but also provided timber for the hand-carved woodwork throughout the house. The home is open April through October 10:00 A.M. to 4:00 P.M., Monday–Saturday and 1:00 to 4:00 P.M. on Sunday. Also open November, December, February, and March 10:00 A.M. to 4:00 P.M. Tuesday through Saturday and 1:00 to 4:00 P.M. on Sunday. Closed holidays and in January. Admission fee. Call (859) 266-8581.

Hunt-Morgan House. 201 North Mill Street, Lexington 40508, at Second Street downtown in Gratz Park. Kentucky's first millionaire, John Wesley Hunt, built this mansion in 1814. Federal in style, it features a circular staircase and fanlight entrance. In the typical Southern style of separating the hot-spot from the rest of the house, the kitchen was built in the cellar, and servants had to hike every meal upstairs to the dining room. The Morgans of Alabama married into the Hunt family before the Civil War, and their progeny included two other famous figures, General John Hunt Morgan, called the "Thunderbolt of the Confederacy," who was the grandson of John Wesley Hunt, and Thomas Hunt Morgan, the general's nephew, who won the 1933 Nobel Prize in physiology for discoveries about the hereditary function of chromosomes. They also lived at Ashland. The Hunt-Morgan House, which still has its original carriage house, is now operated as a museum by the Bluegrass Trust. It is open 10:00 A.M. to 4:00 P.M. Tuesday–Saturday and 2:00 to 5:00 P.M. Sunday. Tours are offered at quarter past the hour; the last tour is at 3:15 P.M. Tuesday–Saturday and 4:15 P.M. on Sunday. Closed Monday, Thanksgiving, and December 23–March 1. Admission fee. Call (859) 253-0362.

Headley-Whitney Museum. 4435 Old Frankfort Pike, Lexington 40510, 4.5 miles west of New Circle Road. This museum features a unique and diverse collection of fine arts, including a world-renowned group of jeweled bibelots, many designed by museum founder George Headley. Open 10:00 A.M.–5:00 P.M. Tuesday–Friday, 12:00–5:00 P.M. Saturday and Sunday. Closed January. Admission fee. Call (606) 255-6653.

WHERE TO SHOP

Civic Center Shops. 410 West Vine Street, Lexington 40507. Located in the heart of downtown in the Lexington Civic Center and Rupp Arena, the area features three levels of specialty shops. Open daily. Call (859) 233-4567.

Victorian Square. 401 West Main at Broadway, Lexington 40507. Located downtown in sixteen Victorian-era buildings renovated into a magnificent shopping area with more than twenty shops of upscale clothing and specialty items. Open daily. Call (859) 252-7575.

WHERE TO EAT

The Coach House. 855 South Broadway (U.S. 68), Lexington 40504. The chef prepares regional and continental specialties at the Coach House, one of Lexington's most popular dining spots. Specialties include chateaubriand, steaks, seafood, and poultry, including wild game birds when available. Weekend reservations recommended. $$. ☐. Closed Sunday. For hours call (859) 252-7777.

Merrick Inn. 3380 Tates Creek Road, Lexington 40500. Situated in the manor house of the old Cal Milam horse farm, this lovely restaurant honors a former resident of the 1920s and 1930s—the racehorse Merrick, who is buried on the property. Southern continental cuisine featuring fried chicken, seafood, steaks, and fresh vegetables is complemented by homemade breads and desserts. Open for dinner Monday–Saturday. Closed holidays. $$. ☐. Call (859) 269-5417.

Dudley's Restaurant. 380 South Mill Street, Lexington 40508. Named after a Dr. Dudley, who chaired the anatomy and surgery departments at Transylvania University in the 1850s, the restaurant is housed in his restored home and offers a dining room and patio. Located in the old South Hill area, the restaurant offers continental dining for lunch and dinner. Reservations recommended. Open daily. $$. ☐. Call (859) 252–1010.

The Mansion at Griffin Gate. 1720 Newtown Pike, Lexington 40511. Located adjacent to the Griffin Gate Marriott, the antebellum mansion is furnished with antiques, silver, and fresh flowers. Gracious continental dining for both lunch and dinner. Open daily. $$$. ☐. Call (859) 288–6142.

WHERE TO STAY

Campbell House Inn & Golf Club. 1375 Harrodsburg Road (U.S. 68), Lexington 40504, southwest of downtown. This gracious old inn has a Southern atmosphere, an 18-hole golf course, and a lobby art gallery. Call (859) 255–4281 or (800) 354–9235.

Gratz Park Inn. 120 West Second Street, Lexington 40507. Adjacent to historic Gratz Park, this luxury hotel is an elegant, small, European-style inn, also offering a lounge and restaurant. Call (859) 231–1777 or (800) 752–4166 from outside the state.

FRANKFORT, KENTUCKY

Frankfort, Kentucky's capital, has long claimed that its chief crop is politics. When Kentucky became a state in 1792, splitting from the old colony of Virginia, Lexington and Louisville were its two largest towns, and both aspired to be its capital. Lexington was the home of some important political figures, but fast-growing Louisville, on the Ohio River, was an important commercial center. Stalemated, the state's fathers chose the village midway between those two towns, Frankfort, in compromise. Frankfort is 24 miles northwest of Lexington via Interstate 64 or U.S. 421 and 56 miles east of Louisville on Interstate 64 or U.S. 60.

Still a relatively small city with a population of about 26,000, Frankfort nevertheless has one of the grandest statehouses in the nation. The city, situated on the Kentucky River, enjoys a large share of the state's bourbon whiskey production because of its natural limestone springs.

Among its other claims to fame is legendary Kentucky frontiersman Daniel Boone, who is buried here.

WHAT TO SEE

The Frankfort Visitors Center. 100 Capital Avenue, Frankfort 40601. The Frankfort/Franklin County Tourist & Convention Commission is located here and offers information about the area. Open 8:00 A.M. to 5:00 P.M. Monday–Friday year-round, and 10:00 A.M. to 2:00 P.M. on Saturday and 1:00 to 5:00 P.M. on Sunday April through October. Call (800) 960-7200.

The Kentucky State Capitol. South end of Capital Avenue. Impressive first because of its size—it is 400 feet long and 200 feet wide and rises 212 feet from the esplanade to the lantern cupola atop its dome—the capitol stands as a work of love by turn-of-the-century Kentucky stonemasons whose only power machinery was a steam-driven concrete mixer.

Completed in 1910, the capitol was inspired by the temples of ancient Greece. The granite edifice has phalanxes of steps and terraces and more than one hundred Ionic columns. Its high central dome is floodlit at night.

The nave contains two huge murals depicting events in the life of Daniel Boone. The rotunda has statues honoring five of the state's most famous native sons: Abraham Lincoln; Jefferson Davis, president of the Confederacy; Henry Clay, orator and statesman; Alben Barkley, vice president under Harry S. Truman; and Dr. Ephraim McDowell, a pioneering physician who performed the world's first abdominal surgery, without anesthetic. Mobs in the street accused him of witchcraft and butchery.

The Capitol Information Desk. Located inside the front entrance. It provides maps, brochures, and tour information for both the capitol and the executive mansion. The capitol also houses the First Lady Doll Collection. Capitol tours are conducted 8:00 A.M. to 4:30 P.M. Monday–Friday, 8:30 A.M. to 4:30 P.M. on Saturday, and 1:00 to 4:30 P.M. on Sunday. Closed major holidays. No admission fee. Reservations for large groups suggested. Call (502) 564-3449.

The Floral Clock. Located on the west lawn, behind the capitol. Visualize a round layer-cake pan 34 feet in diameter and 2 feet deep. A container this size is imbedded in a grassy slope at one end of the capitol's reflecting pool. It is filled with dirt and is planted with whatever flowers or plants are in season, in the design of a clock face, with flowers of a contrasting color for the numerals around the dial.

In the center is a broad steel stem that supports the hands of the clock, which are also planted with flowers matching those of the numerals. Buried beneath this hundred-ton assembly are huge clockworks that move the hands. When the hands are filled with dirt and flowers, they weight nearly half a ton. A busy crew constantly maintains the 20,000 or more plantings needed throughout the year. Call (502) 564-3449.

The Executive Mansion. Located on the east lawn of the capitol grounds. Home of Kentucky's governors since 1914. The mansion was beautifully restored in the early 1980s. It boasts seventy monolithic columns and sculptures of Kentucky dignitaries. The mansion is open to visitors 9:00 A.M. to 11:00 A.M. on Tuesdays and Thursdays. No admission fee. Call (502) 564-3449.

The Lieutenant Governor's Mansion. 420 High Street, Frankfort 40601. This Georgian edifice, which served as the governor's mansion from 1798 to 1914, has been carefully restored and is now the home of the lieutenant governor. A number of illustrious guests have been welcomed here, including seven U.S. presidents and William Jennings Bryan. It can be visited 1:30 to 3:30 P.M. Tuesdays and Thursdays. No admission fee. For information call the Kentucky Historical Society at (502) 564-3016.

The Old State Capitol. Located at St. Clair Street and Broadway. This building, constructed of marble dug from the bluffs of the Kentucky River, served as Kentucky's capitol from 1829 to 1909. It was long a restoration project of the Kentucky Historical Society. The old capitol is now restored and is furnished in period style. Open 10:00 A.M. to 5:00 P.M. Tuesday–Saturday, 12:00 to 5:00 P.M. Sunday. Closed Mondays, Easter, Thanksgiving, Christmas Eve, Christmas Day, and New Year's Day. No admission fee. Call (502) 564-3016.

The Kentucky History Center. 100 West Broadway, Frankfort 40601. This 167,000-square-foot museum and research facility is the cornerstone of the historic cultural corridor in downtown Frankfort. Opened in April 1999, the facility offers genealogical references. It also contains a state art gallery, a gift shop, and the Kentucky Hall of Fame. Guided and self-guided tours are available. The museum is open 10:00 A.M. to 5:00 P.M. Tuesday, Wednesday, Friday, and Saturday, 10:00 A.M. to 8:00 P.M. Thursday, and 1:00 P.M. to 5:00 P.M. Sunday. Closed Monday. The library is open 8:00 A.M. to 4:00 P.M. Monday,

Tuesday, Wednesday, Friday, and Saturday, and 8:00 A.M. to 8:00 P.M
Thursday. Closed Sunday and holiday weekends. Call (512) 564-3016.

The Kentucky Military History Museum. East Main Street and
Capital Avenue. Located in the Old State Arsenal (1850) and operated by the Kentucky Historical Society and the Kentucky National
Guard, the museum emphasizes militia, state guard, and other vol-
unteer organizations from the Revolution to Operation Desert
Storm. Displays include an impressive collection of weapons, uniforms, and flags. Guided and self-guided tours are available. Open
10:00 A.M. to 5:00 P.M. Tuesday–Saturday and 1:00 to 5:00 P.M.
Sunday. Closed Monday. No admission fee. Call (502) 564-3265.

Daniel Boone's Gravesite. 215 East Main Street, in the Frankfort
Cemetery, Frankfort 40601. Boone and his wife, Rebecca, originally
from eastern Virginia, spent most of their lives in the Kentucky
wilderness, then drifted to the Missouri frontier. Boone is reputed to
have said, "When I can see the smoke of a neighbor's chimney, I
know it's gettin' too crowded." He died in Missouri in 1820 at the
age of eighty-six, but the bodies of Boone and his wife were returned
here in 1845 for reburial under a monument dedicated to the state's
most renowned frontiersman. Buses must park at the office. Please,
no tracings or rubbings. Call (502) 227-2403.

The Vietnam Veterans Memorial. Located on Coffeetree Road,
overlooking the beautiful city. The names of Kentuckians who died
in Vietnam are etched in granite beneath the memorial sundial, with
the point of the gnomon's shadow actually touching the veteran's
name on the anniversary of his death. Recognized as one of the most
original and unusual memorials in the nation. No admission fee.

The Salato Wildlife Center. Located at One Game Farm Road,
Frankfort 40601, off US 60, 3 miles west of Frankfort. The farm offers
two public fishing lakes, picnic areas, shelters, and a site for watching
wildlife. Interpretive and interactive displays and exhibits on native
fish, wildlife, and plants are found in the Education Center. Live
exhibits in native habitats, with special events and educational pro-
grams, are mounted year-round. New in 2001 was the University of
Kentucky's live wildcat mascot exhibit. Open 10:00 A.M. to 5:00 P.M.
Tuesday–Saturday, and 1:00 to 6:00 P.M. Sunday, May through
October, and 10:00 A.M. to 4:00 P.M. Tuesday–Friday, 9:00 A.M. to 4:00
P.M. Saturday, and 1:00 P.M. to 5:00 P.M. Sunday, November through
April. Closed Monday. No admission fee. Call (502) 564-7863.

Buffalo Trace Distillery. 1001 Wilkinson Boulevard, Frankfort 40601. Bourbon whiskey has been distilled here since the 1800s and it is known as the oldest continually operating distillery in the United States. Free tours of the aging warehouse, log clubhouse, and scenic courtyard are offered. Samples provided for those who are twenty-one and older. Guided tours are available on the hour, 9:00 A.M. to 3:00 P.M. Monday–Friday, and 10:00 A.M. to 3:00 P.M. Saturday. Hours of operation are 9:00 A.M. to 3:00 P.M. Monday–Friday. Gift shop is open 9:00 A.M. to 4:00 P.M. No admission fee. Call (502) 223-7641.

WHERE TO SHOP

Rebecca Ruth Candy. 112 East Second Street, Frankfort 40601. These are the home kitchens of the bourbon whiskey-candy originators. Tours available Monday through Friday, 9:00 A.M. to 4:30 P.M., January through October. Store is open year-round 8:30 A.M. to 5:30 P.M. Monday–Saturday and 12:00 to 5:00 P.M. Sunday. Call (502) 223-7475 or (800) 444-3766.

WHERE TO EAT

Daniel's Restaurant. 243 West Broadway, Frankfort 40601. Housed in a one-hundred-fifty-year-old historic building, Daniel's Restaurant offers a dining experience unparalleled in the city of Frankfort. Using traditional Kentucky fare, such as catfish and ham, Daniel's creates an upscale dining experience with the flair of a five-star restaurant. Lunch is served 11:00 A.M. to 2:00 P.M. Monday–Friday. Dinner is served 5:00 to 10:00 P.M. Monday–Saturday. Call (502) 875-5599.

Jim's Seafood. 950 Wilkinson Boulevard, Frankfort 40601. Situated on the banks of the Kentucky River, overlooking a dam. Enjoy the scenic view while tasting some of the best seafood the region has to offer. Serving lunch 11:00 A.M. to 2:00 P.M. Monday–Friday and dinner 4:00 to 10:00 P.M. Monday–Saturday. Call (502) 223-7448.

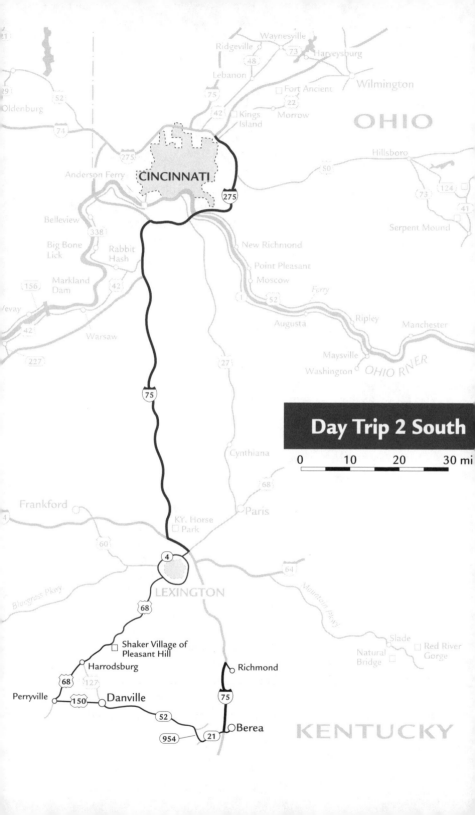

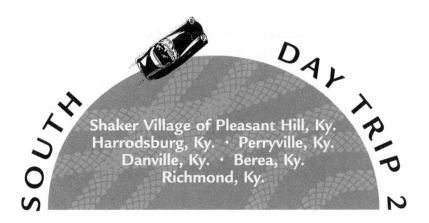

SOUTH DAY TRIP 2

Shaker Village of Pleasant Hill, Ky.
Harrodsburg, Ky. · Perryville, Ky.
Danville, Ky. · Berea, Ky.
Richmond, Ky.

South of the Bluegrass, amid the rolling farmlands and the tortuous course of the Kentucky River, lie fascinating little towns, each one unique. One is a restored Shaker village, another Kentucky's oldest settlement. There is the state's first capital, and yet another that is a center for Appalachian culture. Fine old country inns in the region offer some of Kentucky's very best cooking, and if highly skilled handcraftmanship appeals to your shopping sense, many such outlets can be found.

From Cincinnati take Interstate 75 directly south 73 miles to the northern outskirts of Lexington. After the interstate merges with Interstate 64, watch for exit 115 and take it to Newtown Pike. Follow the pike to K-4 (New Circle Road) westbound. Exit onto U.S. 68 westbound.

Any one of the points on this trip can be visited in a day's time, but if you plan to take on the entire loop, an overnight stop is suggested— urged, in fact—both from the standpoint of safe driving and in view of the wonderful inns recommended here.

Please note that all the towns on this itinerary, except Lexington and Richmond, are in dry counties.

SHAKER VILLAGE OF PLEASANT HILL, KENTUCKY

Soon after leaving the Lexington area via U.S. 68, you are again in the open countryside. Horse farms disappear, replaced by wide fields and meadows and ponds where cattle graze. The play of light across these low hills can be spectacular at certain times of day and after a rain if the sun comes back out.

Actually, you are atop a plateau, a fact that doesn't really become evident until, some 22 miles southwest of Lexington, the highway suddenly begins to descend toward the Kentucky River. Be especially careful here during rain or snow, for the road makes several sharp, unexpected turns. The river, narrow enough at this point to pitch a rock across, is flanked by palisades that rise 400 or more feet above the stream, forming a rocky chasm where water trickles down and where it is always cool.

As the road winds back up to the top of the plateau again, take note of the rock walls, 4 or 5 feet high, that delineate the fields. Most were built by the Shakers, or farm folk they taught, and are stacked together without benefit of mortar. They have lasted many decades.

In the early 1960s Pleasant Hill, Kentucky—then the post-office name for Shaker Village—appeared much the same as many other rural Kentucky towns: a cluster of homes and shops along the highway, with a church and a gas station on the corner. But many preservation-minded individuals were aware that a number of the buildings were part of the original Shaker Village founded here by members of that faith in 1805.

Today, the actual post-office address for Shaker Village is Harrodsburg, Kentucky. Residents continue to refer to the area as Pleasant Hill, however—an apt name for the picturesque setting in which visitors will find Shaker Village.

Several influential Kentuckians founded a corporation and bought the entire town and its 2,800 acres of field and woodland. Then they set about removing all the non-Shaker buildings and restoring the Shaker ones. The result is a virtually complete village of thirty-three Shaker buildings. Amid these handsome structures, one is immersed totally in the nineteenth century. The structures are spaced generously, with wide yards and fine vistas over the countryside creating an idyllic scene in all seasons, even winter. With a snowfall, candles in the windows, holly on the doors, and a carriage in the road with its horse blowing steam, Shaker Village is a Currier & Ives print come to life.

The Shakers, unjustly, were often the subject of derision. This Quaker sect, founded in England, was called "the shaking Quakers" because of the frenzied dancing that accompanied its religious meetings. Shakers disdained sex and rejected marriage as evil, hoping instead to propagate their sect by taking in converts and orphans and the otherwise-homeless. They lived together as "families," but women and men used separate entrances and even separate staircases. Each gender occupied and used only its half of the building, including the dining room. This duality accounts for the sect's architectural trademark—two of everything.

Yet the Shakers, at least in Kentucky, ran a prosperous farm. They made their own clothing, spun their own silk, invented countless gadgets for field and kitchen, and even rigged the first known municipal water system in Kentucky to bring running tap water into every house. The community was governed by elected trustees, who kept a journal of all activities. During the Civil War, armies of both the Blue and the Gray marched down this road, usually prevailing upon these gentle people for food, supplies, and fresh horses. Once, the Shaker women carried tables out into the road and fed 10,000 troops, virtually exhausting their winter supply of food. As industrialization swept the nation after the Civil War, converts became fewer and fewer, and the Shakers dwindled by 1900 to a few aged men and women. The men went about the countryside in wagons, selling seed to farmers. Eventually there were only a few elderly sisters—the last died in 1923.

WHAT TO SEE

Shaker Village is open 9:30 A.M. to 5:30 P.M. April 1 to October 31. From November 1 to March 31 some exhibition buildings are closed and tour hours and admission are reduced. There is a charge for village tours. Special events fill the calendar throughout the year. Call (800) 734–5611 or (859) 734–5411 for details. Some of the unique shops and exhibits that fill Shaker Village include these:

Centre Family House. This is the largest of the Shaker buildings and best exemplifies Shaker family life, with bedrooms, dining room, and kitchen intact and fully furnished with originals or Shaker reproductions made at the village. Displays include fascinating old photographs of the Shakers themselves and some of their writings.

Craft Exhibits. Many of the smaller buildings feature demonstrations by artisans of nineteenth-century crafts as they once were practiced by the Shakers: weaving, spinning, coopering, broom making, and carpentry among others.

The Trustees' Office. Now home to the restaurant operation, the Trustees' Office is the finest of all the buildings and is as sound as the day it was built. Its roof is supported by massive beams that stay in place because of the counterbalance of their own weight. Not a nail or peg was used. The foyer leads to magnificent twin spiral staircases, and beyond, in the dining rooms, huge windows overlook the pastures. Shaker furnishings are used throughout the house, including the guest rooms.

Craft Stores. Two shops feature merchandise such as pottery, hand-made brooms, cookbooks and curios, Shaker reproduction furniture, and other Kentucky-made items.

Dixie Belle Riverboat Excursions. One-hour sightseeing cruises are offered mid-April through October aboard this 149-passenger sternwheeler moored at Shaker Landing. The *Dixie Belle* paddleboat is the only vessel offering public excursions on the Kentucky River. The scenic tour takes you under Kentucky's famous High Bridge, which spans the famous limestone cliffs.

WHERE TO EAT

The Trustees' Office. The dining room is one of the three or four best restaurants in the state for regional specialties, which include Shaker recipes, fried chicken, and fish, accompanied by a cornucopia of vegetable dishes brought around to the table in great bowls throughout the meal. There are homemade breads, corn pudding, eggplant casserole, and green beans, plus the traditional, tart Shaker lemon pie. Especially nice touches are candles ensconced along the walls in big glass chimneys and gracious local women who tend tables in period costume. The restaurant is open daily except Christmas Eve and Christmas Day. No alcohol. Reservations are recommended. $$. For hours and information call (800) 734–5611.

WHERE TO STAY

Inn at Pleasant Hill. This is the collective name for the eighty-one guest rooms located in buildings where Shakers worked and lived. All have modern baths and reproduction Shaker furnishings. Open all year. Call (800) 734–5611 or (859) 734–5411.

HARRODSBURG, KENTUCKY

From Shaker Village continue 7 miles southwest on U.S. 68 into Harrodsburg.

Founded by James Harrod and a group of surveyors in 1774, Harrodsburg is Kentucky's oldest city and the first permanent English settlement west of the Alleghenies. Sulphur springs made the community something of a spa for a while, but harness racing and horse shows proved to be more profitable. Historically, Harrodsburg has amassed a long list of firsts, including the first school, the first mill, and the first corn crop in Kentucky.

WHAT TO SEE

Old Fort Harrod. In a twenty-eight-acre state park in downtown Harrodsburg at the junction of U.S. 68 and U.S. 127 is a full-scale reproduction of the fort, reconstructed near the spot where it stood more than 200 years ago. Assembled here are pioneer structures, including the cabin that was home to Colonel Harrod, the founder, and the Lincoln Marriage Temple, a log cabin where Abe's parents were wed. Among other log homes is the McGinty House. Annie McGinty, wife of Colonel McGinty, drove her own livestock across the mountains, opened a tavern here with all sorts of eastern niceties, and became known as one of the state's first fine cooks. The fort property includes the Mansion Museum, with historic relics from the settlement through the Civil War, and the oldest pioneer cemetery west of the mountains. The fort and the first floor of the museum are handicapped-accessible. The museum is open 9:00 A.M. to 5:30 P.M. mid-March through November. Hours vary the rest of year. Admission fee. Call (859) 734-3314.

Old Mud Meeting House. Four miles south of town via U.S. 68, on Dry Branch Road. Built in 1800, this is the first Dutch Reformed Church in the West. Its mud-and-straw walls are still standing, thanks to occasional patching. Open by appointment only. Call (859) 734-5985 or write P.O. Box 316, Harrodsburg, KY 40330.

Morgan Row. 220-222 South Chiles Street, Harrodsburg 40330. These four brick buildings, erected in 1807, are Kentucky's oldest known examples of row houses—the forerunner of modern townhouses. The complex, operated as an inn and tavern from 1807 to 1830, now houses the offices of the Harrodsburg Historical Society. Open Tuesday through Saturday by appointment. Call (859) 734-9238.

James Harrod Amphitheater. West Lexington Street, Harrodsburg 40330, at the state park. *The Legend of Daniel Boone,* dealing with Boone's adventures in Kentucky, is performed at 8:30 P.M. Tuesday–Saturday and 7:00 P.M. Sunday. The season runs mid-June through August. Handicapped-accessible. Admission fee. Call (800) 852-6665 or (859) 734-3346.

TOURS AND INFORMATION

Harrodsburg–Mercer County Tourist Commission. 103 South Main Street, Harrodsburg 40330. The commission has detailed information on all local attractions. Open 9:00 A.M. to 5:00 P.M. Monday–Friday all year and 10:00 A.M. to 3:00 P.M on Saturday June through October. Call (800) 355-9192 or (859) 734-2364.

Historic Walking/Driving Tour. This is a self-guided driving and walking tour that highlights fifty-two historic sites, including pre-Civil War homes and trails used by James Harrod and Daniel Boone. Maps are available at the Tourist Commission office.

WHERE TO EAT AND STAY

The Beaumont Inn. From U.S. 68 and U.S. 127 in downtown Harrodsburg, follow the signs to Beaumont Drive. The inn was built in 1845 as a private school, but for many years it has been known as a fine old hotel and restaurant that has been owned and operated by four generations of the same family. In its antiques-furnished room, the inn serves, among other country specialties, Kentucky ham and corn pudding. Open daily. $$. ❑. Closed late December–February. For hours and information call (800) 352-3992 or (859) 734-3381.

PERRYVILLE, KENTUCKY

Perryville is the site of the Civil War battle that ended the South's threat to the Ohio Valley and halted the effort to force Kentucky into the Confederacy. From Harrodsburg take U.S. 68 southwest for 10 miles.

WHAT TO SEE

Perryville Battlefield State Site. Two miles northeast of Perryville on K-1920. More than 6,000 men died on this ninety-acre field October 8, 1862, when General Don Carlos Buell's Union troops fought General Braxton Bragg's Confederate forces. Two monuments now mark the principal battle line, one to the 4,241 Union dead and one to the 1,822 Confederate dead. A museum here displays a diorama of the battle and has information on walking and driving tours. There are picnic facilities on the grounds and marked hiking trails. A reenactment of the battle is staged here each year on the weekend closest to the October 8 anniversary of the battle. The park is open all year. Museum hours are 9:00 A.M. to 5:00 P.M. daily April–October. Open by appointment November–March. Admission fee. Call (859) 332-8631.

DANVILLE, KENTUCKY

Danville is 10 miles east of Perryville via U.S. 150 or 9 miles southeast of Harrodsburg via U.S. 127. The city was founded in 1775, just a year after Harrodsburg, while Kentucky was still part of the colony of Virginia. American independence increased migration of settlers across the Appalachians, prompting Virginia, in 1785, to make Kentucky a district and to make Danville its administrative center. Danville, it was thought, could handle the affairs of the frontier and was most nearly in the center of the wilderness population; besides, it had become the most-important and -populous community on the Wilderness Road, the natural trace pounded out by herds of buffalo on their annual migrations through the Cumberland Gap. Such traces were commonly used as pioneer highways.

Even so, governing the territory from the East Coast was cumbersome. A series of conventions held in Danville framed a constitution, and Kentucky was proclaimed a separate commonwealth in 1792. Shortly thereafter Frankfort was chosen as the permanent state capital.

Just as Danville owes its beginnings to the buffalo traces, so too does Kentucky owe its name to the bountiful game once found there. Nearly all the Shawnee villages were built north of the Ohio River so as not to disrupt the wild game so prevalent in Kentucky. Believing the spirits of their dead needed the things of life in the next world, the Indians brought their dead to Kentucky to be buried where game was plentiful.

This land became sacred to them as *Kah-Ten-Tah-Teh,* or "Land of Tomorrow"—the original "Happy Hunting Ground," if you prefer.

Danville, which claims the state's first courthouse, law school, college, and post office, has become a major burley tobacco market, and many Kentuckians have graduated from Centre College, established here in 1819.

WHAT TO SEE

Constitution Square. 134 South Second Street, Danville 40422, in the center of town. This complex includes a reproduction of the old log courthouse as it appeared during the state constitutional conventions. Besides the courthouse, there is a log meetinghouse, a post office, and a jail—the essential ingredients of a pioneer administrative center. Together they are now a state site, housing documentation of events that led to statehood. Also, there are the early 1800s Fisher's Row homes, now a museum, an art gallery, and a museum store. Open 9:00 A.M. to 5:00 P.M. daily. No admission fee. Call (859) 239-7089.

Dr. Ephraim McDowell House and Apothecary Shop. 125 South Second Street, Danville 40422. This was the home and office of Kentucky's most revered physician and surgeon. McDowell performed the world's first successful abdominal surgery without the benefit of anesthesia here. McDowell managed not only to cure his patient but also to overcome much of the superstition about surgery that existed in those days. A statue of McDowell is one of only five enshrined in the Rotunda of the capitol in Frankfort. The McDowell House exhibits medical tools and pharmacy items of the era (circa 1770–1830). It is open 10:00 A.M. to noon and 1:00 to 4:00 P.M. Monday–Saturday and 2:00 to 4:00 P.M. Sunday. Closed Monday November through February and closed Thanksgiving and Christmas. Admission fee. Call (859) 236-2804.

Pioneer Playhouse. A mile south of town on Stanford Avenue (U.S. 150). Broadway productions are presented at this outdoor dinner theater Tuesday–Saturday mid-June through August. The grounds and buildings are designed to represent a Kentucky village of the early 1900s. Theater programs and times are posted. Admission fee. For information call (859) 236-2747.

Penn's Store. Off U.S. 127 and K–37. The oldest country store in America in continuous operation by the same family, Penn's has been open for business since 1850. This American classic comes complete with a potbellied stove, cigar-box cash register, herb garden, and resident dog. Call (859) 332-7715 or (859) 332-7706.

VISITOR INFORMATION

Danville–Boyle County Convention & Visitors Bureau. 304 South Fourth Street, Danville 40422. Open 9:00 A.M. to 4:00 P.M. Monday–Friday. Call (859) 236-7794 or (800) 775-0076.

SPECIAL EVENTS

Historic Constitution Square Festival. This event, held the third week in September, takes visitors back 200 years to the Kentucky that Daniel Boone knew and loved best. Visitors will also see one-hundred juried artisans, strolling minstrels, hammer-dulcimer players, colonial games, a fiddle contest, and continuous live entertainment. Write Constitution Festival, c/o Constitution Square State Historic Site, 134 South Second Street, Danville, KY 40422-1817, or call (859) 239-7089.

The Great American Brass Band Festival. Brass bands of all eras—from Civil War instruments to sophisticated brass ensembles—come together for a weekend in mid-June each year to celebrate the styles of John Philip Sousa, ragtime, and Bourbon Street. For information write The Great American Brass Band Festival, P.O. Box 429, Danville, KY 40423-0429, or call (800) 755-0076.

Forkland Heritage Festival and Revue. Held the second weekend in October, this award-winning event is billed as "the only *true* folk festival in Kentucky." "Folks" can experience the country atmosphere of "the Fork" and take part in heritage displays, old country theater, entertainment, shops, breakfast, and countryside wagon tours. The event is held on K–37 off U.S. 127, and admission is charged. Call (859) 332-7897.

BEREA, KENTUCKY

Two miles south of Danville on U.S. 150, take a left turn onto K–52 east and follow it 22 miles to the tiny town of Paint Lick. There you pick up K–21 southeast (right) for the final 12 miles to Berea.

This route becomes more and more circuitous as the hills become steeper. Farms shrink to garden plots for lack of flat land, and the scenery becomes dominated by woodlands. By the time you reach Berea, you are already in the foothills of the Cumberland Range of the Appalachians.

Berea the town and Berea the college are virtually one and the same. It is difficult to determine where one begins and the other ends. The educational buildings are grouped in vine-covered splendor among magnificent shade trees, but that atmosphere pervades the entire community. At the center of town is a little park, presided over by the big, white-colonnaded Boone Tavern, a delightful old hotel with a wide porch along one side, several shops featuring local crafts, and a restaurant known throughout the state. Except for back-office administration, these operations are run entirely by the students of Berea College.

Berea College originally opened to serve young people from the mountains, but now students come from all over the United States. Still available are tuition-free programs for those with limited funds willing to work at least ten hours a week at any of several jobs.

When a 1954 Supreme Court ruling brought integration to all public schools, it was something of a triumph for Berea College and a cause for jubilation. The college was founded as a nonsectarian, antislavery, integrated school when it first opened its doors in 1855, and it operated that way until a measure called the Day Law in effect segregated it in 1904.

The college runs a 1,200-acre farm for agricultural training and maintains a 7,700-acre forest with lakes, trails, and picnic facilities open to the public year-round. Nearby is Indian Fort Mountain, 1,442 feet high, where prehistoric Hopewell Indians built fortifications.

Designated by the Kentucky legislature as the "Folk Arts and Crafts Capital of Kentucky," Berea has a national reputation as the home and workplace of many professional artists and craftspeople. You can visit numerous working studios, shops, and galleries to see the finest handcrafted work of woodworkers, potters, furniture makers, weavers, and jewelers to be found anywhere.

WHAT TO SEE

Berea Welcome Center. 201 North Broadway, Berea 40403. Located in a restored L&N train depot, the center offers maps, tour information, and crafts displays. Open 9:00 A.M. to 5:00 P.M. weekdays, 10:00 A.M. to 4:00 P.M. Saturday, and 11:00 A.M. to 4:00 P.M. Sunday. Call (800) 598-5263.

Berea College Tours. Main Street. Students serve as guides on the tour of this unique work-study college. Tours begin at the Boone Tavern at 9:00 A.M., 10:00 A.M., 1:00 P.M., and 3:00 P.M. Monday–Friday and 9:00 A.M. and 3:00 P.M. Saturdays. Call (859) 985-3145.

Churchill Weavers. A mile north of town on U.S. 25 at Lorraine Court. Self-guided tours are offered through the vast loomhouse, one of the largest hand-weaving establishments in the nation, established in 1922. Weavers are on duty from 9:00 A.M. to noon and 1:00 to 4:00 P.M. Monday–Friday. Gift shop hours are 9:00 A.M. to 6:00 P.M. Monday–Saturday and noon to 6:00 P.M. Sunday. Loomhouse hours are 9:00 A.M. to 4:00 P.M. Monday–Friday. No admission fee. Call (859) 986-3127.

WHERE TO SHOP

Berea has many shops for mountain crafts and work done by students. The quality and design of the artisanship are superb. Here are but a few of the shops:

Appalachian Arts & Crafts & Quilt Shop. Main and Center Streets. Besides paintings, pottery, wood carvings, and other wares, this shop has the largest selection of handmade quilts in Kentucky, according to its owners. Open 9:00 A.M. to 6:00 P.M. Monday–Saturday and 1:00 to 6:00 P.M. Sunday April 1 to December 31 and 9:00 A.M. to 5:00 P.M. Monday–Saturday January 1 to March 31. Call (859) 986-1239.

Berea College Student Craft Industries. At the Boone Tavern and at the Log House Sales Room on Estill Street, Berea 40403, 1.5 blocks from the tavern. Distinctive gifts include custom furniture, jewelry, hardwood cutting boards, hats and scarves, ceramics, and many other items. The Tavern Shop is open 8:00 A.M. to 8:00 P.M. daily except Sunday, when the hours are noon to 8:00 P.M. The Log House is open 8:00 A.M. to 6:00 P.M. Monday–Saturday and, April through October, 1:00 to 5:00 P.M. Sunday. Call (859) 985-3226.

The Upstairs Gallery. 114 Main Street, Berea 40403, next to the Boone Tavern. The gallery features fine regional art and contemporary Appalachian crafts. From April through December it is

open 9:00 A.M. to 8:00 P.M. Monday–Saturday and noon to 5:00 P.M.
Sunday; the rest of the year, it is open 9:00 A.M. to 5:00 P.M.
Monday–Saturday. For information call (859) 986-4434.

WHERE TO EAT AND STAY

Boone Tavern. K–25 (Main Street), Berea 40403, in the center of
town. You can't miss it. Six two-story columns support the inn's
entrance portico and are floodlit at night. This time-honored hotel
has fifty-seven comfortable rooms, rocking chairs on the porch, a
splendid restaurant, and all the ambience of a premier nineteenth-
century hostelry.

The food invariably gets rave reviews, and the two cookbooks put
out by the hotel are always in short supply. Homemade soups and
such entrees as country ham or chicken flakes in a potato nest are
served, and then great bowls of vegetables and spoonbread are
brought around for endless helpings throughout the meal. All the
hot biscuits, breads, and desserts are prepared from scratch. Boone
Tavern remains among Kentucky's very best restaurants. Open daily
all year. No alcohol. $$. ☐. For hours call (859) 985-3700.

RICHMOND, KENTUCKY

The return route to Cincinnati, north on Interstate 75, takes you
through Richmond, an industrial center and home of Eastern Ken-
tucky University. A downtown walking tour features impressive
nineteenth-century homes. Pick up tour information at the Rich-
mond Tourism Commission, 345 Lancaster Avenue, Richmond
40475. Open all year 8:00 A.M. to 5:00 P.M. Monday–Friday. Call (800)
866-3705.

WHAT TO SEE

Fort Boonesborough State Park. On K–388, 15 miles north of
Richmond. Daniel Boone and his companions erected the state's
second settlement at this site on the Kentucky River. The recon-
structed fort tells the story of Boone's settlement and offers pioneer
craft demonstrations. Camping, picnicking, a museum, and a gift

shop are available. The fort is open daily 9:00 A.M. to 5:30 P.M. April–October except in September and October, when it is closed Monday and Tuesday. Admission fee. Call (859) 527-3131.

White Hall State Historic Site. North of Richmond, off the Winchester-Boonesboro exit of Interstate 75. White Hall is the impressive home of Cassius Marcellus Clay, an outspoken abolitionist and newspaper publisher and friend of Abe Lincoln. The Italianate mansion has many original furnishings. Open daily 9:00 A.M. to 5:30 P.M., April through October; closed Monday and Tuesday after Labor Day. Admission fee. Call (859) 623-9178.

Bybee Pottery. Nine miles east on K-52 in the town of Bybee. The community is named for the family that has operated this pottery since 1845, using the same methods continuously since the mid-1800s. Visitors can see potters at work and can browse among products of the distinctive Bybee line in the sales shop. The heavy kitchen pottery is prized by many chefs because it is ovenproof and inexpensive. The salesroom is open 8:00 A.M. to noon and 12:30 to 4:30 P.M. Monday–Friday. Closed holidays. Call (859) 369-5350.

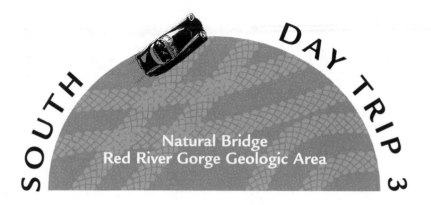

Natural Bridge
Red River Gorge Geologic Area

This is a trip for someone who wants to commune with nature, to wander the majestic wilderness, to breathe the scent of dogwood and wildflowers, and to marvel at the rugged cliffs and natural stone bridges in an area of Kentucky so wild that it has never been settled and, until recent years, has been virtually inaccessible to all except the hardiest of explorers.

Natural Bridge State Resort Park and the Red River Gorge are both part of the Daniel Boone National Forest, which reaches into nineteen counties from east-central Kentucky to the Tennessee border. The forest and the gorge area are administered by the U.S. Forest Service, and the park is maintained by the state. The gorge was to be in the floodplain of a new dam planned in the early 1960s, but thirteen years of public outcry and demonstrations led Governor Julian Carroll to stop the government project in 1975. At the height of the protest in 1967, U.S. Supreme Court Justice William O. Douglas led a Sierra Club excursion into the gorge.

To reach this area from Cincinnati, follow Interstate 75 south to the northern outskirts of Lexington, merge onto Interstate 64 eastbound, and follow this route 17 miles to the entrance of the Bert T. Combs Mountain Parkway. This limited-access road makes a beeline across the wide farm country toward the Appalachian highlands, which soon rise blue and hazy in the distance. It is an easy, 33-mile drive along the parkway to the town of Slade, a veritable outpost at the edge of gorge country. Follow the signs at Slade northeast to the gorge or south to the state park.

NATURAL BRIDGE

The state park and the gorge area share the same natural phenomena—the stone bridges, the cliffs, the woods, and the wildlife—but the state park makes one area of interest immediately accessible and offers creature comforts not available in the gorge.

WHAT TO SEE

Natural Bridge. In the winter this natural sandstone arch can be seen at the head of a 700-foot-deep canyon from the park's lodge. Foliage conceals it the rest of the year. It can be reached by any of four marked trails that begin at the lodge. The shortest, about half a mile, follows the bed of the canyon. The longest, about 4 miles, passes through the hills and emerges atop the bluff. From there it proceeds to the top of the bridge. There are steps to the bottom of the bridge, so you can choose another trail back if you wish. A skylift ride to Natural Bridge operates from mid–April through October and offers a panoramic view of the park.

Although it is not the longest, Natural Bridge is considered the largest such arch in the state because it is more than 6 stories high. The formation results from natural erosion in which rains wash away softer sandstone from under the harder limestone shelf. Trails here and in the gorge reach twelve such bridges.

Late April is the ideal time to visit Natural Bridge. The park is usually not crowded then, and the hills are covered with dogwood, redbud, azaleas, and mountain laurel.

Natural Bridge Nature Center. Near the lodge. The center has displays of local wildlife and the natural history of the gorge area.

For more information write Natural Bridge State Resort Park, 2135 Natural Bridge Road, Slade, KY 40376-9999, or call (606) 663–2214 or (800) 325–1710.

WARNING

Carelessness costs a life or two each year in Kentucky's Natural Bridge and gorge area, mostly in falls from the cliffs. Be sure to stay on marked trails and obey the park's warning signs. Beware of walking on rock with a greenish coloration. This moss, when damp, can make the rock as slippery as wet soap.

WHERE TO EAT AND STAY

Hemlock Lodge. The park headquarters is 2 miles south of Slade on K–11. The lodge is one of only a few places for many miles to eat and sleep. In addition to the thirty-five guest rooms, it offers accommodations in several cabins scattered about the hollow and in four one-bedroom cottages on the grounds, plus a campground. In summer and early fall, it may be difficult to get accommodations unless you call a month or two in advance, but vacancies are more plentiful during winter months. Reservations are a must. Call (606) 663–2214 or (800) 325–1710, or write Natural Bridge State Resort Park, 2135 Natural Bridge Road, Slade, KY 40376-9999.

RED RIVER GORGE GEOLOGIC AREA

This 26,000-acre primitive area lies north of the Mountain Parkway at Slade and is part of the Daniel Boone National Forest. It encompasses the scenic Red River and eighty natural bridges, some of which can be reached by trail.

The gorge area has several archaeological sites, old Indian campsites, a cave with the letters *D Boon* carved in the wall (possibly a Daniel Boone signature), and a wide array of wildlife: some forty-six mammals, sixty-seven reptiles and amphibians, and more than one hundred species of birds. On the endangered-species list are the red-cockaded woodpecker, locally called a woodhen, and the Indiana bat, a cave resident. Wild turkey and white-tailed deer, once endangered, are making a comeback, and grouse, quail, ducks, rabbits, minks, raccoons, squirrels, and foxes are plentiful.

Magnolias, cedars, and sassafras trees mingle with more common varieties, and there are at least 555 species of plants, including some rare ones, and many varieties of ferns. Anthropologists have identified this as one of two unique areas of cultural resources in the eastern United States, saying they have found traces of people here dating to 8000 B.C.

WHAT TO SEE

Visitors Information Center. At the Gladie Creek Historic Site, located in the heart of Red River Gorge. From the Slade exit, take K-15 northwest 1.5 miles to K-77. Turn right on K-77, then right on K-715 to the Visitor Information Center. The U.S. Forest Service command post here oversees 50 miles of scenic drives and trails, plus overlooks, camping areas, and picnic sites. The center has maps of twenty-five numbered scenic trails, one of which, the Swift Camp Creek Trail, passes the remains of a genuine moonshine still. Most trails range in length from 1,100 feet to 8.5 miles, but one, the Shel-towee Trail, ranges 22.4 miles through the gorge area. It is part of a national recreation trail that runs 269 miles through five ranger districts of the Daniel Boone National Forest. The 30-mile Red River Gorge Loop Drive features scenic overlooks and views of several arches and stretches of the Red River in the bottom of the gorge. For a modest fee you can spend the night in one of the first-come, first-served spaces for trailers or tents in Koomer Ridge Campground. Call (606) 663-2852.

Sky Bridge. Reached by several of the marked trails, Sky Bridge is the longest natural arch in the gorge. It is 30 feet high and 90 feet long and is situated at the top of a ridge from which there is a spectacular view of the surrounding countryside.

For more information contact Forest Supervisor, Daniel Boone National Forest, 1700 Bypass Road, Winchester, KY 40391, (606) 745-3100, or Stanton Ranger District, 705 West College Avenue, Stanton KY 40380, (606) 663-2852.

SOUTHEAST DAY TRIP 1

New Richmond, Ohio
Point Pleasant, Ohio · Moscow, Ohio
Augusta, Ky. · Ripley, Ohio
Maysville, Ky. · Washington, Ky.
Manchester, Ohio

Our trips have ranged deep into Ohio, Kentucky, and Indiana, to lakes and plains and mountains, to woodlands and towns and large cities that in their diversity may have but one thing in common. They all lie in the great Ohio River Basin and, in one way or another, are wrapped in its post-Revolutionary frontier history.

It is fitting, then, to end this book with a trip along the majestic Ohio River, which carried the frontiersmen, and the nation's destiny, to the great American West.

Sieur de La Salle and his troop of warriors and missionaries canoed down the Ohio in the 1670s to claim the territory for France. They were the first white men to see this river that the Indians called Oyo. To the French, the word meant *la belle riviere,* the beautiful river. But there was dissatisfaction with so simple a translation, for there were implications in the word not only of beauty but also of heritage, power, and even violence.

Yes, the Ohio can be violent—as the ravages of floods have proved. The peaceful but tenacious little towns along its banks today are the only human settlements known to have existed directly on the river's shores, except for a short-lived Shawnee village near Portsmouth, Ohio, in the 1750s. These villages have changed surprisingly little in the century and a half since the steamboat trade brought them their first measure of prosperity.

Take U.S. 52 east from Cincinnati past old Coney Island, now Riverbend, and River Downs Race Track. A stop at each little river town takes the visitor back a few more years in time.

195

NEW RICHMOND, OHIO

New Richmond, 10 miles east of the racetrack, lies right (south) of U.S. 52. Its Front Street is lined with steamboat-era homes, many of the frame ones decorated with carved wooden ornaments in the style known as Steamboat Gothic. A great many riverboat pilots came from here, and some retired to these homes so they could keep their eyes on the boats. Captain Ernest Wagner, former master of the *Delta Queen* and the new *Mississippi Queen,* made his home here for thirty years. He died in 1978, and the city of New Richmond erected a monument to him near the city's landing.

Take a little time to visit the restored Ross-Gowdy House at 125 George Street, a Greek Revival building listed on the National Register of Historic Places. Ross-Gowdy House is now the home of Historic New Richmond, Inc., an unusual museum housing historic records, memorabilia, and genealogical writings. The museum also includes a tribute to Russian immigrant Brenda Weisberg Meckler, who settled in New Richmond and wrote *Papa Was a Farmer,* as well as some Hollywood screenplays. Open 1:00 to 5:00 P.M. Sundays and other days by appointment. Call (513) 553-9770.

POINT PLEASANT, OHIO

Point Pleasant is 5 miles east of New Richmond on U.S. 52.

WHAT TO SEE

Ulysses S. Grant Birthplace. U.S. 52 in Point Pleasant, at the bridge. The Union's great Civil War general and eighteenth president was born in the three-room, white-frame cottage on the left (north) side of the highway, now listed on the National Register of Historic Places. As a boy he chased tadpoles in Big Indian Creek across from his home. The creek is now crossed by the Grant Memorial Bridge, decorated with an ornamental Civil War cannon. The Grant family moved from here to Georgetown, Ohio, where Ulysses attended elementary school. He was married and living in Galena, Illinois, when he answered the call to arms. The cottage, which contains period furniture, is open 9:30 A.M. to noon and 1:00 to 5:00 P.M. Wednesday–Saturday and noon to 5:00 P.M. Sunday, April–October. Closed Memorial Day and Labor Day. Admission fee. Call (513) 553-4911.

SPECIAL EVENTS

U. S. Grant Birthday Celebration. Annual celebration of U. S. Grant's birthday, held in April at his birthplace. Historical exhibits, entertainment, and presentations. Free admission. Call (513) 553-4911 or (513) 553-3661.

New Richmond Riverdays. Held annually in August on Front Street, Riverdays celebrates the summer and life on the river. Includes rides, games, food, and entertainment. Free admission. Call (513) 684-1253.

MOSCOW, OHIO

Three miles past Point Pleasant on U.S. 52, you will see, to the right, the huge cooling tower of the William H. Zimmer nuclear power plant, which was converted to coal in 1990. The tower overshadows tiny Moscow and can be seen from every street in town. It thus became a striking symbol of contrast between the daily life of a small town and the demands for energy of the growing tri-state area.

In the shadow of the Zimmer power plant are Fee Villa and Spaeth House, both facing the river on Water Street and privately owned. Fee Villa was an important Underground Railroad station and burned candles in the windows to guide slaves across the river. At Spaeth House proslavery sentiment caused the occupants to burn candles in the window to mislead and catch unwary slaves.

WHAT TO SEE

Captain Anthony Meldahl Locks & Dam. U.S. 52, 1.5 miles east of Moscow. There is a parking lot and observation deck here so visitors can watch towboats and their barges lock through.

The dam is just across the highway from Maple Lane Farm, which was purchased by Captain Meldahl in 1895. In 1905, when Meldahl was master of the steamboat *Queen City,* he took the members of the Congressional (House) Rivers and Harbors Committee from Pittsburgh to Cairo, Illinois—the entire 981-mile length of the Ohio River—to prove to them the need for a system of dams to aid Ohio River navigation. Meldahl's winning ways and his vast knowledge of the river must have had an effect. A system of fifty-three dams was completed in 1929, and a parade of steamboats, led by President Herbert Hoover aboard the *Cayuga,* with Captain Meldahl at the wheel, came downriver to Cincinnati for the dedication. After World War II these dams were replaced by twelve high-level dams such as this one, considerably improving navigation.

Along U.S. 52, at places like Eagle Creek and White Oak Creek, you will see backwater marinas that sprang up because the higher water levels created handy coves for mooring boats.

The observation area is open during daylight hours throughout the year. No admission fee. Call (513) 876-2921.

AUGUSTA, KENTUCKY

Continuing east on U.S. 52 is the *Ole Augusta Ferry,* the Ohio landing for the ferryboat across the river to Augusta, Kentucky. You will have to look sharply for the small sign to the right of the highway, for there is nothing else at this point except a farmhouse across the road. The sign says AUGUSTA, KY., 1 MILE and has an arrow pointing toward the river. The procedure is to drive down the road to the water's edge and wait for the boat. This is the only river crossing in the 63 miles between Cincinnati and Maysville, Kentucky. And for Augustans U.S. 52 on the Ohio shore is still the quickest way to get to the rest of civilization. Operated by Donald Bravard, the boat runs year-round 8:00 A.M. to 6:00 P.M. Monday–Friday and 9:00 A.M. to 6:00 P.M. Saturday and Sunday. Admission fee. Call (606) 756-2464.

Except for the city's high school, built in the 1910s, hardly anything has changed in a century in Augusta, and it remains one of the finest examples of an Ohio River town. Note the handsome brick buildings along Riverside Drive. All date to the 1830s and 1840s, and most have been restored.

The city, which dates to the 1780s, was built inadvertently on an Indian burial ground between two creeks. It is said that you still cannot dig a post hole in Augusta without coming up with a shard of pottery or an arrowhead. Human remains found at this site apparently included a vanished tribe of Indians who were of exceptional size. A local legend say that in the 1790s, a jawbone found by an early settler was so large that it would fit over the settler's entire head. The

Shawnee leader of that era, Chief Logan, told townsfolk he knew of no such people ever having lived in the valley.

Augusta is home to the state's first Methodist college and winery that used to produce half the nation's wine. The town has had its share of famous individuals. Residents are proud to show the places where the parents and grandparents of Gen. George C. Marshall lived, where Pres. William Henry Harrison stayed, or where frontiersman Simon Kenton's cabin stands. More currently, Augusta claims fame as the birthplace of Ms. America, Heather Renee French, and the current residence of the famous Clooney family. Rosemary returns every year for the festival in her honor. Tours of Augusta can be arranged by calling Augusta Tours at (606) 756-2603. Additional touring information is available by calling the Augusta Visitors Center at (606) 756-2525 or by visiting www.visitaugusta.net.

WHAT TO SEE

A variety of impressive art galleries and exhibits line the streets of Augusta.

Piedmont Art Gallery. 115 West Riverside Drive, Augusta 41002. This beautifully restored home has become an outlet for the works of regional artists and craftworkers, plus ceramics and American folk art from elsewhere. Open year-round noon to 5:00 P.M. Thursday–Sunday and at other times by appointment. Call (606) 756-2616.

Heritage Hall at the Parkview Inn. 103 West Second Street, Augusta 41002. This pictorial retrospective of Augusta's history is worth the stop. Call (606) 756-2603.

WHERE TO EAT

The Beehive Tavern. 101 West Riverside Drive, Augusta 41002. Marvelous food, a beautiful view of the river, and early 1800s ambience make this a wonderful place to stop or to enjoy the warm bed-and-breakfast accommodations. The 1796 building housing the restaurant was purchased several years ago by Luciano Moral, a native of Cuba, who restored the facility with antiques. Open Wednesday–Sunday. $$. ☐. Call (606) 756-2202.

The Augusta General Store. 109 Main Street and Riverside Drive, Augusta 41002. Historic original general store circa 1850. Offers homemade soups, salads, sandwiches, baked goods, and an old-fashioned ice cream soda fountain. Open daily 8:00 A.M. to 8:00 P.M. and during the summer 8:00 A.M. to 10:00 P.M. $. Call (606) 756-2525.

RIPLEY, OHIO

From Augusta return by ferry to the Ohio shore and continue east on U.S. 52 for 10 miles to Ripley.

Eyewitness accounts found in the form of letters in the early 1970s appear to confirm the tale in *Uncle Tom's Cabin* of a runaway slave girl named Eliza who, with babe in arms, escaped pursuers here by leaping from one ice floe to another across the Ohio River to Ripley and freedom.

The Reverend John Rankin raised twelve children in Ripley in the 1850s and 1860s and, with the aid of a farmer on the Kentucky shore, helped more than 2,000 slaves escape to freedom in the North despite constant harassment by U.S. marshals. Until the Civil War it was against federal law to harbor escaped slaves, but with twelve youngsters Rankin could outdo the marshals in surveillance. Rankin would hang a lantern in his window atop the hill to signal the Kentucky farmer when the coast was clear. The farmer would row the slaves across the river, and the Rankin children would escort them up the hill to the Rankin house. From there, covered by hay in wagons, they were taken to farm hideouts scattered around the county.

Rankin's Cincinnati friend, the Reverend Lyman Beecher, visited often, sometimes with his daughter Harriett—later Harriett Beecher Stowe—who got much of the material for her antislavery book from Rankin's tales.

Ripley is Ohio's only burley tobacco market, and the highway passes two of the big tobacco warehouses. If you come this way between mid-November and early January, except for Christmas week, you can stop by to watch the annual auctions. They usually conclude early in the afternoon.

WHAT TO SEE

The John Rankin House. 6152 Rankin Hill Road, Ripley 45167. The minister's little cottage is high atop a hill overlooking Ripley. As you enter the west side of Ripley on U.S. 52, watch for National Historic Landmark markers and signs to the Rankin house. They will guide you up Rankin Hill Road to the homestead. Open 10:00 A.M. to 5:00 P.M. Wednesday through Saturday, noon to 5:00 P.M. Sunday, Memorial Day–Labor Day. Open 10:00 A.M. to 5:00 P.M. Saturday and Sunday, September and October. Admission fee. Call (937) 392-1627 or (937) 392-4044.

Ripley Museum. 219 North Second Street, Ripley 45167. Originally built in 1836, this ten-room house is packed with memories of all aspects of life for Ripley's earliest residents. Displays include a parlor with Civil War–era furnishings such as a Valley Gem piano, made right in Ripley; oil paintings, writings and documents from famous abolitionists; and military and other period clothing, such as a dress handmade to wear to the 1893 Chicago World's Fair and a woven wedding gown and trousseau from 1875. The garage houses Ripley's first fire engine and an 1890s funeral wagon. Have a seat in original Ripley theater chairs and watch the 1939 film *Life in Ripley.* The second Sunday in December, the museum is the starting point for a spectacular holiday house tour that features several historic homes, including Rankin House, decked out for Christmas. One dollar admission fee. Open Saturday 10:00 A.M. to 4:00 P.M. and Sunday noon to 4:00 P.M. Other times by appointment. Call (937) 392-4660.

Ohio Tobacco Museum. 623 South Second Street, Ripley 45167. Actual historic tobacco farming and curing implements, photos and graphic displays, and Civil War–era tobacco products depict the history of White Burley tobacco in Ohio. Open some Saturdays and by appointment only. Call (937) 392-9410.

Old Piano Factory Shops. 307 North Second Street, Ripley 45167. More than a dozen dealers fill this former Valley Gem Piano Factory, built in 1850. The building's history is as colorful as the antiques found in it today. The Valley Gem Factory closed at the turn of the century and reopened as a shoe factory, then a parachute factory during the Korean War. Now the building is home to a wide variety of antiques and collectibles, including a good selection of antique furniture. An original Valley Gem piano still sits in the lobby. Open 10:00 A.M. to 5:00 P.M. daily and noon to 6:00 P.M. Sunday. Call (937) 392-9243.

The John Parker House. Front Street, Ripley 45167. Home of the African-American abolitionist John Parker, who purchased his freedom for $1,800 in 1845, headed north, and settled in Ripley. He established his own foundry, was a successful businessman, and held several patents for farm-related equipment. Parker was a daring abolitionist and from his home along the Ohio River would make nightly forays across the river and bring escaping slaves across to Ripley. Slated to open in fall of 2001, this National Historic Landmark promises to be worth the stop. Call (937) 392-4188 or (937) 392-4044 for information.

WHERE TO SHOP

River Song Music Shoppe. 19 North Second Street, Ripley 45167. Specializing in dulcimers, this shop is well known east of the Mississippi. (937) 392-9274.

River Valley Trading Company. 19 North Second Street, Ripley 45167. As the name implies, this shop offers both old and new things related to the river and boating. (937) 392-4888.

Rockin' Robin's Soda Shoppe. 8 North Front Street, Ripley 45167. This 1950s-style ice cream shop features a soda fountain that overlooks the river. (937) 392-1300.

WHERE TO EAT

Cohearts Riverhouse. 18 North Front Street, Ripley 45167. The riverfront view from the screened-in front porch of this restored 1840s brick restaurant is delightful. Amid beautiful antiques, diners can try homemade pasta specialties, club sandwiches, cobblers, and brownie pie for lunch and dinner. The restaurant is open daily except Monday and Tuesday and major holidays. Call (937) 392-4819.

MAYSVILLE, KENTUCKY

Nine miles east of Ripley, on U.S. 52 at Aberdeen, are the bridges to historic Maysville, Kentucky, the only span across the Ohio in the 115 miles of river between Cincinnati and Portsmouth.

Maysville, now unfortunately hidden behind a floodwall, is one of the oldest settlements on the Ohio. It was established in 1784 by the Virginia legislature as a supply point for flatboaters moving west from the former colonies along this great waterway to carve new homes from the wilderness. Originally called Limestone, Maysville was renamed in honor of John May. This popular local flatboater and his passengers were slain by the Shawnee after they lured him ashore with a white captive.

Daniel Boone's family operated a tavern here, and some members are buried in small plot behind the Mason County Museum, 215 Sutton Street, Maysville. The old white courthouse tower and several church spires are landmarks to boaters. Quite a few gracious old homes can be seen along Third Street between Market and Sutton Streets, an area called "Little New Orleans." Maps to the historic 24-block downtown area are available at the Chamber of Commerce office located at 15 West Second Street.

Transparent pies, sometimes called puddings, are a specialty of the three-county area around Maysville and are known to exist nowhere else. Usually made in muffin tins, these tiny tarts blend sugar, butter, and eggs in a rich, clear custard baked in a pie crust. They are available at **Magee's Bakery,** 212 Market Street, Maysville 41056. The bakery is open 8:30 A.M. to 5:00 P.M. daily except Sunday and Monday. Call (606) 564–5720.

Maysville is the world's largest burley tobacco market after Lexington, Kentucky, and has several huge warehouses. Auctions, which are open to the public, are conducted from mid-November to mid-January, with Thanksgiving and Christmas week breaks. Sales generally are in the mornings. Call (606) 564–5534.

The Maysville–Mason County Chamber of Commerce at 15 West Second Street has information on what to see. Open 8:00 A.M. to 4:30 P.M. Monday–Friday except major holidays. Call (606) 564–5534.

A welcome center, 115 East Third Street, is located at the foot of the Simon Kenton Bridge. The center houses a small Underground Railroad museum and is open 10:00 A.M. to 4:00 P.M. Monday–Saturday. Here you can pick up brochures, information, and historic walking-tour and covered bridge driving-tour maps. Call (606) 564–6986.

WHAT TO SEE

Mason County Museum. 215 Sutton Street, Maysville 41056. Built in 1876 as the local public library, this restored and enlarged structure is now on the National Register of Historic Places. Inside, local pioneer, river, and tobacco history is chronicled by a number of colorful and hands-on exhibits. The museum also houses a gallery and a genealogical library. Open 10:00 A.M. to 4:00 P.M. Monday–Saturday. Closed Monday January–March. Admission fee. Call (606) 564–5865.

WHERE TO SHOP

Downtown Maysville and Market Street are home to a number of unique shops, including gift and dress shops and a growing number of galleries, including:

Where in the World. 204 Market Street, Maysville 41056. Browse through several rooms of unique gifts, toys, collectibles, and a year-round Christmas collection. Call (606) 564–6815.

The White Gallery. 225 Market Street, Maysville 41056. The White Gallery features award-winning paintings by American artist Steve White, including local scenes of Maysville and neighboring communities. Limited-edition prints, custom framing, note cards, and pottery are available. Call (606) 564–4887.

WHERE TO EAT

Caproni's "On the River." Foot of Rosemary Clooney Street, adjacent to Maysville's railroad depot. (The singer was born and grew up in Maysville.) The riverside restaurant has been in operation for more than forty years and specializes in continental dining. $. ❑. Open 11:00 A.M. to 9:30 P.M. Tuesday–Thursday, 11:00 A.M. to 10:30 P.M. Friday, and 4:00 to 10:30 P.M. Saturday. Call (606) 564–4321.

The Metropolitan Cafe. 2 East Third Street, Maysville 41056. Housed in a lovely old Masonic building, the Metropolitan features gourmet dining and a full beer and wine list. Live entertainment is offered on weekends. Open 5:30 to 9:30 P.M. Tuesday–Saturday. $$. ❑. Call (606) 564–5080.

Izzy B's Coffee Shop. 34 West Second Street, Maysville 41056. Fresh-ground gourmet coffees perfectly complement tasty homemade pastries. A changing selection of soups, salads, and sandwiches is also served. Open 7:30 A.M. to 4:30 P.M. Monday–Friday and 8:30 A.M. to 4:30 P.M. Saturday. $. Call (606) 564–3002.

SPECIAL EVENTS

Rosemary Clooney Festival. Held the first weekend in October, on Third Street. Features performances, including a concert by Rosemary, and a catered dinner. Call (606) 564–9411 or (606) 564–5534.

WASHINGTON, KENTUCKY

Pick up U.S. 62/68 at the Maysville end of the bridge and follow the road 4 miles south to Washington, which lies to the left just before the point where the two federal highways split. The town is not visible from the highway, so watch for the gate to St. Patrick's Cemetery; the entrance road to Washington is immediately past the cemetery.

Even older than Maysville, this hill town began as "Kenton's Station," a wilderness outpost established by Simon Kenton, the first frontiersman to explore Mason County. In August 1782 the fierce Shawnee tribe, inflamed by the British, attacked and decimated a band of frontiersmen 20 miles south of here at Blue Licks, where U.S. 68 now crosses the Licking River. Although Cornwallis had surrendered a year earlier, the Indians hadn't heard about it. This was considered, therefore, the last battle of the American Revolution. A few months later the Shawnee signed a treaty that opened Kentucky to settlement.

The town soon built a stone courthouse to ensure its place as county seat and even put in a bid to become the new nation's capital. It lost on both scores. Although by 1790 Washington had 119 log-cabin homes and a population of 462 and was Kentucky's second-largest town after Lexington, it never grew much after that.

In the late 1960s a Washington resident decided to spruce up his property and remove the clapboard siding from his home. Underneath he found the original home, an eighteenth-century log cabin. Other residents shortly made similar discoveries, and by 1971 restoration was a community project. The town was named a National Historic Place in 1974. All along Main Street—the town's only proper street—historic dwellings, several of them made of logs, have been unsheathed or restored.

Eventually the municipal governments of Washington and Maysville were merged into one entity, with the combined community being called Maysville. Washington, however, still exists as a separate part of the larger community and, because of its rich history, has its own visitors center.

WHAT TO SEE

Visitors Center. Main Street, Washington 41056. Located in the

Cane Brake Cabin, the center offers information, maps, and brochures about the historic district. During May–August costumed guides conduct tours of six museums and the historic village. Fee for tours. Open 10:00 A.M. to 4:30 P.M. Monday–Saturday and 1:00 to 4:00 P.M. Sunday, March 15 through December. Call (606) 759-7411.

Mefford's Fort. Main Street, Washington 41056. An original log cabin with a large fieldstone chimney, this is believed to be one of the last "Flatboat Houses." Boaters normally bought or built their boats near Pittsburgh at the head of the river, floated west with their families and all their possessions, including livestock, then, at their destination, either sold the boat as ready lumber or used the lumber to build a house. Historians believe the floorboards, some paneling, and other wood in Mefford's Fort came from such a boat.

Harriet Beecher Stowe Slavery to Freedom Museum. Main Street, Washington 41056. The former home of Colonel Marshall Key, Harriet Beecher Stowe spent one night here in 1833 at the invitation of Key's daughter, Elizabeth. Elizabeth was a student at a school in Cincinnati where Stowe was teaching. During her visit with the Keys, Stowe witnessed a slave auction where slave Josia Henson was auctioned off. She dubbed Henson "Uncle Tom," and it is reported that this event inspired her antislavery book, *Uncle Tom's Cabin.* Today, this historic piece of the Underground Railroad houses the **Slavery to Freedom Museum** featuring historic documents and objects related to the history of slavery in America. Call (937) 759-4860.

Old Courthouse Lawn. Main Street, Washington 41056. The lawn in front of this edifice, now replaced by a private home, was once the site of slave auctions, probably the northernmost of all such enterprises. Harriett Beecher Stowe witnessed an auction here in 1833, which she recounted dramatically in *Uncle Tom's Cabin.*

Albert Sidney Johnston House. Off Main Street adjacent to the courthouse. First of the restorations, this is the birthplace of the Confederate general who was killed during the Battle of Shiloh in April 1862. The house, once in deplorable condition, was owned by an elderly widow until the Mason County Historical Society acquired it and cared for the widow until her death, then restored the building and opened it as a museum in 1955. The general, educated at West Point, was considered one of the great military minds of the day, and his death was a severe blow to the Confederacy.

WHERE TO SHOP

Main Street has more than twenty little shops here and there featuring paintings, handmade items, custom framing, original silversmith work, yarn and clothing, brass lamps, and crafts. The influx of antique furnishings is growing. Kentucky's early furniture makers were well-known and often copied British, French, and East Coast originals of the late eighteenth and early nineteenth centuries. Original Shaker furnishings also crop up sometimes. Most shops are open all year.

MANCHESTER, OHIO

Return to Ohio via U.S. 68 north through Maysville and across the Ohio River bridge. Turn right onto U.S. 52 and continue east for 6 miles to the Moyer Winery on the right side of the road.

WHERE TO EAT

Moyer Winery. 3859 U.S. 52, Manchester 45144. This former roadside tavern has been transformed into a beautiful dining spot along the Ohio River.

Here, ten acres of vineyards and a winery produce a very creditable selection of white, rosé, and red wines and a good champagne. It is the only winery directly on the banks of the Ohio River. The kitchen staff produces such delicious fare as tournedos of beef, shrimp Creole, king crab Newburg, baked chicken breast with herb stuffing and wine sauce, and other daily specials.

The winery has a beautiful open-air dining deck overlooking the river. It is open 11:30 A.M. to 9:00 P.M. Monday–Thursday and 11:30 A.M. to 10:00 P.M. Friday and Saturday. $$. ☐. Call (937) 549-2957.

Return to Cincinnati by way of U.S. 52 westbound.

DIRECTORY

Restaurants

NORTHWEST

BATESVILLE, IND., AREA CODE: 812; ZIP CODE: 47006
The Sherman House, 35 South Main Street. Old inn features steak Diane, schnitzel, salad bar. Daily. 934–2407 or (800) 445–4939.
BLOOMINGTON, IND., AREA CODE: 812; ZIP CODE: 47401
Fourwinds Resort and Marina, 8 miles south on Ind. 37 and 3 miles east on Smithville Road. Good French menu. Daily. 824–9904.
Lennie's Brewpub, 1795 East Tenth Street. Appetizers, salads, and locally brewed beers. 232–2112.
Mother Bear's, 1428 East Third Street. Campus hot spot. Pizza. 332–4495.
Nick's, 423 East Kirkwood. Old campus watering hole, good sandwiches. 332–4040.
Scholars Inn Dessert Cafe and Wine Bar, 801 North College Avenue. Piano bar. Wines, desserts, full menu. 332–1892.
BROOKVILLE, IND., AREA CODE: 765; ZIP CODE: 47012
The Mounds, U.S. 52. Country-style family fare. Closed Monday and late December to early March. 647–4111.
COLUMBUS, IND., AREA CODE: 812; ZIP CODE: 47201
American Café, in the Ramada Inn, Ind. 46 at Interstate 65. Steaks, seafood, and prime rib. Daily. 376–3051.
Zaharako's Confectionery, 329 Washington Street. Wonderful old-fashioned ice-cream parlor. Closed Sunday. 379–9329.
INDIANAPOLIS, IND., AREA CODE: 317 ZIP CODE: 46204
Buca di Beppo, 35 North Illinois Street. Southern Italian restaurant. 632–2822.

Palomino Euro Bistro. 49 West Maryland Street. Upscale, romantic European bistro serves pizza, fresh salmon. 974-0400.

Peppy Grill. 1004 Virginia Avenue. Breakfast served 24 hours. Home-cooked meals at low prices. 637-1158.

Plump's Last Shot, 6416 Cornell Avenue. Casual pub serving burgers and wings with a full bar menu of tap beers. 257-5867.

Shapiro's Delicatessen. 808 South Meridian. Cafeteria-style Jewish deli is known for generous and excellent food. 631-4041.

Slippery Noodle Inn. 372 South Meridian. Live music nightly and broad menu from bar snacks to full dinners. 631-6974.

METAMORA, IND., AREA CODE: 317; ZIP CODE: 47030
The Hearthstone Restaurant, U.S. 52. Fried chicken and prime rib. Closed Monday. 647-5204.

MORRISTOWN, IND., AREA CODE: 765; ZIP CODE: 46161
The Kopper Kettle, U.S. 52. Family-style meals. Ham, fried chicken, roast beef, seafood. Closed Monday. 763-6767.

NASHVILLE, IND., AREA CODE: 812; ZIP CODE: 47448
Abe Martin Lodge, Brown County State Park, 2 miles east on Ind. 46. Country-style family fare. Daily. 988-7316 or 988-4418.

Brown County Inn, Ind. 46 at Ind. 135. Chicken, steaks, seafood. Daily. 988-2291.

Nashville House, Van Buren and Main Streets. Hickory-smoked ham, fried biscuits. Closed Tuesday except in October. 988-4554.

The Ordinary, Van Buren Street. Colonial menu. Turkey, wild game, beef, pork, seafood. Closed Monday except in October. 988-6166.

OLDENBURG, IND., AREA CODE: 812; ZIP CODE: 47036
Koch's Brau Haus, Wasserstrasse. Chicken, shrimp, pizza. 934-4840.

Wagner's Tavern & Family Restaurant, Main Street. Home cooking, pan-fried chicken. Daily. 934-3854.

NORTH

CLIFTON, OHIO, AREA CODE: 937; ZIP CODE: 45316
Clifton Mill Restaurant, 75 Water Street. Historic gristmill. Serving breakfast and lunch daily. 767-5501.

DAYTON, OHIO, AREA CODE: 937; ZIP CODE: SEE BELOW
Downtown Zip Code: 45409

The Pine Club, 1926 South Brown Street. Fine dining. Steaks, prime rib. 228-7463.

Jay's Restaurant, 225 East Sixth Street. Fine dining. Fresh seafood. 222-2892.

Near Downtown Zip Code: 45404

Elinor's Amber Rose, 1400 Valley Street. American and European cuisine with German and Russian specialties. 228-2511.

Downtown Zip Code: 45403

Thomato's, 110 North Main Street. Fine dining. Mediterranean dishes, sea bass, duck, steaks, and salmon. 228-3333.

South Side Zip Code: 45459

Carver's, 1535 Miamisburg-Centerville Road (Centerville). Hand-cut steaks and chops and a live-jazz and cigar club. 433-7099.

South Side Zip Code: 45429

L'Auberge, 4120 Far Hills Avenue. French country inn decor. Provincial specialties, pâtés. Highly rated. Closed Sunday. 299-5536.

MIAMISBURG, OHIO, AREA CODE: 937; ZIP CODE: 45342

Peerless Mill Inn, 319 South Second Street. Inn dates to 1828. Roast duckling. Closed Monday. 866-5968.

SPRINGBORO, OHIO, AREA CODE: 937; ZIP CODE: 45066

LaComedia Dinner Theater, Interstate 75, Franklin-Springboro exit. Buffet and show. One seating, Wednesday–Sunday. Matinee Wednesday, Thursday, and Sunday. 746-4554.

SPRINGFIELD, OHIO, AREA CODE: 937; ZIP CODE: 45504

Klosterman's Derr Road Inn, 4343 Derr Road. Historic manor, overlooking rolling hills. Daily. 399-0822.

Tapestry & Tales, 14 East Main Street. Victorian tearoom. Lunch Monday–Friday. 322-8961.

URBANA, OHIO, AREA CODE: 937; ZIP CODE: 43078

Mayflowers Chinese Restaurant, 222 North Main Street. Szechwan and Hunan cooking. Lunch and dinner, Monday–Saturday. 652-1050.

Millner's Cafeteria, 1629 East O-29. Family dining. Open daily for lunch and dinner. 653-4411.

Restaurant on the Square, 13 Monument Square. Downtown diner. Open daily for breakfast, lunch, and dinner. 653-9500.

WEST LIBERTY, OHIO, AREA CODE: 937; ZIP CODE: 43357

Liberty Gathering Place, 111 North Detroit Street. Small-town diner. Open daily for breakfast, lunch, and dinner. 465-3081.

YELLOW SPRINGS, OHIO, AREA CODE: 937; ZIP CODE: 45387

The Golden Jersey Inn, 6880 Springfield-Xenia Road. Open daily for breakfast, lunch, and dinner. 324–2050.

Ha Ha Pizza, 108 Xenia Avenue. Vegetarian dishes. Daily. 767–2131.

The Winds Cafe, 215 Xenia Avenue. International menu featuring seafood, chicken, and vegetarian dishes. Daily. 767–1144.

Ye Old Trail Tavern, 228 Xenia Avenue. Historic log tavern offering pizza, wings, and burgers. Daily. 767–7448.

NORTHEAST

COLUMBUS, OHIO, AREA CODE: 614; ZIP CODE: SEE BELOW

Downtown Zip Code: 43215

Gordon Biersch Brewery Restaurant, 401 Front Street. Upscale and imaginative menu, fresh-brewed lagers. 246–2900.

Mitchell's Steakhouse, 45 North Third Street. Art deco decor. Big steaks, memorable potatoes. 621–2333.

Tapatio, 491 North Park Street. Regional Mexican, Latin American, and Caribbean cuisine. Trendy and popular. 221–1085.

German Village Zip Code: 43206

Katzinger's Delicatessen, 475 South Third Street. New York–style deli. Overstuffed sandwiches, soups, salads. Daily. 228–3354.

Lindey's, 169 East Beck Street. Very popular. Progressive American menu. Reservations recommended. Daily. 228–4343.

Schmidt's Sausage Haus, 240 East Kossuth Street. In a restored building; sausage and German pastries. Daily. 444–6808.

North Zip Code: 43212

Buckeye Hall of Fame Cafe, 1421 Olentangy River Road. Casual dining amid sports memorabilia and a video arcade. 291–2233.

Columbus Fish Market, 1245 Olentangy River Road. Fresh seafood in a lively and casual atmosphere. 291–3474.

North Zip Code: 43221

La Chatelaine, 1550 West Lane Avenue. French breads, pastries, salads, soups, and sandwiches. 488–1911.

HILLSBORO, OHIO, AREA CODE: 937; ZIP CODE: 45133

McGee's, 129 West Main. Good home cooking. Wonderful home-made pies. Daily. 393–2014.

LEBANON, OHIO, AREA CODE: 513; ZIP CODE: 45036

Best Cafe, 17 East Mulberry. Cafe offering unique sandwiches and salads and creative American and Continental dinners. 932–4400.

The Golden Lamb, 27 South Broadway. Fine American food in Ohio's oldest inn. Daily. 932-5065.

The Gourmet on Broadway, 20 North Broadway. Mediterranean specialties. Lunch, Monday through Saturday. 933-8377.

Houston Inn, 4026 US 42. Evenings only. Closed Mondays. 398-7377.

Shaker Run Golf Clubhouse and Grille, 4361 Greentree Road. Lunch and dinner. 727-0007.

The Sycamore Tree Tea Room, 3 South Sycamore Street. Lunch in a Victorian setting. 932-4567.

WAYNESVILLE, OHIO, AREA CODE: 513; ZIP CODE: 45068

Der Dutchman, U.S. 42 at Waynesville. Amish family-style dining featuring homemade soups, fried chicken, pies. Daily. 897-4716.

Hammel House Inn, 121 South Main. Restored stagecoach stop. Daily for lunch. 897-2333 or 897-3779.

Village Restaurant, 144 South Main. Down-home cooking for breakfast, lunch, and dinner. Daily. 897-8835.

WILMINGTON, OHIO, AREA CODE: 937; ZIP CODE: 45177

The General Denver Hotel, 81 West Main. Located in General Denver Hotel. Semiformal dining. Lunch and dinner daily. 382-7139.

SOUTHWEST

ANDERSON FERRY, OHIO, AREA CODE: 513; ZIP CODE: 45204

River Saloon & Eatery, 4333 River Road. Pub fare. Live music, sand volleyball, boat dock, full-service bar. Daily. 451-0022.

BARDSTOWN, KY., AREA CODE: 502; ZIP CODE: 40004

Kurtz Restaurant, 418 East Stephen Foster Avenue. Homemade Southern-style cooking. Daily. Closed Christmas. 348-8964.

Old Talbott Tavern, 107 West Stephen Foster Avenue. A 200-year-old tavern. Regional favorites, Old Kentucky ham. 348-3494.

Xavier's Restaurant, 112 Xavier Drive. New American cuisine. Dinner served 5:00 to 10:00 P.M. Tuesday–Saturday. 349-9464.

CLARKSVILLE, IND., AREA CODE: 812; ZIP CODE: 47129

Derby Dinner Playhouse, Interstate 65 Stansifer Avenue exit, next to Holiday Inn Lakeview. Dinner and show. Closed Monday. 288-8281.

FORT KNOX, KY., AREA CODE: 502; ZIP CODE: 40121

Doe Run Inn, 10 miles west of Fort Knox on K-1638. Kentucky ham, fried chicken, lemon pie. Daily. 422-2982.

LOUISVILLE, KY., AREA CODE: 502; ZIP CODE: SEE BELOW
Downtown Zip Code: 40202

English Grill, The Camberly Brown Hotel at 339 West Broadway. Home of the famous "Hot Brown" sandwich. Daily. 583–1234.

The Galt House, River Road and Fourth Street. The Flagship restaurant has a view of the Ohio River; two other restaurants and two lounges offer a variety of dining. Daily. 589–5200.

Kunz's, 115 Fourth Avenue. Excellent steaks, seafood, German specialties. 585–5555.

Oak Room, The Seelbach Hilton Hotel at 500 Fourth Avenue. Elegant, gracious southern dining. Daily. 585–3200.

Vincenzo's, Fifth and Market Streets. Fine dining featuring authentic northern Italian and Continental cuisine. Closed Sunday. 580–1350.

MADISON, IND., AREA CODE: 812; ZIP CODE: 47250

Historic Broadway Tavern & Hotel, 313 Broadway. Steaks, seafood. Barbecued ribs Friday nights. Closed Sunday. 265–2346.

Key West Shrimp House, 117 Ferry Street, at Ohio River bridge. Seafood, chicken, steaks. Closed Monday. 265–2831.

The Pines, 2700 Michigan Road (Ind. 421). Buffet lunch and dinner. Open daily, except Monday and Christmas. 273–4645.

The Wharf, on the river at the end of Vaughn Drive. A floating restaurant offering seafood. 265–2090.

VEVAY, IND., AREA CODE: 812; ZIP CODE: 47043

Belterra Casino Resort, 777 Belterra Drive, 1 mile east of the Markland Dam Bridge. 427–7777.

WARSAW, KY., AREA CODE: 606; ZIP CODE: 41095

Dan's Restaurant, U.S. 42, 1 mile west. Down-home cooking; river view. Daily. 567–7601.

SOUTH

BEREA, KY., AREA CODE: 859; ZIP CODE: 40403

Boone Tavern, Main Street (K–25) downtown. Grand old inn. Kentucky specialties, country ham, spoonbread. No alcohol. Daily. 985–3700.

FRANKFORT, KY., AREA CODE: (502); ZIP CODE: 40601

Daniel's Restaurant, 243 West Broadway. Fine dining. Lunch and dinner. 875–5599.

Jim's Seafood, 950 Wilkinson Boulevard. Seafood. Lunch and dinner. 223–7448.

HARRODSBURG, KY., AREA CODE: 859; ZIP CODE: 40330

The Beaumont Inn, U.S. 68 at U.S. 127 downtown. Gracious dining. Daily. Closed December–February. 734-3381.

LEXINGTON, KY., AREA CODE: 859; ZIP CODE: SEE BELOW

Downtown Zip Code: 40504

The Coach House, 855 South Broadway (U.S. 68). Regional and continental dining. Closed Sunday. 252-7777.

Downtown Zip Code: 40508

Dudley's Restaurant, 380 South Mill Street. In old South Hill area in restored home. Continental dining. Daily. 252-1010.

North Zip Code: 40511

The Mansion at Griffin Gate, 1800 Newtown Pike. Antebellum mansion. Continental dining. Daily. 231-5152.

South Zip Code: 40500

Merrick Inn, 3380 Tates Creek Road. Old manor house on horse farm. Southern continental dining. Closed Sunday. 269-5417.

SHAKER VILLAGE OF PLEASANT HILL, KY., AREA CODE: 859; ZIP CODE: 40330

The Trustees' Office, U.S. 68, 7 miles northeast of Harrodsburg at Shakertown restoration. Old Kentucky ham, Shaker recipes. No alcohol. Daily. 734-5411.

SLADE, KY., AREA CODE: 606; ZIP CODE: 40376

Hemlock Lodge, 2 miles south of Slade on K-11, in Natural Bridge State Resort Park. Standard dining room fare. Daily. 663-2214.

SOUTHEAST

AUGUSTA, KY., AREA CODE: 606; ZIP CODE: 41002

The Beehive Tavern, 101 West Riverside Drive. Restored 1796 building. Closed Monday and Tuesday. 756-2202.

The Augusta General Store. 109 Main Street and Riverside Drive. Historic general store. Homemade entrees and baked goods, and an old-fashioned ice cream soda fountain. Open daily 8:00 A.M. to 8:00 P.M. and in the summer 8:00 A.M. to 10:00 P.M. 756-2525.

MANCHESTER, OHIO, AREA CODE: 937; ZIP CODE: 45144

Moyer Winery, U.S. 52, 3 miles west of Manchester. Family winery and vineyards with dining room. Closed Sunday. 549-2957.

MAYSVILLE, KY., AREA CODE: 606; ZIP CODE: 41056

Caproni's, Rosemary Clooney Street at rail depot. River view, continental dining. Closed Monday and summer Sundays. 564–4321.

Izzy B's Coffee Shop, 34 West Second Street. Gourmet coffees, homemade pastries, soups, salads, and sandwiches. 564–3002.

The Metropolitan Cafe, 2 East Third Street. Historic building. Gourmet dining with full beer and wine list. Live entertainment on weekends. 564–5080.

RIPLEY, OHIO, AREA CODE: 937; ZIP CODE: 45167

Cohearts Riverhouse, 18 North Front Street. River view. Homemade pasta, desserts, sandwiches. Closed Monday and Tuesday. 392–4819.

State Parks and Forests

KEY

BC	Bicycling		**NC**	Nature Center
BR	Boat Ramp		**P**	Picnicking
C	Canoeing		**PL**	Playground
CC	Cross-Country Skiing		**PR**	Provisions Available
D	Outdoor Drama		**S**	Swimming
E	Electrical Hookup		**SH**	Showers
F	Fishing		**SK**	Skiing
G	Golfing Nearby		**SN**	Snowmobiling
H	Hiking		**SR**	Sewer Hookup
HB	Horseback Riding		**T**	Tennis
L	Laundry		**W**	Water Hookup
N	Naturalist on Duty			

INDIANA

Brookville Reservoir, 5 mi N of Brookville on Ind. 101. 16,445 acres of rolling woodland along White River, with several prehistoric Indian mounds. 5,300-acre reservoir. All year. 420 trailer sites. Fee. Write P.O. Box 100, Brookville, IN 47012. (765) 647–6557. BR, C, CC, E, F, G, N, P, S, SH

Brown County State Park, 2 mi E of Nashville on Ind. 46. 15,500 acres of heavily forested hills overlooking two large lakes. Indiana's largest park. 30 tent, 410 trailer sites. Fee. Write P.O. Box 608, Nashville, IN 47448. (812) 988–6406. CC, E, F, HB, N, P, PL, PR, S, SH

Camp Atterbury, 8 mi N of Columbus on Interstate 64 to exit 80 and 1 mi W on Edinburg Rd. 5,500-acre state fish and game area at former military camp. Apr.–Oct. Has 30 primitive tent sites. Primarily used for hunting and fishing, Atterbury also has a 75-acre lake. Fee. Write Edinburg, IN 46124. (317) 232-7535. BR, F, P

Clark State Forest, 19 mi N of Clarksville on Interstate 65 to exit 19 and 3 mi W on Ind. 160. Apr.–Sept. 24,000 acres of wooded hills. 70 primitive sites. Fee. Write Henryville, IN 47126. (812) 294-4306. BR, F, H, HB, P, PL

Clifty Falls State Park, 1 mi W of Madison on Ind. 56. 1,360 acres of Ohio River bluff with deep canyon and waterfalls. 165 sites. Fee. Write 1501 Green Rd., Madison, IN 47250. (812) 265-1331. E, N, NC, P, PL, PR, S, SH, T

Deam Lake State Forest, 13 mi NW of New Albany, Ind., on Ind. 60. Apr.–Sept. 1,300 acres in state forest with 194-acre lake. 286 sites. Fee. Write Borden, IN 47106. (812) 246-5421. BR, E, F, P, PL, S, SH

Fort Harrison State Park. On Indianapolis's east side at 5753 Glenn Road. Year-round. 1,700-acre state park featuring unbroken hardwood forest, nature preserve, several small lakes, miles of creeks and tributaries, trails, golf, and picnic areas. Write 5753 Glenn Road, Indianapolis, IN 46216. (317) 591-0904. BC, F, G, HB, N, NC, P.

McCormick's Creek State Park, 12 mi W of Bloomington on Ind. 46. Forested hills and limestone ravines. 324 trailer sites. 1,800 acres. Fee. Write P.O. Box 82, RR5, Spencer, IN 47460. (812) 829-2235. BC, E, F, HB, N, NC, P, PL, PR, S, SH, T

Morgan-Monroe State Forest, 2 mi W of Bloomington on Ind. 46 and 12 mi N on Ind. 32. 38 sites. More than 23,000 acres. Fee. Write 6220 Forest Rd., Martinsville, IN 46151. (317) 342-4026. BR, F, P, PL

Versailles State Park, 15 mi S of Batesville on Ind. 129 and 5 mi W on U.S. 50. Also 1 mi E of Versailles. Wooded rural setting. 230-acre lake. 225 trailer sites. 5,900 acres. Fee. Write P.O. Box 205, Versailles, IN 47042. (812) 689-6424. BR, E, F, HB, P, PL, PR, S, SH, SR

Whitewater State Park, 2¹/₂ mi S of Liberty on Ind. 101. 1,700 wooded acres with wide sand beach along Brookville Lake. 330 trailer sites. Fee. Write RR 2, Liberty, IN 47353. (317) 458-5565. BC, BR, C, E, F, HB, N, P, PL, PR, S, SH

Yellowwood State Forest, 8 mi W of Nashville on Ind. 46 and 2 mi N following signs. Wooded hills, more than 22,000 acres. 93 tent sites. Fee. Write RR5, Box 390, Nashville, IN 47448. (812) 988-7945. BR, F, HB, PL

Indiana state parks charge $3.00 admission per car, or $18.00 for an annual sticker. Campsites rent for $5.00 to $14.00 a night, with a 14-day limit.

Park Information: Indiana Department of Natural Resources, Division of Parks, 402 W. Washington St., Room W298, Indianapolis, IN 46204. (317) 232-4124.

KENTUCKY

Big Bone Lick State Park, 3 mi W of Beaverlick on K-338. 525-acre park with Indian salt digs and archaeological site where many bones of prehistoric mammals were found. Museum open Apr.-Oct. 62 tent, 62 trailer sites. Year-round camping. Fee. Write Union, KY 41091. (606) 384-3522. E, F, L, P, PL, S, SH, T, W

Blue Licks Battlefield State Park, 21 mi SW of Washington on U.S. 68. 100-acre site of the last battle of the American Revolution in 1782. Apr.-Oct. 51 tent, 51 trailer sites. Fee. Write Mt. Olivet, KY 41064. (606) 289-5507. F, N, P, PL, S

Fort Boonesborough State Park, 7 mi N. of Richmond on Interstate 75 to exit 95, then 7 mi NE on K-338 to 1 mi past Boonesboro. 153 acres of flatland surrounded by hills along Kentucky River, site of Daniel Boone's stockaded settlement, which withstood several Shawnee attacks. Apr.-Oct. 187 tent, 167 trailer sites. Fee. Write RR 5, Richmond, KY 40475. (859) 527-3131. BR, E, F, L, P, PL, PR, S, SH, W

General Butler State Resort Park, 2 mi S of Carrollton on K-227. 800-acre former estate of General William O. Butler, hero of Andrew Jackson's Battle of New Orleans. Includes general's restored home, 30-acre lake, fine lodge, and cottages. Quite popular for snow skiing. All year. 135 tent, 111 trailer sites. Fee. Write Carrollton, KY 41008. (502) 732-4384. CC, E, G, L, NC, P, PL, S, SK, SH, T, W

Kentucky Horse Park, 6 miles north of downtown Lexington on Interstate 75, at Exit 120. All year. 1,032 acres of bluegrass, former standardbred horse farm and the only park in the world dedicated to mankind's relationship with the horse. Many sights, activities related to the horse. The campground has 260 paved RV sites, each with electrical and water hookups. Contact: 4089 Iron Works Parkway, Lexington KY 40511, or call (859) 259-4257 (campground) or (859) 233-4303 (park). E, HB, L, P, PL, PR, S, SH, T, W

Kincaid Lake State Park, from U.S. 27 in Falmouth, 3 mi NE on K-159. Apr.-Oct. 667 acres with a 183-acre fishing lake. Rental boats. 84 trailer sites. Fee. Write Falmouth, KY 41040. (606) 654-3531. BR, C, E, F, P, PL, PR, S, SH, T, W

Koomer Ridge Campground, 3.5 mi SE of Slade, KY, on K-15. Apr.-Nov. 15. 45 acres in primeval Red River Gorge area of Daniel Boone National Forest, operated by U.S. Forest Service. 54 tent, 40 trailer sites. Fee. Write Slade, KY 40376. (606) 663-2852. N

My Old Kentucky Home State Park, 1 mi E of Bardstown on U.S. 150. Near Federal Hill Mansion of Stephen Foster fame. Apr.-Oct. 40 trailer sites. Fee. Write Bardstown, KY 40004. (505) 348-3502. D, E, G, P, PL, SH, W

Natural Bridge State Resort Park, 35 mi SE of Winchester, KY, on Mountain Pkwy. to Slade and 5 mi S on K-11. 1,900 acres of wooded hills and gorges, with Kentucky's largest natural bridge. 95 trailer sites. Fee. Write Slade, KY 40376. (606) 663-2214. BR, C, E, L, N, P, PL, S, SH, T, W

No entrance fee is charged at Kentucky state parks. Campsite rentals are $8.50 to $10.50 per night. Lodges, found at state "resort" parks, are well above average, as are executive and housekeeping cottages. Rates vary. Some of these open all year.

For park information: Kentucky Department of Parks, Capitol Plaza Tower, 500 Mero St., 10th Floor, Frankfort, KY 40601. (502) 564-4930 or (800) 255-PARK.

OHIO

A. W. Marion State Park, 4 mi NE of Circleville on O-188. All year. 454 acres. 60 trailer sites. Fee. Write 7317 Warner-Huffman Rd., Circleville, OH 43113. (614) 474-3386. BR, F, P, PL

Caesar Creek State Park, 5 mi W of Interstate 71 on O-73. All year. 8,000 acres of wooded land surrounding 2,800-acre lake. Boating, waterskiing. Visitors center. Restored pioneer village. 287 trailer sites. Fee. Write 8570 E. State Rte. 73, Waynesville, OH 45068. (513) 897-3055. BR, CC, E, F, HB, N, P, S, SH, SN, SR

Cowan Lake State Park, 5 mi SW of Wilmington on U.S. 68 and 8 mi W on O-350. 1,775 wooded acres on lake. All year. 237 trailer sites. Fee. Write 729 Beechwood Rd., Wilmington, OH 45177. (937) 289-2105. BR, E, F, L, N, P, PL, PR, S, SH

Deer Creek State Park, 25 mi SW of Columbus on Interstate 71, Mt. Sterling exit 84, then 4 mi SE on O-56 to Mt. Sterling and 7 mi

S on O–207. All year. 6,300 wooded acres surrounding 1,300-acre lake. Big lodge with pool and cabins. 232 trailer sites. Fee. Write 20635 Waterloo Rd., Mt. Sterling, OH 43143. (614) 869–3124. BR, E, F, G, HB, L, P, S, SH, SN

Hueston Woods State Park, 4 mi NE of Oxford on O–732. More than 3,500 acres of rolling woodlands with a small lake, lodge, cabins, and woods. All year. 267 tent, 255 trailer sites. Fee. Write RR 1, College Corner, OH 45003. (513) 523–6347. BR, C, E, F, G, HB, L, N, P, PL, S, SH

John Bryan State Park, 10 mi S of Springfield on U.S. 68 to Yellow Springs, then 1 mi E on O–343 and 1.5 mi S on O–370. Camping with 100 sites on 750 partly wooded acres. Spectacular hiking in gorge. All year. Fee. Write 3790 State Rte. 370, Yellow Springs, OH 45387. (937) 767–1274. CC, F, H, P, PL, S, SK

Lake White State Park, 15 mi S of Chillicothe on U.S. 23 to Waverly, then 1 mi SW on O–104. All year. 340 acres on lake. 75 sites. Fee. Write 2767 State Rte. 551, Waverly, OH 45690. (614) 947–4059. BR, F, PL, S

Paint Creek State Park, 3.5 mi W of Bainbridge (13^1/2 mi E of Hillsboro) on U.S. 50 and 1.5 mi N on park road. All year. Large wooded 9,000-acre park on Paint Creek Lake. 199 trailer sites. Fee. Write 7860 Upp Rd., Bainbridge, OH 45612. (937) 365–1401. BR, CC, E, F, L, P, S, SH, SN

Pike Lake State Park, 1 mi W of Bainbridge on U.S. 50 and 6 mi S on unnumbered road, following signs. All year. 600 acres. 112 trailer sites. Cabins. Fee. Write 1847 Pike Lake, Bainbridge, OH 45612. (614) 493–2212. BR, E, F, HB, PL, PR, S

Rocky Fork State Park, 8 mi SE of Hillsboro on O–124 and 1 mi N at sign. 3,500 acres on Rocky Fork Lake. All year. 220 sites. Three marinas, waterskiing. Fee. Write Rte. 4, 9800 N. Shore Dr., Hillsboro, OH 45133. (937) 393–4284. BR, E, F, L, P, PL, PR, S, SH

Scioto Trail State Park, 9 mi S of Chillicothe on U.S. 23 and 1 mi E on O–372. All year. 248 acres. 58 sites. Fee. Write 144 Lake Rd., Chillicothe, OH 45601. (614) 663–2125. BR, CC, F, HB, P

Shawnee State Park, 3.5 mi E of Manchester on U.S. 52 and 6 mi NW on O–125. All year. 1,165 acres of forested hills near Ohio River in the heart of Shawnee country. Lodge and cabins. 107 trailer sites. Fee. Write P.O. Box 68, Portsmouth, OH 45662. (614) 858–6652. BR, CC, E, F, G, H, HB, L, N, P, S, SH

There is no admission fee to Ohio's state parks. Campsites rent for $6.00 to $15.00 a night. For park information: Ohio Division of Parks and Recreation, Fountain Square, Bldg. C, Columbus, OH 43224. (614) 265–7000.

Celebrations and Festivals

By no means comprehensive, this list is a representative sampling of some of the more important and unusual events. All information is subject to change.

FEBRUARY

NORTHWEST

NASHVILLE, Ind.—Winterfest. Early February. Bikini races for men and women, snow sculpting contest, and races for kids. Ski World, P.O. Box 445, Nashville, IN 47448. (812) 988–6638.

MARCH

SOUTHWEST

LOUISVILLE, Ky.—Humana Festival of New American Plays. A six-week extravaganza of new plays. Plays are produced by the renowned Actors Theater of Louisville. (502) 584–1265; www.actorstheatre.org.

APRIL

NORTHWEST

BLOOMINGTON, Ind.—Little 500 Bicycle Race. Late April. Bike and tricycle races. Golf tournament. Entertainment. (812) 334–8900 or (800) 800–0037.

SOUTHEAST

POINT PLEASANT, Ohio—U.S. Grant Birthday Celebration. April. Annual celebration of U.S. Grant's birthday, held at his birthplace. Historical exhibits, entertainment, and presentations. Free admission. (513) 553–4911 or (513) 553–3661.

SOUTH

KENTUCKY HORSE PARK—Kentucky Rolex Three-Day Event and High Hopes Steeplechase. Late April. North of Lexington on Interstate 75. The three-day event is an Olympic-level equestrian trial. The steeplechase is a series of races with jumps over brush and timber. (859) 233-4303; www.kyhorsepark.com.

LEXINGTON, Ky.—Bluegrass Stakes. Late April during Spring Race Meet. Important thoroughbred racing preliminary to the Kentucky Derby. Juleps and burgoo. Keeneland Race Course, 6 mi west on U.S. 60. P.O. Box 1690, Lexington, KY 40592. (859) 254-3412.

MAY

NORTHWEST

INDIANAPOLIS, Ind.—"500 Festival." All month. Series of events leading up to the Indianapolis 500 race on Memorial Day weekend. Parade, Family Float Night, minimarathon. Indianapolis City Center/Visitors Center, 201 S. Capitol Ave., Indianapolis, IN 46225. (317) 237-5200; www.indy.org. For festival events: (317) 636-4556; www.500festival.com. For race information: Indianapolis Motor Speedway, 4790 W. 16th St., Indianapolis, IN 46222. (317) 241-2501.

METAMORA, Ind.—May Day. First weekend of May. Maypole dancing highlights festivities at old canal village. Whitewater Canal State Memorial, Metamora, IN 47030. (765) 647-6512 or 647-2109.

NASHVILLE, Ind.—Spring Blossom Festival. First weekend in May. Parade leads list of events as art colony kicks off its summer season. (812) 988-6647.

SOUTHWEST

LOUISVILLE, Ky.—Kentucky Derby Festival. "Thunder over Louisville" kicks off two weeks of festivities leading up to Derby, held the first Saturday in May. Pegasus Parade, Great Steamboat Race between the *Delta Queen* and the *Belle of Louisville* on the Ohio River, hot-air balloon race, musical events, minimarathon, etc. (502) 584-2121 or (888) LOUISVILLE; www.gotolouisville.com or www.kdf.org.

SOUTH

BEREA, Ky.—Kentucky Guild of Artists and Craftsmen's Fair. Mid-May (also mid-October). Indian Fort Theater. Mountain artisans and Kentucky crafters display their works. Music, dancing. (859) 986-3192.

NORTHEAST

CHILLICOTHE, Ohio—Feast of Flowering Moon. Late May. At Yoctangee Park in Chillicothe. A Native American Indian Powwow and mountain man rendezvous. (614) 775-0900.

JUNE

NORTHWEST

INDIANAPOLIS, Ind.—Talbot Street Art Fair. Mid-June. Fine artists and craftsworkers from all over the United States, food, strolling minstrels. (317) 745-6479.

BATESVILLE, Ind.—Batesville Music and Arts Festival. Third week in June at Batesville High School. This celebration of musical entertainment has been a Batesville tradition since 1975. Entertainment begins on Wednesday with the Cincinnati Pops and fireworks and continues through Friday. Performances nightly from 7:30 to 10:00 P.M. No admission fee. (812) 934-7675.

NORTHEAST

COLUMBUS, Ohio—Columbus Arts Festival. First Thursday through Sunday of June. Downtown riverfront, Broad and High Streets. Artists and craftsworkers exhibit their works. Music, food. (614) 221-6623 or (800) 345-4FUN.

   WILMINGTON, Ohio—Banana Split Festival. June. J. W. Williams Park. Music, food, games. (937) 382-1965.

SOUTH

DANVILLE, Ky.—The Great American Brass Band Festival. Mid-June. From Civil War-era bands to sophisticated ensembles, performers gather to play ragtime, John Philip Sousa works, and traditional music. The Great American Brass Band Festival, P.O. Box 429, Danville, KY 40423-0429. (800) 755-0076.

   FRANKFORT, Ky.—Capital Expo Festival. First weekend in June. Artists and artisans from Kentucky assemble at Capitol Plaza. Dancing, games, contests, ethnic foods, balloon racing, and entertainment. (502) 875-8687.

JULY

NORTHWEST

OLDENBURG, Ind.—Freudenfest. Late July. Street fair with carnival rides, game booths, German and other food specialties.

NORTH

DAYTON, Ohio—United States Air & Trade Show. Four days, mid- to late July. Air show and stunt flying at Dayton International Airport. Demonstrations and exhibits. (937) 898-5901.

URBANA, Ohio—Marketplace Days. Third weekend in July. A typical hometown celebration complete with street vendors, sidewalk sales, 5K race, and Main Street parade. (937) 653-5764.

NORTHEAST

COLUMBUS, Ohio—Budweiser Jazz and Ribs Festival. Last weekend in July. Downtown riverfront. Local, regional, national jazz artists. Ribs from Ohio's top ribs restaurants. (614) 221-6623 or (800) 345-4FUN.

SOUTHWEST

FORT KNOX, Ky.—Armored Division Demonstration. July 4. From Patton Museum, Fayette Drive, Fort Knox. Armor rolls out for a mock tank battle to celebrate the Fourth. Public Affairs Office, U.S. Army Armor Center, P.O. Box Y, Fort Knox, KY 40121. (502) 624-3812 or 624-3051.

MADISON, Ind.—The Madison Regatta. Early July. Hydroplane races on the Ohio River. Week-long celebration draws nationally known pilots in the world's fastest boats. (812) 265-2956.

SOUTH

LEXINGTON, Ky.—Junior League Horse Show. Six days in mid-July. World's largest show of standardbred horses at the Red Mile Race Track, 847 S. Broadway, Lexington, KY 40504. (859) 252-1893.

PARIS, Ky.—Steam and Gas Engine Show. Weekend after July 4. Old farm machinery, steam engines, tractors, flea market, and country music performances. (606) 987-3205.

AUGUST

NORTHWEST

INDIANAPOLIS, Ind.—Indiana State Fair. Ten days in late August at the state Fairgrounds, E. 38th St. and Fall Creek Pkwy. Major agricultural and livestock exhibits, horse races, and entertainment. Indiana State Fairgrounds, 1202 East 38th St., Indianapolis, IN 46205-2869. (317) 927-7500; www.indianastatefair.com.

INDIANAPOLIS, Ind.—RCA Tennis Championships. Early August. Top tennis pros compete in a week-long tourney at the Indianapolis Tennis Center, 725 W. New York St., P.O. Box 26035, Indianapolis, IN 46226. (317) 632-8000.

NORTH

VANDALIA, Ohio—Amateur Trapshooting Tournament. Ten days in August. Competition held daily from 8:00 A.M. to 8:00 P.M. by the Amateur Trapshooting Association, 601 W. National Rd., Vandalia, OH 45377. (937) 898-1945.

NORTHEAST

COLUMBUS, Ohio—Dublin Irish Festival. First weekend in August at Coffman Park. One of the top Irish festivals in the country. Eight music stages feature Irish dance and music. Food, shopping, cultural exhibits, and demonstrations. Admission fee. (614) 410-4545 or (877) 674-7336; www.dublinirishfestival.org.

COLUMBUS, Ohio—Ohio State Fair. Early to mid-August. Ohio Exposition Center, 717 E. 17th Ave. Established more than a century ago, with extensive agricultural, livestock, and homemaking competitions, daily live entertainment and fireworks, harness racing, carnival rides, and a wide variety of food concessions. (614) 221-6623 or 644-3247.

WAYNESVILLE, Ohio—Ohio Renaissance Festival. Five miles east on O-73. Eight weekends late August through mid-October. Sixteenth-century English village fair. Music, food, entertainment. (513) 897-7000.

SOUTHWEST

ELIZABETHTOWN, Ky.—Kentucky Heartland Festival. Late August. Parade, arts and crafts displays, food concessions, antique auto show, canoe races, and country music. From Louisville 33 mi south on Interstate 65. From Bardstown 23 mi southwest on Bluegrass Parkway. (502) 765-4334.

LOUISVILLE, Ky.—Kentucky State Fair. Ten days in mid-August. Kentucky Fair and Exposition Center, Louisville, KY 40214. (502) 367-6700. State fair events include a rodeo and a champi-

onship horse show. (502) 584–2121 or (888) LOUISVILLE; www.
gotolouisville.com.

SOUTHEAST

NEW RICHMOND, Ohio—New Richmond Riverdays. Annual
August event on Front Street. Riverdays celebrates the summer and
life on the river. Includes rides, games, food, and entertainment. Free
admission. (513) 684–1253.

SEPTEMBER

NORTHEAST

COLUMBUS, Ohio—Greek Festival. First weekend in September
at the Greek Orthodox Cathedral, 555 North High St. A Columbus
tradition since 1972, the Greek Festival offers food, music, dancing,
shopping, and tours of the church. Admission fee. (614) 224–9020.

COLUMBUS, Ohio—German Village Oktoberfest. Weekend
after Labor Day. Beer, brats, and "oom-pa-pa" fill the Old Brewery
District next to German Village. (614) 221–6623 or (800) 345–4FUN.

NORTHWEST

BATESVILLE, Ind.—Apple Fest. Last weekend in September in
Liberty Park. Enjoy local crisp, juicy apples, cider, and sweet apple
butter. Family fun, games, music, fine arts, crafts, food, and entertainment. No admission fee. (812) 933–6103.

MORROW, Ohio—Valley Vineyards Wine Festival. Last
weekend in September. 2276 U.S. 23 just outside Morrow. Grape
stomp, entertainment, winery tours, food, music. (513) 899–2485.

WILMINGTON, Ohio—Clinton County Corn Festival. Second
weekend in September. Parade, antique farm machinery, wheat
thrashing, meal grinding, apple butter making, quilt demonstrations, music, food, antiques, contests, and crafts. Corn Festival, 69
N. South St., Wilmington, OH 45177. (937) 382–2737.

NORTH

SPRINGFIELD, Ohio—Fair at New Boston. Labor Day weekend.
Hundreds of pioneer-day aficionados create a raucous pioneer town
festival complete with blacksmiths, weavers, and gunsmiths. Admission fee. George Rogers Clark Heritage Association, P.O. Box 1251,
Springfield, OH 45501.

SOUTHWEST

JEFFERSONVILLE, Ind.—Steamboat Days. First weekend after Labor Day. Along riverfront. Parade, talent show, rides, arts and crafts exhibits, and entertainment. Howard Steamboat Museum is in this area. (812) 284-2628.

LOUISVILLE, Ky.—Bluegrass Music Festival. Weekend after Labor Day. Riverfront Amphitheater. One of the country's best. Musicians from all over the country throng to Louisville for this event. (502) 584-2121.

LOUISVILLE, Ky.—Corn Island Storytelling Festival. Third weekend in September. Held at the E.P. "Tom" Sawyer State Park. Visitors from nearly 50 states and several countries attend the "Woodstock of Storytelling," as it is the largest storytelling gathering in the world. Admission fee. (502) 245-0643.

MADISON, Ind.—The Madison Chautaqua Festival of the Arts. Fourth weekend in September. One of the Midwest's premier art exhibits for more than 200 artists and crafters in 6-block area in restored historic district. (812) 265-2956.

DANVILLE, Ky.—Historic Constitution Square Festival. Mid-September. Colonial-era games, a fiddling contest, and eighteenth-century food. Constitution Square State Historic Site, 105 E. Walnut St., Danville, KY 40422-1817. (606) 236-5089.

OCTOBER

NORTHWEST

COLUMBUS, Ind.—Ethnic Expo. Mid-October. Downtown festival celebrates town's cultural diversity with food, dance, music, parade, kite flying. (812) 376-2500 or 372-1954.

OXFORD, Ohio—Apple Butter and Fall Festival. Mid-October. Apple butter is made in kettles over open fires at Pioneer Farm and House Museum. Doty and Brown Roads, at south entrance to Hueston Woods State Park. (513) 523-6347.

NORTH

DAYTON, Ohio—Oktoberfest. Dayton Art Institute, Forest and Riverview. Fine arts, crafts, entertainment, food. (937) 223-5277.

URBANA, Ohio—Oktoberfest. First Sunday in October. On the lawn of the Champaign County Historical Society, with more than seventy artists and food vendors. (937) 653-6721.

NORTHEAST

BAINBRIDGE, Ohio—Fall Festival of Leaves. Third weekend in October. Children's carnival, flea market, art shows, log-sawing contest, muzzle-loaders shoot, auction, parade. Self-guided scenic driving tours. Festival of Leaves, P.O. Box 571, Bainbridge, OH 45612. (614) 634-2997.

CIRCLEVILLE, Ohio—Circleville Pumpkin Festival. Third weekend in October, for four days. Classic small-town fair. Annually features the world's largest pumpkin pie, plus displays of squash, gourds, and pumpkins. Rides, games, music, Miss Pumpkin event, hog-calling contest, and pumpkin products. Pumpkin Show, 135 W. Main St., Circleville, OH 43113. (614) 474-4923 or 474-4224.

LEBANON, Ohio—Applefest. Downtown Lebanon. Third Saturday in October. Street fair with arts and crafts, apples fixed every way imaginable, a 5K race, entertainment. (513) 932-1100.

WAYNESVILLE, Ohio—Ohio Sauerkraut Festival. Second weekend in October. Main Street. Regional artists and crafts fair. Sauerkraut food items, music, entertainment. (513) 897-8855.

SOUTHWEST

HODGENVILLE, Ky.—Lincoln Day Celebration. Second weekend in October. Parade, rail-splitting contest, puppet show, arts and crafts exhibits celebrate Abe Lincoln's birth here in 1809. (502) 358-3411.

LOUISVILLE, Ky.—St. James Court Art Show. First full weekend in October. Fine arts and crafts show held on the streets and courts of historic Old Louisville. (502) 635-1842.

LOUISVILLE, Ky.—Oktoberfest and St. James Art Fair. Early October. Former German neighborhood of Butchertown comes to life in music, dancing, and beer drinking, with most activities centering upon Bakery Square. Street fair at St. James Court in Old Louisville area includes art exhibits, entertainment, food concessions. Some local homes are open to visitors. (502) 584-2121 or (888) LOUISVILLE; www.gotolouisville.com.

SOUTH

BEREA, Ky.—Forkland Heritage Festival and Revue. Second weekend in October. *True* folk festival, country atmosphere of "the Fork," heritage displays, old country theater, entertainment, shops, breakfast, and countryside wagon tours. The event is held on K-37 off of U.S. 127 and admission is charged. (859) 332-7897.

SOUTHEAST

MAYSVILLE, Ky.—Rosemary Clooney Festival. First weekend in October on Third Street. Features performances, including a concert by Rosemary, and a catered dinner. (606) 564-9411 or (606) 564-5534.

DECEMBER

NORTHWEST

METAMORA, Ind.—Christmas Walk. First three weekends following Thanksgiving. Candlelit canal, streets, and buildings. Music, caroling, entertainment. Whitewater Railroad runs special trains from Connersville to Metamora. (317) 647-2109 or 825-2054.

NORTH

URBANA, Ohio—Annual Candlelight Tour of Homes. First Saturday in December. Tours of unusual or historic homes in Urbana. All money aids local cancer patients through the Cancer Association of Champaign County. (937) 653-7207.

NORTHEAST

WAYNESVILLE, Ohio—Christmas in the Village. Each weekend between Thanksgiving and Christmas. Horse-drawn carriage rides, historic walking tours, strolling carolers, town crier. (513) 897-8855.

SOUTHWEST

BARDSTOWN, Ky.—Christmas 'round Bardstown. Late November through December. Historic home tours, concerts, candlelight tours of nearby distilleries, live nativity. (502) 348-4877.

MADISON, Ind.—Nights Before Christmas Tour. First two weekends after Thanksgiving. Guided tour visits historic public and private homes, decorated for holidays in Victorian style. Caroling. (812) 265-2956.

SOUTH

BEREA, Ky.—Christmas in Berea. Late November through December. Open houses, craft demonstrations, Christmas parade, special sales, decorated shops. (859) 986-2540 or (800) 598-5263.

Additional Information

INDIANA

Indiana Department of Commerce Tourism Development Division
One N. Capitol St., Suite 700
Indianapolis, IN 46204
(317) 232-8860 or (800) 289-ONIN.

KENTUCKY

Kentucky Department of Travel Development
500 Mero St., Suite 2000
Frankfort, KY 40601
(502) 564-4930 or (800) 255-TRIP

OHIO

Ohio Division of Travel & Tourism
P.O. Box 1001
Columbus, OH 43266-0101
(800) BUCKEYE